LUTHER AND THE
STORIES OF GOD

LUTHER AND THE STORIES OF GOD

Biblical Narratives as a Foundation for Christian Living

Robert Kolb

Baker Academic

a division of Baker Publishing Group
Grand Rapids, Michigan

© 2012 by Robert Kolb

Published by Baker Academic
a division of Baker Publishing Group
P.O. Box 6287, Grand Rapids, MI 49516-6287
www.bakeracademic.com

Printed in the United States of America

Library of Congress Cataloging-in-Publication Data

Kolb, Robert, 1941–
   Luther and the stories of God : biblical narratives as a foundation for Christian living / Robert Kolb.
      p.   cm.
   Includes bibliographical references and indexes.
   ISBN 978-0-8010-3891-4 (pbk.)
      1. Luther, Martin, 1483–1546. 2. Bible—Use—History—16th century. 3. Storytelling—Religious aspects—Christianity—History—16th century. 4. Bible stories. 5. Christian life—Lutheran authors. I. Title.
   BR333.5.B5K65 2012
   230′.41092—dc23   2011041160

Unless otherwise indicated, Scripture quotations are translated by the author from Luther's German text.

Scripture quotations labeled NIV are from the Holy Bible, New International Version®. NIV®. Copyright © 1973, 1978, 1984, 2011 by Biblica, Inc.™ Used by permission of Zondervan. All rights reserved worldwide. www.zondervan.com

Scripture quotations labeled NKJV are from the New King James Version. Copyright © 1982 by Thomas Nelson, Inc. Used by permission. All rights reserved.

Scripture quotations labeled NRSV are from the New Revised Standard Version of the Bible, copyright © 1989, by the Division of Christian Education of the National Council of the Churches of Christ in the United States of America. Used by permission. All rights reserved.

12   13   14   15   16   17   18   7   6   5   4   3   2   1

CONTENTS

ABBREVIATIONS

ARG   *Archiv für Reformationsgeschichte* [journal]. Gütersloh.

BoC   *The Book of Concord.* Edited by Robert Kolb and Timothy J. Wengert. Minneapolis: Fortress, 2000.

BSLK   *Die Bekenntnisschriften der evangelisch-lutherischen Kirche.* 11th ed. Göttingen: Vandenhoeck & Ruprecht, 1992.

CP   *The Sermons of Martin Luther* [the Church Postils]. Edited and translated by John N. Lenker. 8 vols. 1905; Grand Rapids: Baker Book House, 1983.

EA²   *Dr. Martin Luther's sämmtliche Werke* [Erlangen Ausgabe]. Erlangen ed., 2nd. ed. Frankfurt am Main and Erlangen: Heyder & Zimmer, 1862–85.

FS   *Festival Sermons of Martin Luther: The Church Postils.* Translated by Joel R. Baseley. Dearborn, MI: Mark V, 2005.

HP   *Sermons of Martin Luther: The House Postils.* Edited and translated by Eugene F. A. Klug. Grand Rapids: Baker Books, 1996.

LQ   *Lutheran Quarterly.* Gettysburg, PA.

LuJ   *Lutherjahrbuch.* Göttingen: Vandenhoeck & Ruprecht.

LW   *Luther's Works.* Edited by Jaroslav Pelikan and Helmut T. Lehmann. St. Louis: Concordia; Philadelphia: Fortress, 1958–86.

TR   Martin Luther. *Tischreden* [Table Talk]. 6 vols. in WA.

TRE   *Theologische Realenzyklopädie.* Edited by Gerhard Krause and Gerhard Müller. Berlin: de Gruyter, 1977–2004.

WA   *D. Martin Luthers Werke* [Weimarer Ausgabe]. Weimar: Böhlau, 1883–1993.

INTRODUCTION

Luther the Storyteller and His Cultivation
of the Christian Life

All books in the entire Scripture are either reports or historical narratives; they offer examples, sometimes of laws, sometimes of the activities of God, and they all teach faith. The Pentateuch, in which the law is comprehended, reveals the origin of the human creature and sin. The prophets identify sin and pray to Christ, who takes sin away. John points to Christ as the Lamb of God. Christ takes away sin and brings salvation.[1]

Early in his career as reformer, Martin Luther wrote these words as he prepared to preach on Genesis 14 in 1521. By that time a veteran preacher and somewhat seasoned university lecturer, he had already defined the nature of God's revelation as centered on his actions in the form of speech (heard, or unheard as in Genesis 1) and his mysterious guidance of human and natural events, all embedded in human history, and interpreted authoritatively by the prophets and apostles in the Holy Scriptures. Luther recognized that God's unfolding plan for his human creatures constituted what today is labeled a "metanarrative," a master narrative that makes sense of incorporated specific stories. This metanarrative—beginning with creation and the fall into sin in Genesis, focused on Christ's incarnation, death, and resurrection, ending with his return at the end of time—guided and framed the history of God's people as it was reported in both broad strokes and minute, personal details throughout the Bible.

1. *D. Martin Luthers Werke* [WA = Weimarer Ausgabe] (Weimar: Böhlau, 1883–1993), 9:353.8–10.

Luther used several rhetorical forms in his preaching and exegetical lectures to expose the meaning of the text and apply it. Sometimes he presented careful exposition of the biblical text; at other times he employed a catechetical approach, organizing his discourse to teach the truths and applications of the truth he found in a text. But the Wittenberg exegete also believed that God had created human beings to experience reality in the flow of history. Luther believed that the stories constituting this flow reveal something of the larger story of God's creation and preservation of his world. Therefore the retelling of biblical stories, supplemented on occasion with other stories, both from his own experience and reading and from the experiences of his congregation, enriched his conveying of the biblical text. This volume focuses particularly on Luther's recounting stories as he cultivated the Christian way of living, providing instruction and direction for his hearers' and readers' participation in the unfolding drama of God's governance of human history.[2]

Martin Luther as Storyteller

Luther indeed recognized not only the usefulness but also the ambiguity of the biblical stories. In 1532 Conrad Cordatus recorded his mentor's observation that "the stories of the Old Testament are particularly clear, but to those who read them superficially, they are deadly. To the faithful they are alive." To support this observation, Luther used the rather peculiar example of the resultant childlessness of Jephthah (Judg. 11), who sacrificed his only child to fulfill a vow. Luther contrasted Jephthah's fate with that of Hannah, who received a child, Samuel, as a gift from God (1 Sam. 1–2).[3] The example may be curious, but the point of the reformer's observation—that readers should not, like Jephthah, take matters into their own hands, attempting to control or set the rules for their own lives—remained the underlying guideline for his use of stories, biblical and nonbiblical, in his bringing the Word of God to hearers and readers. In his *Preface to Galeatius Capella's History* (1538), and on the basis of the ancient Roman historian Marcus Terentius Varro's statement, Luther thus declares: "The best way to teach is to add an example or illustration to the word, to aid understanding and retention. Otherwise, when a speech without examples is heard, no matter how appropriate and good it may be, it does not move the heart as much and is not as clear and easy to remember."[4]

2. Compare Kevin J. Vanhoozer, *The Drama of Doctrine: A Canonical-Linguistic Approach to Christian Theology* (Louisville: Westminster John Knox, 2005), 102–10.

3. WA TR 2:632, §2753a. On treatments of Jephthah, cf. John L. Thompson, *Reading the Bible with the Dead: What You Can Learn from the History of Exegesis That You Cannot Learn from Exegesis Alone* (Grand Rapids: Eerdmans, 2007), 33–47.

4. WA 50:383.1–8; *LW* 34:275. See John A. Maxfield, *Luther's Lectures on Genesis and the Formation of Evangelical Identity* (Kirksville, MO: Truman State University Press, 2008), 155–56.

Fifteen years earlier the same theory of narrative had guided his treatment of biblical texts in his preaching in Wittenberg. Mary and Joseph had not understood what their twelve-year-old had meant when he explained that he had to be about his father's business. They had despaired of finding him and had questioned God's love for them. "Such examples are very useful for us. We need them to show us how also among the saints, who are God's children and are above others given God's favor, weakness nonetheless remains, so they often stray and make mistakes. Sometimes they stumble badly, although not intentionally or willfully, but from weariness and misunderstanding." The apostles had such experiences. These stories teach God's people to find comfort in God and to cling to his Word.[5]

The biblical accounts of God's action and the actions of both saints and sinners need to be interpreted and applied within the context of the contemporary proclaimer's hearers and readers. With that provision, Luther was convinced that these accounts of human experience and God's intervention in history are valuable means for demonstrating who God is and what it means to be human. He also was convinced that such stories need to be interpreted within the context of the larger framework of God's revelation—Luther's metanarrative.

Indeed, Luther used a variety of stories to explain his larger vision of God's revelation of himself and what it means to be human. These include references to experiences from Luther's own life and memory. Such recollections occurred more frequently, to be sure, at the supper table than in the lecture hall or pulpit. His stories also include tales from ancient myths and classical history, as well as from the history of the church, and even from its tradition of the legends of the saints. His narrative depictions of God in action include also the professor's own fables, such as scenes from Christ's battle against Satan, that have an almost Tolkienesque ring. But in addition, Luther fostered faith and piety from the pulpit and in his exegetical exposition through the retelling of biblical stories. He often imaginatively filled in details in a way he believed was consistent with what was happening in the text, details that provided his hearers and readers with special insight into its significance for their lives.

Luther and the Bible

Although he left few reports of the initial impact that hearing its accounts made upon him, Luther experienced the Bible early in his life. Undoubtedly, he heard its stories first as a child. His student and amanuensis Veit Dietrich recounted the professor's supper-table telling of his fascination, while still a

5. WA 17.2:26.38–27.9; CP 2:46.

"boy," with the story of "Samuel's mother."[6] The Latin *puer* can be a fairly young boy but may also refer to an adolescent. Dietrich's first comment might imply the former: "The book made him marvel, and he thought he would be very happy if he could possess such a book." But his recollection continues, "A little later [Luther] bought a postil [sermon collection]; it did please him a great deal because it contained so many Gospel stories";[7] such a purchase seems unlikely for a younger child. Whatever the age, one of Luther's earliest encounters with Scripture involved a story of God's calling a servant to the ministry of his Word.

The Bible confronted the young Martin above all in liturgies that echoed psalms and other parts of Scripture. He heard some preaching as a child, not exclusively on the biblical texts but also on the tales of the saints and their adventures. Once he began his schooling, biblical texts formed part of the reading material that brought him ever deeper into the Latin language. His entry into the monastery propelled him into reciting psalms daily, hearing Scripture read frequently at meals, and reading the Bible itself on occasion. In pursuing theological study as a monk, he became familiar with more of Scripture. As a member of his monastic community, he began to preach on it to his fellow Augustinians and lecture on it in their monastic program of instruction. By the time he reached the apex of his study of theology and the Doctor in Biblia degree was bestowed upon him in 1512, he knew the sweep of divine revelation well. Emanuel Hirsch, a prominent scholar of the twentieth-century Luther renaissance, has noted the rhetorical and theological develop-ment revealed by Luther's sermons. His first sermons were topical, following a certain medieval model common within scholastic circles, but during the 1510s his biblical studies turned him into an expository preacher.[8] He was not the first: older contemporaries, such as Johann Geiler von Kaisersberg, had renewed a much older tradition of using an expository method alongside a topical focus. In medieval religious practice, however, the sermon did not serve as a medium of grace, as the sacraments did. Sermons functioned at best as a warm-up for the reception of sacramental grace, argues David Steinmetz.[9] Luther incorporated the sacraments into his broader concept of the forms of the Word of God, which arose from the biblical page in oral, written, and sacramental modes of divine power and presence.

The exact progress of his growth in biblical knowledge is not clear; it also is hard to precisely trace Luther's move from more typical medieval conceptions of authority and sources of truth to his confidence in Scripture alone as the

6. WA *TR* 1:44, §116; Heinrich Bornkamm, *Luther and Old Testament*, trans. Eric W. Gritsch and Ruth C. Gritsch (Philadelphia: Fortress, 1969), 8–9.

7. WA *TR* 1:44, §116.

8. Emanuel Hirsch, "Luthers Predigtweise," *Luther* 25 (1954): 1–2.

9. David Steinmetz, "Luther, the Reformers, and the Bible," in *Living Traditions of the Bible*, ed. James E. Bowley (St. Louis: Chalice, 1999), 164–66.

only and unchallenged authority for faith and life. Whatever this chronology might be, however, it is important to recognize that absolute biblical authority never meant that Luther excluded a wide variety of other authors from his quiver of citable authorities so long as they confirmed what he believed stands in Scripture. Against Satan's lies, everything that could serve to convey God's will and ways to his people could be drafted into the battle for God's truth, which the Wittenberg reformer perceived to be taking place whenever preachers of the gospel of Christ bring his Word to his people. Yet all other sources stood under the ultimate and absolute authority of Scripture.

The role of narrative and metanarrative in systematic theology—as well as in biblical studies and several elements of practical theology, especially preaching—has attracted scholarly treatment in the past three decades. In this period Luther's various means of communicating—including his rhetoric,[10] preaching,[11] and lecturing[12]—have been studied from a variety of angles. But in view of how important "narrative" has been in recent scholarly discourse, amazingly little attention has been paid to his use of storytelling apart from Michael Parsons's monographic study of Luther's and Calvin's treatments of Old Testament stories[13] and a few periodical articles.[14]

Most helpful is a 1983 essay by Richard Lischer, which noted that Luther's use of storytelling did not fit into three of the five categories in current discussion of narrative.[15] In his public utterances the reformer did not focus on his own biography: occasional references to his own memories and experiences are rare apart from his Table Talks. He did not use parables to convey images from Scripture to an audience with little sense of the biblical story, as do many modern "narrative preachers." He did not see narrative as "an aesthetic form [that] represents the linguistic confines of Christian existence." However, Luther did, according to Lischer, display two other characteristics that mark the work of twentieth-century narrative theologians: (1) He elaborated biblical

---

10. Ulrich Nembach, *Predigt des Evangeliums: Luther als Prediger, Pädagoge und Rhetor* (Neukirchen-Vluyn: Neukirchener Verlag, 1972).

11. Fred W. Meuser, *Luther the Preacher* (Minneapolis: Augsburg, 1983); Elmer C. Kiessling, *The Early Sermons of Luther and Their Relation to the Pre-Reformation Sermon* (Grand Rapids: Zondervan, 1935); Harold J. Grimm, *Martin Luther as a Preacher* (Columbus, OH: Lutheran Book Concern, 1929); and Eberhart Winkler, "Luther als Seelsorger und Prediger," in *Leben und Werk Martin Luthers von 1526 bis 1546*, ed. Helmar Junghans (Göttingen: Vandenhoeck & Ruprecht, 1983), 1:253–78.

12. Maxfield, *Luther's Lectures on Genesis.*

13. Michael Parsons, *Luther and Calvin on Old Testament Narratives: Reformation Thought and Narrative Text* (Lewiston, NY: Edwin Mellen, 2004).

14. E.g., Mark Ellingsen, "Luther as Narrative Exegete," *Journal of Religion* 63 (1983): 394–413; Ellingsen focuses particularly on the place of Luther's use of narrative within the context of "Yale school" discussions of the time, including the critique of Luther's use of narrative under the domination of his metanarrative.

15. Richard Lischer, "Luther and Contemporary Preaching: Narrative and Anthropology," *Scottish Journal of Theology* 36 (1983): 487–504.

stories and dialogue in contemporary terms to convey their message to his hearers; and (2) he used the larger biblical history as a "plotted sermon structure, an unfolding over time which results in concrete, vivid, and novel expressions of God's relationship with human beings." This structure framed his sermons with "a dramatic or narrative logic by which the sermon begins in the midst of some human ambiguity and proceeds through complications to a moment of insight (or recognition) and on to a resolution."[16] This metanarrative guided the Wittenberg expositor not only in his general approach to Scripture but also in his application of individual accounts within it to his hearer's lives.

Luther drew individual reports from the lives of biblical figures, connecting them to the larger framework and sweep of God's history of interacting with his human creatures. These stories served to cultivate the faith and piety of parishioners, whose religion and fundamental view of reality Luther wished to change. He gradually came to believe that the religious way of life in which he had grown up had so seriously misrepresented God's will for his people that it needed reform and reconstitution at its very base. Luther perceived that the direction of medieval piety ran from the human performer of God-pleasing actions—above all, ritual actions in the sacred realm—to the Creator. His earliest extant sermons attack false confidence in practices that he regarded as superstitious, among which ritualistic observances were prominent.[17] Whatever role the word "grace" may have played in the various theological systems he encountered from his boyhood instruction and from his scholastic professors at the university, the belief of his contemporaries focused largely on what they did to please God and thus secure human well-being. Yet not every medieval theologian thought of humans as initiating God's goodwill. Luther believed that, from Genesis 1:1 and throughout the entire Bible, God is in charge. He never denied that God had created human beings to be responsible, obedient, loving human beings: that is their God-given design and God's expectation of them, he tirelessly taught. But he believed that to be human involves first of all the receptivity of creatureliness, the trust that comes from experiencing God's love, which creates the only true relationship between the divine Creator and the human creature.

Luther's Cultivation of a New Christian Worldview

Throughout his career as reformer, Luther strove to cultivate this relationship between God and those who heard his lectures and sermons or who read his works. Among his many rhetorical devices for delivering the metanarrative, his refashioning of the biblical reports of God's intervention in human history did not predominate. But his rehearsing the stories did form one vital element

16. Ibid., 488–89.
17. Kiessling, *Early Sermons*, 111–19.

of his cultivation of a godly way of life among the people of God; it was an effective tool for fostering faith and piety. The retelling became a key tool in what contemporary communication theorist Charlotte Linde calls "narrative induction": "a process of being encouraged or required to hear, understand, and use someone else's story as one's own."[18] She defines this as "the process by which people come to take on an existing set of stories as *their own* story." Memory, she contends, is "a social process of construction and reconstruction" and thus serves as "a key to identity and to the acquisition of identity."[19]

Luther strove to place the personal memory of each person who heard or read his proclamation within the context of the story of God's people from Adam and Eve through his own time, particularly from creation to the time of Christ and the apostles. What John Maxfield says about Luther's university lectures—"Luther attempted to form in his students a new identity"—describes the preacher's goal for those who heard him from the pulpit as well. Maxfield continues, "Luther's Genesis lectures shed light on how he used scripture to instill in his students a worldview that reflected the ideals of the Lutheran Reformation and that, therefore, contributed to the break between Evangelicals and those who remained within the papal church."[20]

Linde's own work focuses on how commercial and industrial firms build an esprit de corps and how they model, for instance, good salesmanship and dedication to the firm and its goals. But she views that process as akin to "religious conversion narratives."[21] Indeed, Luther's stories told what Linde labels a "non-participant narrative," which delivers the story of another person, such as the founder of a sales firm. Such a narrative functions as a "paradigmatic narrative": it "offers the framework for understanding life and interpreting reality apart from the actual presence of that person." The process includes coming to learn the institution's story and throughout one's career being reminded of "both facts and their official meanings," which are the larger framework for interpreting the institution's reality, the metanarrative. This process also incorporates this larger story into one's own biography, one's own way of life.[22] "Paradigmatic narratives" represent "the ideal life course within an institution" and present the stories of others as exemplary.[23]

Not all of Luther's retellings of biblical stories directly convey a positive paradigmatic narrative, which instructs hearers in how to conduct their lives. Indeed, some warn against sin or provide consolation for sinners when they see the mercy of God toward the likes of Abraham, even when he sinned. But

18. Charlotte Linde, "The Acquisition of a Speaker by a Story: How History Becomes Memory and Identity," *Ethos* 28 (2000): 608–32, here 608, 613.

19. Ibid., 608.

20. Maxfield, *Luther's Lectures on Genesis*, 2; cf. 216–21.

21. Linde, "Acquisition," 609.

22. Ibid., 614–15.

23. Ibid., 621.

the Wittenberg professor strove through nonparticipant narratives to foster a new historical memory and identity for his hearers and readers. This historical memory was intended to lead them to place their own lives within the context of the biblical paradigms for faith in God and obedience to him and love for their fellow human beings. Luther wanted to give them a new sense of group identity, not merely as religious pilgrims who must find their own way to God or as religious athletes who must continually improve their performance to gain and retain God's favor but as children of God, who could approach God as "beloved children approach a beloved father," as he said in explaining the introduction to the Lord's Prayer in his Small Catechism. He was cultivating a worldview centered on God's conversation with his people, in contrast to the attempt to approach God through ritual performance, which had informed much of the piety with which he had grown up. Paul Hiebert defines the oft-used but not always precisely defined concept of "worldview" as "the assumptions underlying a culture [which] provide a more or less coherent way of looking at the world," "models *of reality,* . . . which describe and explain the nature of things—and models *for* action," which "provide us with mental blueprints that guide our behavior."[24] This was Luther's purpose in retelling the stories of biblical figures as set in his own context: to lay a new foundation for his hearers' and readers' viewing of reality and their conduct of daily life, centered in trusting God and being his children in his world.

Luther's Use of Oral and Printed Communication

Like most human beings, Luther first learned to communicate orally. He was raised and educated in an oral culture. As a monk who was assigned to preach, he learned the art of homiletics in the fashion of the late Middle Ages. As an instructor who was assigned to teach, he learned to seek the truth in academic disputations, which matched wits, and he judged them on the basis of oral performance. He was assigned to convey the truth in lectures, which gave a living voice to the written texts of medieval theologians like Peter Lombard, ancient fathers such as Augustine, as well as the prophets and apostles.

The oral vehicles were not only the media of choice for Luther, but they fit his theological perception of God and his human creatures as well. He believed that God is a God of conversation and community and that God fosters community among his human creatures by having them communicate with himself and also with each other face-to-face. Gerhard Forde reflects Luther's understanding, even if not his general practice in preaching, in stating that the native form of God's speaking his word of new life is in the "I" to "you" language of absolution: "I forgive you your sins in the name of

24. Paul G. Hiebert, *Transforming Worldviews: An Anthropological Understanding of How People Change* (Grand Rapids: Baker Academic, 2008), 28.

the Father, the Son, and the Holy Spirit."[25] When Luther told stories about others and through them explained in the third person what God was accomplishing for his hearers, he often made it explicitly clear that God was acting "for you." When he did not repeat this "for you" or "for me" explicitly, he usually led the congregation to understand the implication that their lives paralleled that of the biblical persona whose experience with God and the world he was depicting. They heard a living voice that was conveying the Word of God to them.

That living voice addressed both the Wittenberg populace and the Wittenberg students, the former only in the worshiping congregation, the latter both there and in the lecture hall. The German Reformation scholar Heinrich Bornkamm describes the challenge of Luther's "acclimatizing" the people of Wittenberg to the Bible and what he perceived the biblical view of reality to be—in contrast to medieval conceptions of religion:

> Medieval preaching was overrun by playing around with allegorical interpretations, the legends of the miracles of the saints, the extolling of the church's means of cultivating piety such as indulgences, the rosary, and other forms of prayer, and moralizing. All that vanished in Luther's sermons. He preached precisely and exhaustively on the text, not on a dogmatic topic at hand in the text. To be sure, he did not just stay with the exegesis or exposition of the text, but he led his hearers into the enduring truths in and behind each word of Scripture that were still applicable even as they had been when they were written.[26]

He intended that this message would effect a revolution in the way his audiences perceived God and themselves.

Luther's Audience

The medieval age is often called an age of faith, but a closer glimpse at records of all kinds indicates that that was not the case. The population of medieval Europe may seem gullible and superstitious to modern eyes, as we also may appear to a later generation. But most people were hardheaded survivors, forced by the exigencies of disease, weather, and other human personalities to calculate carefully how the family and the village might survive the near future. In that day as well as in the twenty-first century, heaven could wait. In a sermon on those who blasphemed by accusing Christ of casting out devils by Beelzebub (Luke 11:14–23), Luther himself observes that three kinds of hearers receive the proclamation of the gospel:

25. Gerhard O. Forde, *Theology Is for Proclamation* (Minneapolis: Fortress, 1990), 146–90.
26. Heinrich Bornkamm, "Erneuerung der Frömmigkeit: Luthers Predigten, 1522–1524," in *Wahrheit und Glaube: Festschrift für Emanuel Hirsch zu seinem 75. Geburtstag*, ed. Hayo Gerdes (Itzehoe: Die Spur, Dorbandt, 1963), 50–51.

Some stand in wonder before him. They are the pious, true Christians, who take him so seriously that they are just beside themselves. Others blaspheme, as did the Pharisees and learned of his day, who were annoyed that they were not able to do as much as he and were worried that he would be more highly respected by the people than they. Still others tested him, wanting signs. He was supposed to perform them, as they thought he should. They are just making a game of what he was doing, just as Herod desired such a sign from Christ (Luke 23:8).[27]

Luther wanted to converse with the first category in communicating the teaching of Scripture, but he was well aware that his congregation in Wittenberg contained many who fit the other two categories, or were at best lukewarm to his proclamation. Thus Ulrich Nembach's judgment that Luther's sermons addressed "the not quite serious Christian" often seems to be true,[28] although it is a presupposition that the reformer probably did not carry into his lecture hall. However, he conceived of his lectures as preparing his students to preach to those same not-quite-serious Christians, a fact that the homiletical quality of his lectures often reveals.[29] Furthermore, although he may have presumed that his hearers were not all taking his message as seriously as they should, he did have confidence that God's presence in the proclamation of his Word was conveying his power and promise. He was convinced that God works through human speech as he created it, in its natural forms of communication, to people in a variety of situations. Nembach has shown that Luther's sermons follow the form of Quintilian's address to a popular, unlearned audience that needed to be taught. Critical in such speech is the "detailed concretization" of the lessons to be learned.[30] Narrative serves as an effective tool for focus on the concrete failures of sinners, the concrete promise of God in Christ and his faithfulness to his people in daily life, and God's concrete plans for their actions in daily life. Therefore Luther believed that his preaching was making a significant difference in the hearers' lives. Both lectures and sermons give us some indication of how he thought he might use "narrative induction" to cultivate the identity of "child of God" in his hearers.

The reformer himself expressed his desire to have Christians go directly and only to Scripture, but he recognized, as he wrote his first model sermons for parish priests in 1521, that many needed help in reading the text. His intention in this postil was to depict the Christian life in such detail

27. WA 17.2:215.9–16; CP 2:156–57.

28. Nembach, *Predigt des Evangeliums*, 68, 82.

29. On the similarities between Luther's lectures and sermons, see Ulrich Asendorf, *Die Theologie Martin Luthers nach seinen Predigten* (Göttingen: Vandenhoeck & Ruprecht, 1988), 17–18.

30. Nembach, *Predigt des Evangeliums*, 139–42. See also Gerhard Heintze, *Luther's Predigt von Gesetz und Evangelium* (Munich: Kaiser, 1958), 50–65. Neither Nembach nor Heintze comments specifically on the pedagogical or proclamatory use of stories in Luther's preaching.

that enough is said to inform a Christian individual of what is necessary for salvation. Would to God that my interpretation and those of all other teachers would perish and every Christian take the Scripture alone and just God's Word for themselves. You see from my verbosity how immeasurably different God's Word is in comparison to every human word, how no human being can sufficiently grasp and explain with all his words what is there. . . . Therefore, into the Scriptures, dear Christians, and let my interpretation and those of all other teachers be only a scaffolding for the building itself, that we may grasp the simple Word of God itself, taste it, and remain in it.[31]

This volume focuses on cultivating the identity of God's children as Luther pursued it through the particular instrument of the narrative, especially the retelling of biblical stories. To listen to Luther's practicing the task, we turn to his printed works, which purport to offer what he said in lectures and sermons. Of course, they do not do so precisely. They are not recordings by electronic means but rather are filtered through the brains and pens of his students and amanuenses, sometimes touched up by his own editorial oversight, sometimes not. Lischer bemoaned this fact. He recognized the "problem of accessibility to an oral event," which "makes it impossible for us to reproduce Luther's preaching through characterizations of his voice and bearing, as well as of the congregation's response."[32] As regrettable but also inevitable as that is, marks of orality do indicate that editors did not intend to eliminate the experience of hearing the reformer completely. These marks of orality included references to current events, among others. The reformation that arose in Wittenberg, while indeed an oral happening, also exploited the medium of print in revolutionary ways.

Luther's concept of authorial authority differs from that of the twenty-first century. He regarded himself and an extensive group of colleagues as members of a team: for the most part he apparently trusted his colleagues and presumed their reworking of his material would serve the common cause. In addition, it is certain that he knew well the difference between the impact his writings made in print and the impact his speaking made in person. Both served the cause: Luther's retelling the stories of Scripture provided a new paradigmatic narrative for the lives of his contemporaries.

His recitations of these stories took place within the framework of what scholars in the last quarter century have come to call a "metanarrative." This volume begins with a brief attempt to summarize the Wittenberg hermeneutic that may define the term for Luther. The following chapter provides an overview of how Luther fits into the conception of narrative theology set forth by a few of its leading proponents these past three decades. Five chapters follow,

31. WA 10.1.1:728.5–22; CP 1:455.
32. Lischer, "Luther and Preaching," 487.

studying Luther's telling of stories in order that his hearers and readers might trust God well, view suffering well and put their sinful desires to death well, obey God in praising him and praying to him well, obey God in loving the neighbor well, and die well. This is the story of a preacher and teacher who believed that the Holy Spirit was aiding him as he strove to tell God's story well as a means of cultivating such a life through the paradigmatic patterns that Scripture presents.

This study began in the preparation for a lecture at the eleventh International Congress for Luther Research, held in Canoas, Brazil, in July 2007. The Congress Continuation Committee invited the author to explore the topic "Models of the Christian Life in Luther's Genesis Sermons and Lectures." This lecture appeared in the 2009 *Lutherjahrbuch*, volume 76, much improved by the editorial insight and guidance of Helmar Junghans, whose friendship and support since 1981 have contributed a good deal to my work as a student of Luther's life and thought. He has been a model of good scholarship and of the kind of life described in this volume. With his encouragement and that of his successor as editor of the *Lutherjahrbuch*, this study has emerged.

This volume also incorporates, sometimes rather directly, material from other article-length studies written by the author: "David: King, Prophet, Repentant Sinner: Martin Luther's Image of the Son of Jesse," *Perichoresis* (2010), 203–32 (in chaps. 4 and 6 below); "Luther's Recollections of Erfurt: The Use of Anecdotes for the Edification of His Hearers," *Luther-Bulletin* 20 (2010): (forthcoming) (in several chapters below); "Die Josef-Geschichten als Fürstenspiegel in der Wittenberger Auslegungstradition: 'Ein verständiger und weiser Mann' (Gen. 42, 33)," in *Christlicher Glaube und weltliche Herrschaft: Zum Gedenken an Günther Wartenberg*, edited by Michael Beyer, Jonas Flöter, and Markus Hein (Leipzig: Evangelische Verlagsanstalt, 2008), 41–55 (in chap. 6 below); "'Life Is King and Lord over Death': Martin Luther's View of Death and Dying," in *Tod und Jenseits in der Schriftkultur der Frühen Neuzeit*, edited by Marion Kobelt-Groch and Cornelia Niekus Moore (Wiesbaden: Harrassowitz, 2008), 23–45 (in chap. 7 below); "'Ein kindt des todts' und 'Gottes Gast': Das Sterben in Luthers Predigten," *Lutherische Theologie und Kirche* 31 (2007): 3–22 (in chap. 7 below); "'The Noblest Skill in the Christian Church': Luther's Sermons on the Proper Distinction of Law and Gospel," *Concordia Theological Quarterly* 71 (2007): 301–18 (in chap. 1 below). Thanks go to the editors of those periodicals or volumes for their help as well.

1

THE WHOLE LIFE OF A CHRISTIAN AS A LIFE OF REPENTANCE

Luther's Metanarrative

The word *metanarrative* cannot be found in dictionaries even a quarter century old. The term was invented to designate the framework of the narrator's thinking and the skeleton for the construction of the stories being told. A metanarrative constitutes a fundamental view of reality; it lays down principles of interpretation; it forms the hermeneutic that guides the composition of new stories and the manner in which old stories are re-presented. It is not only, as a literalist might interpret "meta," *after* the story, although it does help the narrator summarize what has been told and indicate to the hearers what they should make of the story. It also takes place *before* the story: it is a perception of ultimate truth that shapes the narrator's selection of the stories to be recited, the emphases on various elements within them, and the significance assigned to the story and its parts.

The narrator is first of all the hearer or reader of the story; as one who repeats or recasts the story, the narrator always speaks from one's own social location. In Luther's case that meant that he recounted his stories out of his own personal piety and out of his calling to proclaim God's Word, a calling that came to him as a monk and was intensified by his reception of the doctorate, as a "teacher of the Bible."[1] Thus the location from which Luther told the story embraced his concerns, as a university lecturer and preacher, to deliver the message of Scripture and to change his hearers' and readers' false perceptions of how to live the Christian life, to change their orientation for life into faithfulness to God and service to his creatures. Luther's concerns certainly reflected his larger social, political, and economic environment, which shaped, limited, and defined his horizon for thinking. This location helped form his expression of what scholars today might label his metanarrative, because metanarratives are always in dialogue with the circumstances of daily life. It provided a path along which he strove to connect God's revelation in Scripture with the daily life of his contemporaries.

God Reveals Himself and His Human Creatures in History and Stories

Viewing the Christian hermeneutic as narrative or metanarrative recognizes a key part of the biblical writers' perceptions of reality. They all ground their truth and its expressions in the dynamic, interactive person of God. What all of them have to say relates to the unfolding course of human life, which takes place in the series of happenings labeled "history." From Genesis's garden of Eden to the streets of gold over which the saints will tread in the new Jerusalem, the biblical message is grounded in place and time. No biblical writer conceived of the subject matter under consideration apart from the historical unfolding of the story of who God is and what it means to be human.

So it was for Martin Luther. He had no concept of God apart from God in relationship to his human creatures. In April 1518, as he first explained his theology to his Augustinian brothers from across Germany in a meeting held in Heidelberg, he distinguished between God "hidden" and God "revealed." This distinction formed a part of his "theology of the cross," which teaches that coming to know God's true nature requires the crucifixion of human reason's attempts to fathom the Divine. It also teaches that the climax and apex of God's revelation of his nature came on Christ's cross.[2]

---

1. See Luther's comment in 1530 in his lecture on Psalm 82: WA 31.2:212.12–18; *LW* 13:66.
2. A sampling of the rich literature on the "theology of the cross" begins with Walther von Loewenich's *Luther's Theology of the Cross*, trans. Herbert J. A. Bouman (Minneapolis: Augsburg, 1976), first published in German in 1929, which treats, above all, Luther's concept of faith and reflects the context of the discussion of existentialism at that time. Philip S. Watson, *Let God Be God! An Interpretation of the Theology of Martin Luther* (Philadelphia: Muhlenberg, 1947), focuses more on what this *theologia crucis* means for Luther's concept of divine revelation and of the atonement of Christ for sinners. Further bibliography may be found in Robert Kolb and Christian Neddens, *Gottes Wort vom Kreuz: Lutherische Theologie als kritische Theologie* (Oberursel: Lutherische Theologische Hochschule, 2001); and in Robert Kolb, "Luther's Theology of the Cross Fifteen Years after Heidelberg: Luther's Lectures on the Psalms of Ascent," *Journal of Ecclesiastical History* 61 (2010): 69–85. The topic is also treated in standard overviews of Luther's theology.

Because Luther did not know he was inventing terminology that would be used for generations as technical theological vocabulary, he was not always careful when he used these terms. Thus the "hiddenness" of God is defined in three different ways in his writings. It sometimes refers to God as he exists in human imaginations, refashioned by sinful and thus inadequate, if not rebellious, fantasies about a manageable deity who fits the sinner's needs and demands. In its first sense, however, it refers to the aspects of God that lie beyond human grasp, in part because the sinful mind is no longer able to see God as he really is, and in part because by definition the creature simply cannot grasp the whole of the Creator. In Heidelberg (April 1518), that use of the term stands over against the "revealed" God, meaning God as he lets himself be known, and lets himself be known by his human creatures precisely through his interaction with them. However, Luther inadvertently muddied the waters by pointing out that God's revelation of himself takes place in ways that human reason cannot understand (1 Cor. 1:18–25). Therefore the revealed God is hiding from falsely functioning human reason in (from reason's perspective) highly unlikely places, such as "crib" and "cross."

This revealed God reveals himself in human history, through the message of the prophets and the proclamation of the apostles and through the written record from both. Kevin Vanhoozer explains that God unfolds his own story in a drama that is composed of word and deed, a drama that actually reveals both who God is and what it means to be human.[3] In this written form, Luther was convinced, God's people hear God's voice.[4] Luther moved beyond what medieval theologians understood to be the Bible's ultimate authority for the teaching of the church within the context of the church's formal authority to interpret Scripture and set forth its only meaning. He was able to do so because he could capitalize on the rich resources he carefully mined from its mother lode as a monk, as a reluctant but dedicated student climbing the academic ladder from degree to degree, as lecturer and preacher. His command of Scripture and his multifaceted exposure to its contents in the monastery could not help but lead his mind into formulating operating summaries to guide his interpretation, and they arose out of the biblical narrative, filtered through his Ockhamist education, his sensitive spirituality, and his experiences within the church and in the society of his time. His own formulations fulfilled Alister McGrath's prescription, "The genesis of doctrine [or metanarrative] lies in the uncritical repetition of the narrative heritage of the past," only if it can be conceded that he did indeed receive

3. Kevin J. Vanhoozer, *The Drama of Doctrine: A Canonical-Linguistic Approach to Christian Theology* (Louisville: Westminster John Knox, 2005), 39, cf. 37–56.

4. Robert Kolb, "The Relationship between Scripture and the Confession of the Faith in Luther's Thought," in *Kirkens bekjennelse I historisk og aktuelt perspektiv: Festskrift til Kjell Olav Sannes*, ed. Torleiv Austad, Tormad Engelviksen, and Lars Østnor (Trondheim: Tapir Akademisk Forlag, 2010), 53–62.

the medieval tradition critically in his effort to return to a straightforward repetition of the biblical message.[5]

Gordon Wenham identifies a fundamental presupposition behind the stories in Genesis that helps clarify the significance of Luther's understanding of the revealed God: the presumption that humankind is "intended to enjoy such intimacy (as described in Psalm 84:2) with God. In the garden of Eden story Adam and Eve and their creator seem to be on the friendliest terms until the serpent upsets it. The LORD worries about Adam's loneliness. He brings the animals to him, and then having created Eve out of a rib, presents her to him as a benevolent father-in-law would. Their intimacy is perpetuated by them all walking together in the cool of the day. Expulsion from Eden ends this age of intimacy."[6] Luther certainly shared this presupposition, and God's efforts to restore that intimacy of Eden in creating faith in Jesus Christ did guide and direct his delivery of the biblical message.

Luther believed that the culmination of God's revelation of himself and his re-creating, salvific restoration of humanity came in the person of Jesus Christ, truly God and at the same time truly a human being. Christ and his impact on the life of the sinner whom he transforms into God's child form the center and framework for Luther's reading of Scripture and communication of its message. Preparing sermons on Genesis in 1521, he comments, "The first chapters of the book of Genesis embrace the full message of the entire Scripture, . . . [which] contains the incarnation of the eternal Son, the mortification of the old nature, and the life of the one who has been resurrected, that is, the new person."[7] God the Son, incarnate as this human being, Jesus, thoroughly historical, was born, matured, spent time with disciples, died, and—rewriting the history of his human family—rose from the dead, body and all, retaining the scars of his death and the ability to eat fish. But as God reveals himself in history, he is hiding himself from sinful reason by coming in forms that do not match the sinful imagination's projection of what the Ultimate and Absolute, the pinnacle of reality, should act like and be like. For no one should expect to find God in a crib, on a cross, in a crypt. It is this third use of the "hiddenness" of God in Luther's usage that sometimes confuses scholars and diverts their view from one or both of the first two. All three are vital for an understanding of Luther's teaching regarding God.

Luther presumed that the revealed God reveals himself from the beginning— in the beginning (Gen. 1:1)—as a person who is speaking. God creates through speaking, and he begins conversation with his human creatures immediately. When they sinned, the first human creatures heard God, heard his sound as he

---

5. Alister E. McGrath, *The Genesis of Doctrine: A Study in the Foundation of Doctrinal Criticism* (Oxford: Blackwell, 1990), 7, 58–59.

6. Gordon J. Wenham, *Story as Torah: Reading Old Testament Narrative Ethically* (Grand Rapids: Baker Academic, 2004), 81.

7. WA 9:329.10–14.

was walking, apparently to the place where they usually met to converse (Gen. 3:8). When they were not there, he called to them, asking not what they had done but where they were (3:9). The problem was that this God of conversation and community (community almost always involves conversation) wanted to be in relationship with his human creatures, and that involves meeting as well as conversing. Luther made a great deal out of both God's conversation with human beings and his community with them as he preached (early in his reforming career, 1523) and lectured (in the last years of his career, 1535–45) on Genesis.[8] The entire biblical record that follows rehearses conversations and communications of God with human beings. The only God whom Luther can discuss is God in relationship to his human creatures.

The Creator and His Human Creatures

Likewise, the relationship of the human being to God is at the core of Luther's definition of what it means to be human. Relationship offers a good vantage point from which to assess how God, his human creatures, and indeed his whole creation actually function and therefore what the foundation or structure of reality is. On the basis of Luther's exegesis of the Psalms, Brian Brock states, "All creatures, says Luther, participate in a great cosmic web of reciprocal relations. The sun does not shine for itself, water does not flow for itself, plants do not give fruits for themselves; every creature lives by the law of love, sharing freely of itself with its neighbors."[9] The relationship between God and his human creatures is not only, but most importantly, a matter of conversation. "If God is a speaking God, then we are always in the midst of learning from him what our grammar is about. Language is not simply 'there,' but we are learning what it means, and thus what it is, by listening in the form of prayer" and, looking beyond the psalm text on which Brock is commenting, above all by listening to preaching or proclamation in any form. "Language is the place God has given so that he can use it to claim us"[10] and the place where we respond.

The human being is first and foremost a creature of God.[11] In the Wittenberg reformer's basic instruction for children, they learn before all else that the first commandment of the Decalogue means that "we are to fear, love, and trust in God above all things."[12] In his Large Catechism this first command of God

---

8. The sermons are found in WA 14:97–488 (printed versions, 1527, in WA 24:1–710); the lectures in WA 42–44; *LW* 1–7.

9. Brian Brock, *Singing the Ethos of God: On the Place of Christian Ethics in Scripture* (Grand Rapids: Eerdmans, 2007), 188.

10. Ibid., 177.

11. Gerhard Ebeling, *Lutherstudien*, vol. 2, *Disputatio de homine*, part 3, *Die theologische Definition des Menschen* (Tübingen: Mohr/Siebeck, 1989), 92–96, 545–622.

12. *BSLK* 507; *BoC* 351.

for his people means that "you are to regard me alone as your God." Like psychological theorist Erik Erikson more than four hundred years later,[13] Luther defined trust as fundamental to human personality. In contrast to Erikson, Luther applied this observation to the human creature's relationship to God. Gods of any sort are "that to which we are to look for all good and in which we are to find refuge in all need. Therefore, to have a god is nothing else than to trust and believe in that one with your whole heart; . . . it is the trust and faith of the heart alone that make both God and an idol."[14]

The distinction between Creator and creature structured Luther's thinking about both God and the human being. As Jewish exegete Meir Sternberg has observed about the Old Testament record, the Bible "directs much of its narrative energies" "against [a] humanizing conception of the divine order." Instead, it "inculcates a model of reality where God exercises absolute sway over the universe (nature, culture, history) in conspicuous isolation and transcendence."[15] But this absolute Lord of creation is, also in Sternberg's view, a God who desires conversation and community with the people he has made. "God shapes the world plot with a view to getting his creatures to 'know' him. Biblical history therefore stretches as a long series of demonstrations of divine power followed by tests of memory, gratitude, inference from precept and precedent, or, in short, of 'knowledge,' with further demonstrations staged in reward or punishment."[16] Luther defined the content of the demonstrations as both divine punishment and the display of God's mercy and love; yet he also understood that the "metanarrative" guiding human history is above all God's desire to be known by his human creatures and to enjoy a relationship of love and trust with them. Retelling stories of God's dealings with his people repeats his promise to be their faithful God in the future, to be the same God for them tomorrow as he was yesterday for patriarchs, disciples, and all their successors among the people of God.

Luther believed that all stories in Scripture occur, as all other events in human history, in a sequence that began with creation and will end with Christ's return to judge. He "experienced history as a movement or progress in which God was ever active" as he led his human creatures through time. History on the move, as the ever-changing chain of divine and human actions and interactions, has its ultimate purpose, John Headley argues, in bringing human beings "to a knowledge of God through His works." Even though historical knowledge

13. Erik Erikson, *Child and Society* (New York: Norton, 1950); Erikson, *Insight and Responsibility* (New York: Norton, 1964), esp. 81–107; Erikson, *Identity, Youth, and Crisis* (New York: Norton, 1968), esp. 91–141; Erikson, *Life History and the Historical Moment* (New York: Norton, 1975).

14. *BSLK* 560–61; *BoC* 386.

15. Meir Sternberg, *The Poetics of Biblical Narrative: Ideological Literature and the Drama of Reading* (Bloomington: Indiana University Press, 1985), 101.

16. Ibid., 48.

apart from God's revelation provides only indirect and often obscure glimpses of God's presence in the world, God, according to Luther, is present in the course of human events. Based on what Scripture reveals, his people could gather some sense of what he was about through observing these events.[17] Since history "is God's work," the historical accounts of Scripture reveal what God was doing in behalf of his people, alongside telling the story of human action, in sin and in trust and obedience toward God. Therefore the reformer's treatment of such biblical accounts, in commenting on them or in reshaping them with pointed detail, reflects his convictions about both God and human creatures, at the time of the accounts and in his own day.[18] According to Headley, "faith and unbelief" constitute the history of humankind, particularly of the church. "And at the vortex is the Word, this veritable attack of God upon human history" and sinful rebellion against God. This attack creates the church and leads it into the struggle against all that opposes God.[19]

The oft-repeated judgment that "Luther was not a systematic theologian" must be qualified in the light of what has been observed here. He may not fit the twenty-first-century definition of the systematic theologian, and he certainly departed from the medieval model for constructing a theological system, a system governed by Aristotle and Peter Lombard. But Luther worked with the inner logic and coherence of a worldview that flowed from the personal claim he experienced in the Bible, the claim of the person of God upon his human creatures, expressed throughout human history and above all in the incarnation of Christ.

With this understanding of God's revelation as embedded in history, the Wittenberg reformer fits the Yale school's systematic theologian Hans Frei's observation about the long succession of biblical commentators that Augustine also exemplifies: they "envisioned the real world as formed by the sequence told by the biblical stories . . . from creation to the final consummation to come."[20] The Wittenberg reformer believed, as Frei's colleague George Lindbeck expresses it, that the Bible is "a canonically and narrationally unified and internally glossed (that is, self-referential and self-interpreting) whole centered on Jesus Christ, and telling the story of the dealings of the Triune God with his people and his world in ways which are typologically . . . applicable to the present."[21]

That sequence began with creation, God's act that set the framework for all reality, including the unfolding of human history. In the beginning was

---

17. John M. Headley, *Luther's View of Church History* (New Haven: Yale University Press, 1963), 42.

18. Ibid., 42–55.

19. Ibid., 55.

20. Hans W. Frei, *The Eclipse of Biblical Narrative: A Study in Eighteenth and Nineteenth Century Hermeneutics* (New Haven: Yale University Press, 1974), 1.

21. George A. Lindbeck, "Scripture, Consensus, and Community," in *Biblical Interpretation in Crisis*, ed. Richard John Neuhaus (Grand Rapids: Eerdmans, 1989), 75.

God, it is stated in Genesis 1:1, and everything that constitutes reality flows from his saying, "Let there be. . . ." His speaking in Genesis 1 was speaking that determined reality: creative speaking. The next significant milestone in the unfolding of the human story was the fall into sin. For Luther, as for the apostle Paul (if Ben Witherington's analysis is correct), history repeated a cycle of apostasy, repentance, and obedience that can be seen in Genesis 1–11, repeated in the entire history of Israel, a third time in Jesus's encounter with the world, and finally in the lives of Paul and of every other person among God's faithful.[22] The fall determined that sinners hear God's speaking only in terms of his anger over their not being what he had created them to be. They hear only the demands of the law and its diagnoses of their state apart from their Creator. The center of the story comes with the interruption of this sinful rebellion by the appearance of Jesus Christ on earth. Clearly Luther viewed the incarnation of the Second Person of the Trinity as the key, the turning point in the world's history.

In composing his Wartburg Postil in late 1521, Luther prepared a letter of dedication to Albert, count of Mansfeld. It provides "instruction on what to look for and expect in the Gospels" and focuses on the gospel as "a discourse or story about Christ, just as happens when someone writes a book about a king or prince, telling what he did, said, and suffered in his day." Some tell the story succinctly, others not. In whatever form, this gospel "is supposed to be nothing but a chronicle, a story, a narrative about Christ, telling what he is, what he did, said, and suffered; . . . in briefest form, the gospel is a discourse about Christ, that he is the Son of God and became human for us, that he died and was raised, that he has been made Lord over all things."[23] Luther's "summary" of the gospel repeats these thoughts: "It is the story . . . of Christ, God's Son, David's son, who died and rose and was placed as Lord" at God's right hand.[24] Christ's restoration of human life through his death for sin and his resurrection to restore righteousness (Rom. 4:25) enables human history to proceed, with his faithful people trusting in him and serving him as they love his other creatures.

They are, however, involved in a lifelong struggle with the person of Satan and his forces. Luther taught that human history after the fall takes place on the battlefield between God and Satan, between truth and deception. John Maxfield's reading of Luther's Genesis lectures concludes that he "reconstructed the Christian past in such a way as to provide a clear picture of how Christian existence, caught in the cosmic battle between God and the devil, had endured since the beginning and would endure until the last day."[25] Indeed,

---

22. Ben Witherington III, *Paul's Narrative Thought World: The Tapestry of Tragedy and Triumph* (Louisville: Westminster John Knox, 1994), 5.

23. WA 10.1.1:9.11–20; *LW* 35:117–18.

24. WA 10.1.1:10.6–11.

25. John A. Maxfield, *Luther's Lectures on Genesis and the Formation of Evangelical Identity* (Kirksville, MO: Truman State University Press, 2008), 179.

this recital of the history of God's people encourages believers in the midst of present conflict. This story supports and sustains them amid strife. In that struggle preaching played a key role, as the proclamation of God's law (revealed not only against the backdrop of human sin but also of the devil's lies) and as the gospel of salvation through faith in Christ. The sword of the Holy Spirit (Eph. 6:17) counters Satan's claims on the sinner with God's re-creative action in Christ's death and resurrection.[26] "As Luther exercised himself and his students in the word of God from the book of Genesis, he utilized the narrative to develop in his students a perception that the present, like the past, is caught up in apocalyptic warfare, and the future is to be placed in God's hands."[27] This eschatological battle will find its end, nonetheless, when Christ comes to judge the living and the dead and to consummate the restoration of the righteousness of his chosen people. This sequence outlined the biblical view of human history, which Luther accepted and used.[28]

The grand sweep of human history repeats itself, Luther observed, in the daily lives of all God's chosen people. By delivering the metanarrative, and all the brief narratives that make up the Scriptures, Luther strove to bring God's active and re-creative Word into the heart of his hearers' and readers' lives. In 1531, when Luther reflects on the "success" of his efforts over the past decade, he comments, "It has, praise God, come to this, that men and women, young and old, know the catechism and how to believe, live, pray, suffer, and die."[29] In *Two Kinds of Righteousness*, written in 1519, he outlines the Christian life on the basis of Titus 2:12. That life consists of living soberly (crucifying the flesh), justly (in regard to the neighbor), and devoutly (in relationship to God).[30] Said another way: in 1525, in his work *Against the Heavenly Prophets*, he outlines the five chief parts of Christian teaching for parish pastors:

1. preaching the law to reveal sin and terrify the conscience,
2. preaching the gospel to bestow the forgiveness of sins,
3. putting to death sinful desires,
4. encouraging works of love toward the neighbor, and
5. continuing to emphasize the law for those without faith.[31]

Scott Hendrix has found a worthy summary of Luther's goals in pulpit and lectern in his book *On the Two Kinds in the Sacrament* (1522): the reformer

---

26. See Fred Meuser, *Luther the Preacher* (Minneapolis: Augsburg, 1983), 25–27.

27. Maxfield, *Luther's Lectures*, 212.

28. Headley, *Church History*, 1–55, 224–65.

29. "Aber nu ists / Gott lob / dahin komen / das man vnd weib / jung vnd alt / den Catechismum weis / Vnd wie man gleuben / leben / beten / leiden / vnd sterben sol"; in *Warnung an seine lieben Deutschen*, 1531: WA 30.3:317.32–34; LW 47:52.

30. WA 2:147.4; LW 31:299.

31. WA 18:65.9–66.11.

sought "to provide a religious environment in which believers would develop as fully as possible into the model Christians described by him in *Freedom of a Christian*: free through faith to serve others in love. The creation of these 'real Christians' [as the sense of Luther's phrase is effectively rendered with the addition of the adjective] took precedence over other agendas that interpreters have occasionally tried to impose on Luther."[32] Hendrix quotes Luther: if his readers would abandon "unfaithfulness, hatred, envy, wrath, and unbelief," then "we would at last become again a group of real Christians, whereas at present we are almost completely pagan and only Christian in name."[33]

With two words Hendrix aptly recapitulates what Luther meant when he talked of Christians as those who have been restored to their true humanity. The first is *righteousness*—Luther's conception of what one is supposed to be and only is by faith—a sense of identity in relationship to God and a sense of identity in relationship to God's creatures, human and other. The second word is *piety*: Luther himself transformed "piety," the German word *Frömmigkeit*, from a term for general upright and honorable living to a designation for living a life of faith in God that produces love and service to others.[34] Helmar Junghans has aptly deemed Luther's "Christianization" of German culture as the exercise of the Christian "office of salting," of being the salt and light of which Christ speaks in Matthew 5:13.[35]

On the basis of the linguistic theory he had learned from his Ockhamist instructors, Luther presumed that God's Word does not merely provide information or point to a reality in heavenly forms. God's Word for Luther is active and serves as God's tool to achieve certain goals in human history. Luther's use of that Word presumed that "in the beginning there was not a big bang but the creative word, not a mute principle, an idea, existence in general, mere material, but living speech, communication that creates understanding, the creative and liberating devotion in this word from the Creator. This word is to be treasured so highly because it is the divine coming together of meaning and power and action."[36] Scripture engaged him, Luther believed, not as "true information about, or even an accurate running commentary upon, the work of God in salvation and new creation, but as taking an active part *within* that ongoing purpose. . . . Scripture is there to be a means of God's action in and

---

32. Scott Hendrix, *Recultivating the Vineyard: The Reformation Agendas of Christianization* (Louisville: Westminster John Knox, 2004), 37.

33. Ibid., 41; *Von beider Gestalt des Sakraments zu nehmen*, WA 10.2:39.1–14; LW 36:264.

34. Hendrix, *Recultivating the Vineyard*, 59–60; cf. Walter Sparn, "'Wahrlich, dieser ist ein frommer Mensch gewesen!' Überlegungen zu einem evangelischen Begriff von Frömmigkeit," in *Post-Theism: Reframing the Judeo-Christian Tradition*, ed. Henri A. Krop, Arie L. Molendijk, and Hen de Vries (Louvain: Peeters, 2000), 447–65.

35. Helmar Junghans, "Luther und die Kultur," *LuJ* 52 (1985): 164–83, here 172–83.

36. Joachim Ringleben, "Die Bibel als Wort Gottes," in *Die Autorität der Heiligen Schrift für Lehre und Verkündigung der Kirche*, ed. Karl-Hermann Kandler (Neuendettelsau: Freimund, 2000), 21.

through us."[37] More than the "performative" speech of contemporary literary scholars,[38] God's promise of a restored relationship with himself is creative, or re-creative, speech. On the basis of Romans 10:17, "faith comes by hearing, and hearing by the word of God" (NKJV), Luther formulated a concept of the prevenient Word: "The Word has to come first, and it initiates salvation."[39] God's Word, Luther believed, continued to foster trust, fight evil lusts, and activate the God-pleasing life of service and love.

The "righteousness" that God's Word creates in the sinner establishes a new identity in a manner similar to that described by Charlotte Linde's "narrative induction."[40] The rebel becomes a child of God; the person infatuated with and possessed by Satan's lies becomes Christ's disciple. Luther's perception of how God works in his Word anticipated the assertion of David Kelsey that "God 'uses' the church's various uses of scripture in her common life to nurture and reform the self-identity both of the community and of the individual persons who comprise it."[41] From different angles Luther set forth his understanding of how the Word of God actually accomplishes the creation of a righteous, pious person in the context of daily life and how it fosters the expression and practice of one's new identity. His understanding of the nature of that Word, as it becomes concrete in oral, written, or sacramental forms in the mouths or hands of Christians, approximates the analysis of human speaking as "deputized discourse," as advanced by Nicholas Wolterstorff. Luther believed that God, in order to convey his will to his chosen people, had placed his own authority in the words of preachers. God gave his own words via Scripture to the church, Luther taught, in the manner of Kevin Vanhoozer's "canonical-linguistic" perception of how the Holy Spirit works.[42] Luther believed that the Spirit entrusts something to the preachers ordained to deliver his promises and commands to the people publicly, and to all Christians in personal conversation—namely, a measure of "superintendence" over the formulation of the message that God speaks in Scripture in their delivery of the message to others.[43]

The Christian life that Luther strove to cultivate involved first of all trust in God—Creator, Redeemer, and Sanctifier. As Wolterstorff states, a system of

37. N. T. Wright, *The Last Word: Beyond the Bible Wars to a New Understanding of the Authority of Scripture* (San Francisco: HarperSanFrancisco, 2006), 22.

38. Especially J. L. Austin, *How to Do Things with Words* (Oxford: Oxford University Press, 1961); and John R. Searle, *Speech Acts: An Essay in the Philosophy of Language* (Cambridge: Cambridge University Press, 1969).

39. WA 17.2:201.5–7; CP 2:149.

40. See Introduction: "Luther the Storyteller and His Cultivation of the Christian Life."

41. David Kelsey, *Proving Doctrine: The Uses of Scripture in Modern Theology* (Harrisburg, PA: Trinity Press International, 1999), 214.

42. Vanhoozer, *Drama of Doctrine*, 15–25, and passim.

43. Nicholas Wolterstorff, *Divine Discourse: Philosophical Reflections on the Claim That God Speaks* (Cambridge: Cambridge University Press, 1995), 42–51.

relationship based upon speaking requires the hearer's trust in the truth and reliability of what is said.[44] Luther's examples from biblical figures served to nurture dependence on God and confidence in his merciful disposition toward his baptized children.[45] Luther took for granted that suffering of all kinds determines much of life on earth, and so he turned to the likes of Abraham and Joseph, for example, to demonstrate how his hearers and readers could flee to the refuge and haven of their providential Creator and Savior for support and comfort in times of suffering. Such a daily life embraces two aspects of righteous or pious activity for a preacher with convictions about sin as strong as Luther had. He emphasized the need to "mortify the flesh," to continue to beat back and defeat the temptations to stray from trusting in God and loving the neighbor. Such mortification aimed toward the practice of humanity as God had designed it, toward worship of God and love for other people. That love proceeds out of the trust that God gives in reestablishing the relationship between himself and his human creatures. Luther found a natural part of trusting in God to be in conversing with this God who created through his Word and proved himself to be a God of conversation and community. Thus Luther looked to patriarchs and prophets as models of hearing God's Word, of repeating it to others, and of praying. Luther also regarded the God-pleasing conduct of daily life as a significant element of piety. That conduct expresses itself in the practice of community, of mutual love and support, with other human beings and the whole of creation. Included in such exemplary living is exemplary dying. For Luther, as for medieval pastors, preparation for dying belongs to the rhythm of daily life. To be sure, Luther treated these aspects of pious living on the basis of a variety of biblical genres, but important among them were the models for such living that sprang from the biblical narratives on which Luther preached and lectured.

The Hermeneutical Functions of Luther's Metanarrative

The first of his postils, the Wartburg series of sermons (1521–22), begins with an introduction that explains what the gospel is and how to proclaim it effectively to God's people. In it Luther borrows language from Romans 12:7–8: preaching involves "teaching and admonition. Teaching is when one preaches on what is not known, in order to bring the people knowledge and understanding. Admonition is when one urges them and encourages them to do that which everyone already knows. Both are necessary for the preacher."[46] As Luther later developed his insights, teaching concentrates on the delivery

44. Ibid., 89–93.
45. Heinrich Bornkamm, *Luther and the Old Testament*, trans. Eric W. Gritsch and Ruth C. Gritsch (Philadelphia: Fortress, 1969), 23–24.
46. WA 10.1.2:1.18–2.3.

of the gospel that creates or restores new life in Christ, while admonition applies both consolation and instruction to daily Christian living. Eberhard Winkler describes how Luther practiced both proclamation and pastoral care in view of these parallel biblical claims: "The decisive priority of God's action in no way excludes the appeal to human insight. The pastoral comfort [that stems from God's commitment to love his people] therefore . . . points to a component that sets [human] activity in motion."[47] Together these two activities constitute the good work that God has called preachers to perform. Preaching was the most important good work that Christ performed in his earthly ministry. Where Christ is present, the gospel will certainly be preached. When preachers proclaim Christ, they make him present for their hearers.[48]

Luther presumed that Scripture held the ultimate authority for the proclamation of God's Word. The fact that Luther and his followers did not fix a definite list of canonical books officially changes nothing in that observation.[49] The Bible held that authority because the Holy Spirit had given it and because God is present in it and in the message that arises from its pages. Fred Meuser speaks of Luther's belief in "the real presence of Christ in proclamation."[50] The reformer informed readers of his Church Postil that "God is everywhere, but he is really to be found in the Holy Scriptures, in his Word, more than anywhere else."[51] For Scripture is "the Holy Spirit's own special book, writing, and word."[52] William Graham interprets Luther's correlation of these three terms as asserting that the book, which originated from the act of writing, nonetheless is designed to issue into "oral speech or spoken message."[53] Thus for Luther this "book" becomes more than pages within a binding: it is an event in God's care for his people on earth. Graham admits that "Luther's statements about the word of God . . . take on a concreteness and immediacy that most of us today are able to grasp only with difficulty, if at all." He continues, "Nevertheless, if it was natural to him and his audience for the written word of scripture to be experienced and conceived of as an oral word, it was also much more natural to them than to us today to conceive of and perhaps to experience God's direct speech in the reading of scripture (or in the preaching of a sermon)."[54] Graham also

47. Eberhard Winkler, "Luther als Seelsorger und Prediger," in *Leben und Werk Martin Luthers von 1526 bis 1546: Festgabe zu seinem 500. Geburtstag*, ed Helmar Junghans (Berlin: Evangelische Verlagsanstalt, 1983), 1:228.

48. WA 10.1.2:154.10–15; CP 1:94.

49. William A. Graham (*Beyond the Written Word: Oral Aspects of Scripture in the History of Religion* [Cambridge: Cambridge University Press, 1987], 121) asserts that Calvin and Zwingli were like Luther in this regard. This does not alter the fact that the churches of the Reformed tradition generally did fix the canon in their confessional documents.

50. Meuser, *Luther the Preacher*, 13.

51. WA 12:413.32–34; CP 2:23.

52. WA 54:474.4.

53. Graham, *Beyond the Written Word*, 152.

54. Ibid., 153.

observes, "Luther's understanding of the word of God, that most central theme of Reformation thought, was indissolubly bonded to the role of scripture as the tangible embodiment of the Word. If he commonly juxtaposed 'the spirit' (*spiritus / der Geist*) and 'the letter' (*litera / der Buchstabe*) of scripture, to the advantage of the former as the ultimate source of Christian faith and life, this in no way lessened his concern with the written word of scripture as the palpable authority for that faith and life."[55] Medieval preachers had largely followed the definition of the preaching task as "instruction for morals and faith," as set forth by Alan of Lille at Paris in the late twelfth century.[56] Luther likewise believed that preachers taught and admonished with those goals in mind. In addition, Luther's sense of God's performative Word, as the instrument of his accomplishing his creative and re-creative will, indeed posited God's presence in both its oral and written forms, albeit in a different way and different form than he viewed God's gift of the true presence of Christ's body and blood for the forgiveness of sins in the Lord's Supper. But God's presence made itself known in the power of the gospel for the salvation of those who trust it (Rom. 1:17), according to Luther. This proclamation engages God's chosen people in conversation with their Creator, Luther believed, and that conversation creates the trust in God that permeates and transforms life. As Vanhoozer notes, "Scripture, in addressing our imaginations, speaks to our minds, wills, and emotions alike."[57] Therefore, preaching God's promise generates the assurance that God is and will remain present in the hearer's life. In his analysis of Augustine's and Luther's ways of "singing the ethos of God," Brian Brock states that "the preoccupation of antique conceptions of ethics with individual flourishing is displaced in Luther by an inquiry into what it means to live with God, in which the dramatics of fellowship are emphasized. . . . Luther's emphasis is on transformation into the form of Christ understood in terms of *Nachfolge*, the following of . . . a God who is leading in time. . . . Luther's is a dialogical ethic of hearing and speaking *with* God."[58]

Critical, then, is the question of how God and his human creatures conduct this dialogue. Early in his ministry, Luther departed from a medieval precedent that saw the spirit/letter distinction as a contrast between inner and outer forms of communication, especially written words. Instead, he interpreted "spirit" in terms of his own definition of "gospel" in contrast to his understanding of "law."[59] This means that the Wittenberg reformer took for granted what

---

55. Ibid., 145.

56. Mark Zier, "Sermons of the Twelfth Century Schoolmasters and Canons," in *The Sermon*, ed. Beverly Mayne Kienzle (Turnhout: Brepols, 2000), 325.

57. Vanhoozer, *Drama of Doctrine*, 12.

58. Brock, *Singing the Ethos*, 165–66.

59. Erik Herrmann, "'Why then the Law?' Salvation History and the Law in Martin Luther's Interpretation of Galatians 1513–1522" (PhD diss., Concordia Seminary, St. Louis, 2005), passim, esp. 236–47.

Graham calls the "relational" aspect of sacred writings. God speaks from the pages of the Bible and through those who present its message. He is a God of conversation, who through the word that he speaks in Scripture creates community, the "sensual" or "affective" aspects along with the cognitive that foster and structure them.[60] God the Holy Spirit transforms the spirit of his chosen children as he repeats his words found on the biblical page, whether through its reading or through hearing it—in preaching, conversation, or in connection with the material signs of the sacraments. "The oral dimension [of the use of Scripture] is, however, the one most intimately bound up with the major personal communal roles of scripture in religious life, especially those that move not only in the intellectual or ideational realm but also in that of the senses—as, for example, in ritual or devotional use,"[61] both in the home or private use and in public worship.

There was never a time when God's written message for his people—at first in the reading of the Old Testament, then in Gospels and Epistles of the New—did not occupy a central place in Christian worship and congregational life: not a single Sunday in the history of the church passed without reading the Scripture in public worship.[62] But that reading, in oral form itself, always led to proclamation, applying the message that the preacher found in the pages of the Bible to the concerns of the audience in the midst of life as its members were experiencing it. As Graham observes, "The Protestant Reformation in Europe was in many ways a conscious effort to recover the early Christian kerygmatic orientation—the direct preaching and teaching of the word of God to all who would listen."[63] That orientation, of course, never completely disappeared from the medieval church, though it was often lacking on the local level.

Despite God's presence in the pages of the Bible, its text could be misinterpreted. Therefore the preacher had to depend on the guidance of the Holy Spirit. That is necessary, Luther told the Wittenberg congregation, because every biblical teaching had been attacked and rejected by heretics.[64] His recounting of Herod's encounter with the wise men led Luther to point out that the king made it look as though he wanted to learn the truth as he gathered the learned to search the Scriptures (Matt. 2:4). But he did so deceitfully, seeking to accomplish what he wanted and intended, not what Scripture commanded. He desired to do the opposite of what God's Scriptures said: he sought to muffle God's Word. This treatment of his Word served as an example that should bring fear to the consciences of Christians so that they might avoid this kind

---

60. See Graham, *Beyond the Written Word*, 6.
61. Ibid., 155.
62. Contra Graham, *Beyond the Written Word*, 123.
63. Ibid., 120.
64. WA 21:230.21–38; CP 2:293.

of abuse of the Bible, Luther observed.[65] For "the spiritual Herodians do not deny the gospel outwardly but learn it from true Christians, but only with the intention of using it for their own wanton purposes."[66] On Easter Monday 1523 Luther reminded his hearers that "the Word without the Spirit is useless. But God almighty himself says . . . that his Word which he has preached will not return empty. Therefore we cannot be indifferent to preaching since it is God's will that the Holy Spirit be given us through the Word, and he will not stand for our shutting our traps and waiting until he sends miracles from heaven while the Word and the Sacrament just sit there."[67]

Luther's presumption that God is present in Scripture created the reformer's conviction that the divine Word there is powerful. In 1523 he told his audience that Isaiah 55:11, with its promise that God's Word will not return empty, "should make us bold and joyful when we are already cold. We have by God's grace the very Word of God, for which we should raise our hands in thanks to God." Because God promises that his Word will bear fruit, "you will undoubtedly feel and experience something when you take it in hand and not make a mockery of it but deal with it seriously. You cannot have such evil thoughts in your heart if you take something from Scripture and read it or go to someone else and talk with him about it. That will calm your evil desires and your flesh."[68] Luther cultivated his new piety of conversation with God in this way.

Luther came to define the ultimate purpose of the daily use of God's Word in teaching and admonition as the fostering of the life of repentance. For his entire life he wrestled with the mystery of how sin and evil continued in the lives of those who trusted in Christ. He became convinced that the pattern Paul defines as dying to sin and being raised to walk in the footsteps of Christ, set in baptism (Rom. 6:3–11; Col. 2:11–15), takes place on a daily basis through the use of other forms of God's Word. He begins his 1517 attack on indulgence practices in his Ninety-five Theses with the sentence "The whole life of the Christian is a life of repentance."[69] Scholars differ on the extent to which, at this point in his theological development, he was only echoing the words of Johann Tauler and other medieval theologians who stressed the continuing need for sorrow over sin, and to what extent his exegetical studies were bringing him to a new perception of repentance.[70] He expresses his new understanding best when he claims in his Small Catechism that the Holy Spirit's baptismal

---

65. WA 10.1.1:632.6–10; 10.1.1:633.14–19; CP 1:376–77.

66. WA 10.1.1:668.15; CP 1:407.

67. WA 12:503.33–504.6; CP 2:278–79.

68. WA 12:500.33–501.17; CP 2:275–76.

69. "The Ninety-Five Theses on Indulgences," 1517, in WA 1:233.10–11; *LW* 31:25.

70. Theo Bell, *Divus Bernhardus: Bernhard von Clairvaux in Martin Luthers Schriften* (Mainz: Zabern, 1993), 62–71, 124–33; Volker Leppin, "'Omnem vitam fidelium penitentiam esse voluit': Zur Aufnahme mystischer Tradition in Luthers erster Ablaßthese," *ARG* 93 (2003): 7–25; Leppin, "Transformationen spätmittelalterlicher Mystik bei Luther," in *Gottes Nähe unmittelbar erfahren: Mystik im Mittelalter und bei Martin Luther*, ed. Bernd Hamm and Volker Leppin

action is repeated in daily repentance: "The old Adam in us with all sins and evil desires is to be drowned and die through daily contrition and repentance, and on the other hand, a new person is daily to come forth and rise up to live before God in righteousness and purity forever."[71] Luther firmly believed in the continuity of God's promise of salvation, no matter in what form it first claimed the sinner. He did not attempt to explain why that promise does not come to perfect fruition when it is made. He only knew that sinfulness still besets those who have the promise of salvation, and so he dedicated his every sermon to addressing the need to die to sin and be raised to the life of God's promise day in and day out.

The Three Distinctions of Luther's Hermeneutics

Guiding Luther in his study and proclamation of the biblical message were three essential distinctions that clarified what the writers of Scripture were saying. These three points of orientation included a description of what God says to his human creatures (the distinction of law and gospel), a description of what it means to be human (the distinction of two kinds of righteousness), and a description of the two realms or relationships in which God speaks and human identity is displayed (the distinction of the vertical and horizontal realms. [Luther himself did not use the terms "vertical" and "horizontal" but instead spoke of the "heavenly" and "earthly/temporal" realms, or the realm of God's right hand and the realm of his left hand.]).[72]

The story of Jesus presented the Messiah as both "sacrament" or "gift"— as Savior from sin and evil (which is God's action)—and as example (which reveals the requirements for human performance). "When you have Christ as the foundation and chief benefit of your salvation, then comes the other part, that you grasp him as example and dedicate yourself to serving your neighbor, since you see that God has given you this neighbor. So faith and love work together."[73] Luther tells his postil readers that the gospel for Oculi (third Sunday in Lent), Luke 11:14–23, "like all the gospels, teaches us faith and love, for it presents Christ to us as a most loving savior and helper in every need on the basis of his great love." He pours out his love on believers "so that, according to the nature of love, we should do to others what he has done for

---

(Tübingen: Mohr/Siebeck, 2007), 165–85; and Martin Brecht, "Luthers neues Verständnis der Buße und die reformatorische Entdeckung," *Zeitschrift für Theologie und Kirche* 101 (2004): 281–91.

71. *BSLK* 516–17; *BoC* 360.

72. See summaries of these distinctions in Robert Kolb and Charles P. Arand, *The Genius of Luther's Theology: A Wittenberg Way of Thinking for the Contemporary Church* (Grand Rapids: Baker Academic, 2008), passim; and Robert Kolb, *Martin Luther, Confessor of the Faith* (Oxford: Oxford University Press, 2009), 50–55, 64–68.

73. WA 10.1.1:12.12–15.

us."[74] Christ brings both the free gift of salvation and the renewal of the life that God designed for us to serve the neighbor. This "teaching" could find its proper expression, Luther believed, only if preachers can distinguish what God does for his human creatures and what he expects them to do themselves. He designated these two divine actions as gospel and law respectively. Luther could use the two words in different senses, but when they appear together, they are inseparable yet sharply distinct: what God gives to his human creatures dare never be confused with what he demands from them: their performance. He gives life and core identity as his children; he requires obedience to his plan for human life.

Law and Gospel

This distinction between God's creative, life-bestowing word or way of acting and his prescribing word, which expresses his design for life, guided and framed all of Luther's use of God's Word. He bestows believers' core identity as his children upon them through the gospel, which restores humanity to its original relationship of love and trust in God. In that relationship God expects his children to perform the activities he has designed them to do. Luther began to employ this distinction as his formal hermeneutical guide to biblical interpretation by 1519,[75] and in his lectures on Galatians in 1531 he observed, "Whoever knows well how to distinguish the gospel from the law should give thanks to God and know that he is a real theologian."[76]

Luther does not elaborate on the distinction between law and gospel in his Smalcald Articles of 1537, a programmatic writing setting forth his agenda for discussion at the ecumenical council called by the pope. Yet he does define each word in such a way that its text provides a basis for perceiving how he understands these two inseparable but distinct messages from God. God's law, his expression of his expectations for human performance, has two purposes: to keep order in society through threats of punishment and promise of reward, and to reveal the root of our sin and all its fruits in the sins we commit. The law that keeps order in society often has other than the intended result: it provokes some people to sin worse to prove that they are in charge of their own lives, and it encourages others to rely on their works to please God rather than to use them to love the neighbor.[77] The law's most

74. WA 17.2:214.30–215.3; CP 2:156.
75. See Lowell C. Green, *How Melanchthon Helped Luther Discover the Gospel: The Doctrine of Justification in the Reformation* (Fallbrook, CA: Verdict, 1980), 201–3; Uuras Saarnivaara, *Luther Discovers the Gospel: New Light upon Luther's Way from Medieval Catholicism to Evangelical Faith* (St. Louis: Concordia, 1951), 43–46, 68–71.
76. WA 40.1:207.3–4; *LW* 26:115.
77. Smalcald Articles 3.2; in *BSLK*; and in *BoC* 311–12.

significant function is to reveal God's wrath as the "thunderbolt of God, by means of which he destroys both the open sinner and the false saint and allows no one to be right but drives the whole lot of them into terror and despair." Luther sees the law as the hammer that breaks the rock in pieces (Jer. 23:29). To those whom the law drives to repentance, the Holy Spirit sends the gospel, "the consoling promise of grace," for which the law, like John the Baptist's preaching, has "prepared the way for the Lord, so that they could receive grace and await and accept from him the forgiveness of sins." Luther bases this distinction on Luke 24:47, Christ's command to preach repentance and the forgiveness of sins.[78]

The Wittenberg reformer repeated his contrast often to make it clear to his students and to his lay hearers as well. The distinction of law and gospel as such never became the subject of a major work of his, but he did publish two sermons he had preached at two critical points in the 1530s on this distinction: the first in 1532, when the pure proclamation of the gospel seemed at stake anew in polemics with Roman Catholic theologians, and the second in 1537, amid heated dispute with his own student Johann Agricola, whose dismissal of the role of the law in the Christian life seriously threatened the proper understanding of both law and gospel, in Luther's opinion.[79] He depicted the contrast in various ways throughout his life, but with a great deal of consistency. Quotations from the 1532 sermon may illustrate this: "The law is for the old Adam, the gospel for the troubled conscience."[80] "The law makes me a sinner. The gospel says, 'Your sins are not to harm you, but rather you shall be saved.'"[81] From Galatians 3:23 Luther reminded his hearers that the law had made them its prisoners.[82] Luther's amanuensis and editor Georg Rörer expands the text in the Jena edition of the reformer's works: "The law demands perfect righteousness from everyone." The law tells us "what he commands us to do, what we should do. It demands works from us." That, Luther judged, was easy to accomplish *in causa formali* but very difficult *in causa finali*: it is easy to ascertain what should be done and make some token show of obedience, but it is difficult to fulfill the law's true goal, obedience with a heart that loves God without reservation.[83]

Five years later Luther was deeply concerned about a proper understanding of the law in the face of Agricola's antinomianism. In a 1537 sermon he states that the law reveals "what the human being is, what he was, and what he will

78. Smalcald Articles 3.2; in *BSLK*; and in *BoC* 312–13.

79. See Robert Kolb, "'The Noblest Skill in the Christian Church': Luther's Sermons on the Proper Distinction of Law and Gospel," *Concordia Theological Quarterly* 71 (2007): 301–18, from which much of the following material is taken.

80. WA 36:22.28–30; cf. 36:41.13–14, 30–32.

81. WA 36:19.35–36.

82. WA 36:21.4–25.

83. WA 36:13.25–27; cf. 36:30.19–35.

become once more." Its first description and prescription is "'You shall love God with your whole heart.' . . . You had this treasure in paradise and were created so that you could love God with your whole heart. You have lost that and must return to it. Otherwise you cannot come into God's kingdom." Luther then addresses what he fears—perhaps falsely—is a libertine streak in his disciple's thinking. He rejects the idea that a person who loves neither God nor neighbor and commits grievous sin will suffer no spiritual harm "if you just believe." Sin brings condemnation; to confirm this, Luther cites Galatians 5:19–21; Matthew 5:17–18; 12:36; and Romans 8:3–4; 3:31.[84] Luther's experiences with God's demands continued to make their mark on him: "When I measure my life against the law, I see and feel all the time its opposite in my life."[85] Even believers battle their own sinful desires and therefore need the law's calling them to Christ as "helper and Savior."[86]

Christ helps sinners in two ways. First, he takes our part against God and serves as "the cloak that is thrown over our shame—ours, I say, the cloak over our shame because he has taken our sin and shame upon himself—but in God's sight he is the mercy seat, without sin and shame, pure virtue and honor. Like a brooding hen, he spreads his wings over us to protect us from the hawk, that is, the devil with the sin and death that he causes. God has forgiven this sin for Christ's sake."[87] But the gospel does not only effect the removal of sin. It also bestows upon the believer the power and strength to live as a child of God. By means of that forgiveness, God has bestowed on sinners this new identity as his children. "He not only covers and protects us, but he also wants to nourish and feed us as the hen nourishes and feeds her chicks. That is, he wants to give us the Holy Spirit and the strength to begin to love God and keep his commandments. When Christ demanded that the man give up everything to follow him (Matt. 19:16–25), he was saying that keeping God's commandments involves knowing and having Christ."[88]

The gospel does not demand our works or tell us what to do, Luther proclaimed in 1532. Instead, it tells us to receive, to accept a gift, so that we are passive. That is, the gospel affirms that God promises and says to you:

"This and that I impart to you. You can do nothing for it; you have done nothing for it, but it is my doing." Just as in baptism I did nothing; it is not of my doing in any way. It is God's doing, and he says to me, "Pay attention. I baptize you and wash you of all your sins. Accept it, it is yours." That is what it means to receive a gift. This is the distinction of law and gospel. Through the law a demand is made for what we should do. It presses for our activity for God and

84. WA 45:146.25–147.33.
85. WA 45:151.5–9, 26–28.
86. WA 45:153.26–32.
87. WA 45:153.33–154.14.
88. WA 45:153.15–154.36.

the neighbor. In the gospel we are required to receive a gift. . . . The gospel is pure gift, freely bestowed, salvation.[89]

Because Luther believed that theology is a discipline that trains for practical application, he developed this hermeneutical approach to interpreting God's Word while being quite sensitive to the pastoral care it provided, particularly for anxious consciences. Faith receives a message from heaven so that "the law cannot make its demands on the troubled heart any longer; it has tortured and smothered us enough and must now give place to the gospel, which God's grace and mercy gives us."[90] The gospel directs its hearers to Christ,

> your treasure, your gift, your help, comfort, and Savior. When the conscience weighs heavy upon sinners, forcing them to despair, they cannot tell the difference between God's promises and his command, between what he gives and what he expects. The consciousness of sins or impending death, the stresses of war, pestilence, poverty, shame, and the like, all amplify the voice of the law: "You are lost. I demand this and that from you, but you have not done it and cannot do it." When it comes to this, it terrifies people to death, stomps on them, and they must despair. Whoever can make the distinction in this situation, make it! For here this distinguishing is absolutely necessary![91]

"War, pestilence, poverty, and shame" along with guilt impress upon sinners their need for God and the necessity of fearing, loving, and trusting in him above all that he has made. Every form of evil—whether the misdeeds that sinners perpetrate or the wicked works through which others make them sufferers and victims—terrifies those who have strayed from God and makes them feel the despair and hopelessness of death.[92] Rörer described the goal of the law as pointing to Christ by "terrifying the unrepentant with God's wrath and displeasure."[93] At the end of this sermon Luther speaks of the terrified conscience facing the demands of the law. "Performance is very difficult, particularly when the law wants to put its claim on the conscience. Then a person must grasp the promise, and so that you do not fall under his justice, do not leave it with the law, for whoever denies the gospel must thrash about in the hope that God does have a gospel, that he will not play with me according to the standards of justice but rather will deal with me on the basis of grace for Christ's sake, that he forgives you all that you have failed to do out of grace, and that he will give you what you cannot do."[94] Rörer paraphrases the text: "See to it that you grasp the promise and not let the law gain the upper hand

89. WA 36:14.22–34; cf. 36:31.16–31.
90. WA 36:22.18–21.
91. WA 36:15.30–16.25.
92. WA 36:17.23–24; cf. 36:1–35.
93. WA 36:26.19–20.
94. WA 36:22.30–23.12.

and rule in your conscience. That will bring you under judgment if you deny the gospel. You must cast yourself upon and grasp the word of grace or the gospel of the forgiveness of sins."[95]

Luther practiced this distinction throughout his preaching and teaching. Already in 1518 he had reoriented the pious practice of meditation on Christ's passion toward producing sorrow over the believer's sinfulness and faith in Christ's redeeming death and resurrection.[96] The two sermons found their place in his Church Postil for Good Friday, instructing readers on how to read the story of Christ's suffering. Proper meditation on Christ's suffering begins with terror that brings the conscience to despair because of sin. A sense of personal responsibility for Christ's death arises out of hearing the story of the week before the crucifixion. But the resurrection of Easter morning frees the conscience and cultivates the faith that clings to Christ and rests assured in his forgiveness and love. This comfort fosters a life lived following Christ's example in the battle against all vice and bad habits.[97] To the end of his career, as the two sermons from the 1530s indicate, this pattern of law and gospel shaped and guided Luther's application of the biblical message.

Two Kinds of Righteousness

God's two words, the first that gives life and the second that reveals its shape or proper form, described both his disposition and his mode of acting toward his human creatures. Therefore law and gospel reveal something, though not everything, of God's nature. Luther's corresponding view of what it means to be human expressed itself also in the inseparable but distinct dimensions that he first labeled human righteousness from "outside oneself" (*justitia aliena*) and righteousness that the person practices in his own actions (*justitia propria*). Later he used the terms "passive righteousness" and "active righteousness" for these two dimensions of the human creature. Passive righteousness is what makes people who they are at their core, their fundamental identity. The Creator gives them this identity, and from it proceeds their character. Their character shapes their decisions and actions, which constitute the active righteousness, the actions that God designed them to perform. Luther also calls this distinction of two kinds of human righteousness "our theology" in his Galatians lectures of 1531. As part of his initial orientation to the lectures

95. WA 36:41.37–42.21.

96. *Two Sermons on Christ's Passion*, 1518, WA 1:336–49; and *A Sermon on the Meditation on the Holy Sufferings of Christ*, 1519, WA 2:136–42; *LW* 42:7–14. See Martin Elze, "Das Verständnis der Passion Jesu im ausgehenden Mittelalter und bei Luther," in *Geist und Geschichte der Reformation: Festgabe Hanns Rückert*, ed. Heinz Liebing and Klaus Scholder (Berlin: de Gruyter, 1966), 127–51.

97. WA 2:137.10–142.8; *LW* 42:8–14.

for the students, he explains: "By this we teach a precise distinction between these two kinds of righteousness, the active and the passive, so that morality and faith, works and grace, secular society and religion may not be confused. Both are necessary, but both must be kept within their limits."[98] A simple illustration explains this to the students: "As the earth itself does not produce rain and is unable to acquire it by its own strength, worship, and power but receives it only by a heavenly gift from above, so this heavenly righteousness is given to us by God without our work or merit. As much as the dry earth of itself is able to accomplish and obtain the right and blessed rain, that much can we human creatures accomplish by our own strength and works to obtain that divine, heavenly, and eternal righteousness. Thus we can obtain it only through the free imputation[99] and indescribable gift of God."[100] Indeed, as the dry earth then produces its fruits when the rain empowers it, so the Christian produces the fruits of good works. But for the conscience, especially when it is oppressed by guilt, Luther adds the reminder that it should tell itself, "I do not seek active righteousness. I ought to have and perform it; but I declare that even if I do have and perform it, I cannot trust in it or stand up before the judgment of God on the basis of it. Thus I put myself beyond all active righteousness, all righteousness of my own or of the divine law, and I embrace only the passive righteousness, which is the righteousness of grace, mercy, and the forgiveness of sins."[101]

From his first postils in 1521/22 to his last lectures and sermons in 1545, Luther devoted much of his proclamation of God's Word to the preaching of the law as a call to repentance, as an instrument of death for the sinful identity, to be sure, but also as instruction for the living of daily life. Likewise, during this entire quarter century, he continued distinguishing the two dimensions of what it means to be human, and his focus fell first on the gift of the Christian's identity as child of God: passive righteousness provided the foundation

---

98. WA 40.1:45.24–27; *LW* 26:7. The observation of Emanuel Hirsch ("Initium theologiae Lutheri," in *Der Durchbruch der reformatorischen Erkenntnis bei Luther*, ed. Bernhard Lohse [Darmstadt: Wissenschaftliche Buchgesellschaft, 1968], 75, from Hirsch's *Lutherstudien, II* [Gütersloh: Mohn, 1954], 9–35) that Luther first spoke of passive righteousness after 1525 can only be true in a very literalistic sense. The concept is present from 1519 onward and very apparent in *The Freedom of the Christian* (1520) and *Judgment on Monastic Vows* (1522); see Robert Kolb, "Die Zweidimensionalität des Mensch-Seins: Die zweierlei Gerechtigkeit in Luthers *De votis monasticis Judicium*," in *Luther und das monastische Erbe*, ed. Christoph Bultmann, Volker Leppin, and Andreas Lindner (Tübingen: Mohr Siebeck, 2007), 207–20.

99. Luther appropriated the previously relatively seldom used verb *imputare* from scholastic vocabulary to express what God does in creating a new reality by assigning through his re-creative word a new identity, existence, or persona—righteous child of God—to the sinner. God's imputation, whether interpreted as his regard or way of viewing a person or as his word that creatively assigns a new status or identity, is the basis of reality in Luther's ontology of God's Word.

100. WA 40.1:43.18–25; *LW* 26:6.

101. WA 40.1:42.26–43.15; *LW* 26:6.

for active righteousness. In the mystery of the continuation of sin and evil in believers' lives, the active righteousness was always imperfect, not always visible. In spite of that, passive righteousness, confidence in God's promise of this new identity in Christ, could not help but move those who trust the promise to obedience, the performance of the fruits of faith.

The stories of this relationship between Creator and creature take place within a framework that Luther found in his reading of Scripture. His paradigmatic narrative leaves unanswered precisely *how* the responsibility that God assigns to himself and the responsibility that he assigns to his human creatures fit together, but he attributed to God the almighty power and total responsibility for his world of which his Ockhamist instructors had spoken.[102] At the same time, Luther found—in God's address to the creatures to whom he had given identity as his children and creatures—the demand for performance that expresses that unconditionally and freely given identity. Meir Sternberg has posed the problem: "Does the Almighty control the human heart? If no, where is his omnipotence? If yes, where is man's free will, hardly less novel in terms of ideology and equally underscored at the beginning of Genesis? Biblical narrative gives no straightforward answer because the question is unanswerable, and no consistent treatment except for the consistency of maneuvering between the two extremes."[103]

Luther's sense of the mystery of what it means to be human plotted another solution to the tension between narratives that focus on God's power and responsibility and those that focus on human responsibility and calling to obedience in God's world. Occasionally he at least glanced at this tension as he presented the biblical stories to students and parishioners. He did not presume to unravel the mystery of how God and human creature can both be responsible within the functioning of God's creation, but he did believe that God is at work when it appears as though human agents are in charge. At the same time he nonetheless insisted that God requires human beings to carry out the responsibilities he has given them. Luther found concrete stories to be a suitable way of exploring this tension between God's giving of life and his expectations that human creatures produce the fruits he created them to produce.

The Two Realms

These fruits occur in two realms or relationships, Luther taught, often with the expression "two kingdoms [*Reiche*]." That working terminology was dogmatized by scholars in the nineteenth century, but its usage has been problematic

102. Heiko Augustinus Oberman, *The Harvest of Medieval Theology: Gabriel Biel and Late Medieval Nominalism* (Grand Rapids: Eerdmans, 1967), 36–47.
103. Sternberg, *Poetics*, 110.

for two reasons. Some scholars seriously misinterpreted it as grounds for a separation, not merely a distinction, between the human relationship with God and the human relationship with God's creatures, especially the human. But Luther, unaware that he was fashioning technical vocabulary, did not use the term consistently. Occasionally he could talk about the institutions of church and temporal political government as "two kingdoms." Much more frequently he designated the rule and manner of rule exercised by God and by Satan as the conflict of "two kingdoms." But Luther also quite often used the word "kingdom" to refer to God's design for human life in the inseparable but distinct spheres or realms of the vertical relationship with God and the horizontal relationships with all his other creatures, especially the human ones.[104]

The vertical realm, the relationship between the human creature and God, is the sphere of the human being's core identity. God's chosen children receive their core identity from God's word of gospel. It constitutes their passive righteousness. God's law commands these children to respond to God in this realm with faith, praise, and prayer, and these human "actions" constitute the active righteousness of the vertical sphere. The horizontal realm, the relationship between the individual human creature and all other creatures, is the sphere of the individual's own performance. God's chosen children are moved by the gospel to love God with their obedient response to his commands, which they receive in his law. The passive righteousness that motivates them displays their faith in God's gospel and identifies them as God's children as they act like his children, as they learn the godly pattern of life from the instruction of God's law.

The Distinctions as Key to the Eschatological Conflict

As simple as the relationship between parent and child, as complex as the intricate nature of daily experience in this world, Luther's three distinctions (see above) never earned in his own writings extensive abstract treatment or the kind of theoretical formulation presented here. Yet from some time around 1520 to the end of his life a quarter century later, these distinctions framed and guided his preaching and teaching. Rather than a "breakthrough to the gospel," it is better to speak of his "evangelical maturation." By 1520 this maturation solidified the reformer's framework for biblical interpretation and its application for those under his tutelage. It arose out of his personal experience; his lectures on the Psalms, Romans, Galatians, and Hebrews in the 1510s; and his conversations, academic and pastoral, in those years. These tools served to take the story of God's love in Christ for sinners and convey it to the hearers and readers whose lives the reformer strove to shape in what he

104. Kolb, *Luther, Confessor*, 176–77; Kolb and Arand, *Genius*, 55–71.

perceived to be biblical fashion. These tools convey God's Word as the sword of the Spirit against Satan on the battlefields of human lives. Throughout his career Luther continued to refine and sharpen that sword, but he did not depart from the basic framework for teaching that he had formulated by about 1520.[105]

Luther's metanarrative not only had a plot that focused the audience's attention on the biblical text and on life; it also had a setting. Luther believed that the fall of Satan with his crew and the fall of Adam and Eve with all their descendents had placed the history of humanity within a setting of conflict. This eschatological battle between life-giving truth and deadly deception was ultimately—as is all reality—personal: the clash between God, whose essence is love and mercy, and Satan, who is hell-bent on deceiving and murdering God's human creatures (John 8:44). Because at the root of his creative nature God is a speaker, the war is conducted first of all with words, with truth and deception. God's law continually labels the devil's way of life fraudulent and fatal; his gospel continually re-creates those caught in its death grip. This means that every day once again brings the necessity of dying to sin and being raised to new life in Christ.

This story Luther told each time he mounted the pulpit and entered the lecture hall, and frequently also in conversations. "Luther's style of preaching," according to Elmer Kiessling, combined expository and topical methods. "Rarely is there a really exhaustive textual exposition even in his homilies." Individual lessons, verses, and words of Scripture became "signposts pointing the way to what he considered the great central fact of Christianity, justification by faith."[106] "Justification by faith" in this case stands for the metanarrative that is grounded in God's creating human beings and re-creating sinners into his children through Christ's death and resurrection, which integrates these sinners into God's family through a life-transforming trust in Christ. To be sure, each element of the "metanarrative" can be (and was) used quite apart from the telling of a particular story or repeating a biblical account of God's interaction with his people. But the metanarrative—which stands behind all other forms of Christian proclamation, whether expository or catechetical or admonitory—does assist in applying these accounts from Old and New Testaments to the concrete situation of the hearers in new historical circumstances, as their present or their future makes specific claims on them or subjects them to specific problems. Michael Parsons correctly observes that "'story' as a theological category probably cannot sustain the weight sometimes placed upon it." He notices that Luther and Calvin did not make that clear since for them narrative was not a theological category; rather, they worked with the presupposition that they needed to move beyond the text, "allowing the nar-

105. Kolb, *Luther, Confessor*, 42–71.
106. Elmer C. Kiessling, *The Early Sermons of Luther and Their Relation to the Pre-Reformation Sermon* (Grand Rapids: Zondervan, 1935), 62.

rative to point beyond itself to theology and further to experience of God. . . .
What matters is that believers are pointed beyond the narrative *per se* to their
own encounter with the living and faithful God, through the Word by the
Holy Spirit."[107]

Thus Luther transformed the past of the Bible into a confrontation with
the contemporary sinfulness of hearers and readers and into an encounter
with the love and mercy of their Creator, who had come as their Redeemer,
and who was in the process of sanctifying them through his Word. He illustrated and modeled how faith receives the gift of passive righteousness and
how it shapes the Christian's way of thinking using stories of the people of
faith, such as Abraham and Sarah. The reformer illustrated and modeled how
faith acts out its trust in obedience to God's commands within the structure
of his callings with the stories of these people, such as Joseph and David.
All these elements, or members, of God's story had their specific places and
functions in God's address of the human situation. Re-membering places the
parts of the story in the new context of the present. This recombination of its
elements for relevance to living hearers requires analysis that identifies what
is true and significant, both in the setting of the biblical account and in the
lives of the preacher's contemporary hearers or readers. To this task Luther
dedicated his life.

107. Michael Parsons, *Luther and Calvin on Old Testament Narratives: Reformation Thought and Narrative Text* (Lewiston, NY: Edwin Mellen, 2004), 230–31.

2

LUTHER THE STORYTELLER

The Reformer's Use of Narrative

Martin Luther talked for a living. As professor and as preacher, he mastered the arts of oral communication, a wordsmith whose ear for the German tongue carried onto the printed page. Even if the degree of his influence on the development of modern German is often exaggerated, he set the tone and tenor for his language in ways that few others have done for theirs. This command of the language embraced a feeling for the common vocabulary, for the rhythm, elegance, and turn of phrase that conveyed his intent and perhaps above all demonstrated his eye and ear for the real-life story. In the more than thirty years from which we have Luther's lectures and sermons, his thought matured and the expressions of his ideas changed in some instances; he was constantly experimenting with the proper formulations for addressing new problems and articulating new perspectives. Nonetheless his use of artful language and his telling of stories remained a part of his way of communicating throughout this period. Furthermore, from 1520 or so to the end of his life, his fundamental insights remained in place even though changing circumstances and challenges, along with his own deepening command of the biblical text and the church's tradition, altered the ways in which he verbalized and applied these insights.

History and Humanity—Orality and Textuality

As important as Luther's lectures were for the development of his theology, the sermon may well have served as the medium for his most daring and

constructive experiments in formulating his thought and his interpretation
of Scripture and of daily life. His own sermons come down to the present
in notes recorded by several amanuenses, above all, the official scribe whom
Elector Johann Friedrich appointed and salaried for the task, Georg Rörer,
and by editors—for the most part students who knew the professor's mind
rather well and who fashioned the notes into publishable works. In decisive
fashion his preaching shaped the faith of Wittenberg citizens and hundreds
of students who passed through the city. His published sermons, particularly
the postils—collections of sermons on the appointed lessons for Sundays and
festivals—also became the models for evangelical preaching, the homilies pulled
into the pulpit in a pinch, and the devotional reading of lay families not only
in Luther's own time but even into our own.

Luther therefore took his own sermons seriously and tried to conform them
to the ideal that he once gave his students at the supper table. Good preachers,
Luther told them, are effective teachers, good thinkers, with rhetorical skills,
a good voice, a good memory, and the ability to recognize when to stop. They
are diligent in their preparation, throwing heart and soul into their sermons,
and they must be ready to take criticism, even unfair criticism. They should
remember that they must patiently bear such criticism and dissatisfaction with
their preaching.[1] But above all, preachers must know that the Word of God has
taken them captive and that God has called them to serve him by proclaiming that Word.[2] In his own execution of these guidelines, Luther prepared
an outline before he mounted the pulpit: in Fred Meuser's words, "[Luther's
sermons] were conceived in the study and born in the pulpit." Meuser cites
Paul Althaus, "The [typical sermon of Luther taken as a] whole is not undis-
ciplined, but it is unregulated, uncalculated, alive, like a free-flowing stream."[3]
Just as Luther found himself in conversation with God when he read the text,
so he continued the conversation as he stood between God and his hearers,
with a lively facility for stimulating the conversation about God and human
life, about the course of human history, which is also God's history. God is
present in the story and speaking; he is also present alongside the hearers or
readers, with their hurts and doubts.

In writing and orally, in the pulpit and at the lectern, Luther repeated the
grand narrative that reaches from creation through fall and atonement to the
final judgment. He often did so in simple, careful exposition of the text, often
in a catechetical manner that drew other passages into the interpretation of
a text, but also sometimes with his own way of telling and retelling stories
from several sources, first of all from the Bible itself. Scholars of folklore
initiated the exploration of the telling of stories, a wide range of stories, in

---

1. WA TR 2:531, §2580.
2. Fred Meuser, *Luther as Preacher* (Minneapolis: Augsburg, 1983), 41–42.
3. Ibid., 57, citing Paul Althaus, "Luther auf der Kanzel," *Luther* 3 (1921): 18.

medieval and early modern literature. In their studies Luther often commanded attention, particularly as the originator of a rich tradition that drew upon certain medieval forms, such as the mirror genre (a type of presentation of "examples," models for proper behavior, focused on one particular walk of life), as an organizing framework for stories and observations that cultivated virtues and pious practices. The narrative tradition that Wittenberg instructors bequeathed their students shaped and enriched their preaching as it developed into the Baroque period.[4]

Luther knew that human beings experience life in narrative form. The biblical stories present a picture of human life that can be described in other forms, but the narrative form conveys a special sense of reality as it records the events in which God interacts with his human creatures. The stories of Scripture beg for comparison with the lives of its readers. These readers are invited into the stories of Abraham, Isaac, and Jacob; the lives of Sarah, Rebekah, Leah, and Rachel; the lives of John and Peter, Mary and Mary Magdalene. Luther's Genesis lectures, for example, "reveal that present-day concerns were his primary focus."[5] As a narrator or reteller of the biblical stories, Luther presumed that only an osmotic membrane separated Jerusalem from Wittenberg, ancient Israel from contemporary Saxony.[6] He lost the perceived need to find meaning through allegorizing as his theological conviction grew that the Creator was comfortable with his creation and that real human life, experienced in communion with the Creator, was the place where God's reality rests. He hauled public perceptions of reality out of Plato's ideal, heavenly realm onto the solid ground of the earth and its experiences. So he retold the biblical stories in order to recall and recount what human life is, as God initiates and sustains it.

Mickey Mattox has aptly observed that Luther accepted the invitation of the biblical text to enter into its world of thought "enthusiastically, never hesitating to imagine the biblical characters into his world or himself into

---

4. See the essays in the volume edited by Wolfgang Brückner, *Volkserzählung und Reformation: Ein Handbuch zur Tradierung und Function von Erzählstoffen und Erzählliteratur im Protestantismus* (Berlin: Erich Schmidt, 1974), especially Brückner's own essay, "Historien und Historie: Erzählliteratur des 16. und 17. Jahrhunderts als Forschungsaufgabe," 13–123; also in this volume, on the trajectories launched in Luther's and Melanchthon's Wittenberg, see Bernward Deneke, "Kaspar Goltwurm: Ein lutherischer Kompilator zwischen Überlieferung und Glaube," 124–77; Heidemarie Schade, "Andreas Hondorffs Promptuarium exemplorum," 646–703; and Herbert Wolf, "Erzähltraditionen in homiletischen Quellen," 704–56.

5. John A. Maxfield, *Luther's Lectures on Genesis and the Formation of Evangelical Identity* (Kirksville, MO: Truman State University Press, 2008), 24.

6. What Kathryn Green-McCreight says about Calvin is equally true for Luther: "The absorptive capacity of the biblical text is multi-directional from Jacob to Christ, from Christ to Jacob, from both to us. The multi-directional flow is from the Christ-story outward, both backward and forward." See "'We Are Companions of the Patriarchs' or Scripture Absorbs Calvin's World," *Modern Theology* 41 (1998): 221.

theirs."[7] The reformer presumed that a fundamental resemblance existed between himself and all other readers of Scripture whom the Holy Spirit guided as they read the text. He assumed the role of guide for other readers, whether present parishioners or future preachers, believing that they were joining this company of hearers of prophetic and apostolic proclamation. In that way he replicated the role of the biblical narrator at the same time he examined the text literarily and theologically. Meir Sternberg conjectures that for the biblical narrator "the intervention of the Holy Spirit levels all the barriers that normally divide the far from the near, the private from the public, the interior from the exterior."[8] Luther seems to have presumed something similar. American homileticist John McClure contends that preachers should "*both* 'textualize experience,' thereby inviting their hearers to see their lives on the terms of the biblical narrative, *and* 'experientialize the text,' thereby allowing current experience to illustrate the meaning and ongoing significance of the text."[9] Luther did both.

Heinrich Bornkamm contended that Luther could do so because he experienced in Old Testament texts a "mirror of life" as it took place in sixteenth-century Germany: "He was very much at home [in the Old Testament] because it was a peasant world with many characteristics which he knew full well. It had breadth of scope and varied folk life and genuine folk religion. This setting gave him much livelier examples, warnings, and admonitions for the proclamation of his message to his own people than the New Testament setting did."[10] In fact, however, passages from the gospel lessons did supply him with many concrete insights directly applicable as both consolation and warning for his "beloved Germans." Michael Parsons declares that, like Calvin, Luther believed that "the way in which [God] is portrayed in [Old Testament] narratives is *actually* the way he is in his economic relations in the sixteenth century. . . . The way in which God is in present experience is the way he is in Old Testament history. . . . Both Reformers can assume that the Old Testament believer and the New Testament believer together with their contemporary believers in the sixteenth century (and beyond) have virtually the same relationship to God in Christ through the Word."[11] Therefore Luther explained biblical texts

7. Mickey Leland Mattox, *"Defender of the Most Holy Matriarchs": Martin Luther's Interpretation of the Women of Genesis in the "Enarrationes in Genesin," 1535–45* (Leiden: Brill, 2003), 1.

8. Meir Sternberg, *The Poetics of Biblical Narrative: Ideological Literature and the Drama of Reading* (Bloomington: Indiana University Press, 1985), 76.

9. John McClure, in a review of *Preaching Jesus*, by Charles Campbell, *Journal for Preachers* 21, no. 2 (1998): 36; as quoted by David J. Lose, *Confessing Jesus Christ: Preaching in a Postmodern World* (Grand Rapids: Eerdmans, 2003), 123.

10. Heinrich Bornkamm, *Luther and the Old Testament*, trans. Eric W. Gritsch and Ruth C. Gritsch (Philadelphia: Fortress, 1969), 11; cf. 11–44.

11. Michael Parsons, *Luther and Calvin on Old Testament Narratives: Reformation Thought and Narrative Text* (Lewiston, NY: Edwin Mellen, 2004), 229.

out of contemporary German life, as in the case of Lot's incest in a drunken state (Gen. 19:31–33). With a rather untypical indulgence, he regarded Lot's indiscretion as an inadvertent rather than a purposeful sin, similar to a young boy's imprudently setting a fire and being spared by the law because he clearly was not an arsonist. Lot reminded Luther of those involved in "a brawl in which angry people engage in a fight" and are then excused by civil authorities for an imprudent sin due to circumstances. The report records not "impossible things" but rather things that are "natural and in harmony with experience."[12] Likewise, Luther evaluated or explained contemporary German life on the basis of biblical texts. The coexistence of evil with the appearance of the good in Noah's time, implied in Genesis 6:11–12, should not surprise students, who could recognize the same pattern in the Roman church.[13]

To be sure, Luther had not always read the Bible in this manner; he thought that he could remember a time when he could not bring the stories into real life but regarded them as no different from Livy's historical accounts.[14] As his written legacy began to take shape, however, his lively recollections of the stories from Scripture usually demonstrated this similarity of ancient Israel and contemporary Germany. He fashioned credible comparisons and correlations between his own world and that of the prophets or apostles. Bornkamm argues that Luther's projection of his own struggles into the events of the Old Testament stand in contrast to Puritan attempts to impose Old Testament models rigidly upon their own time, a contrast of "creative spirit and artificial reconstruction."[15] That judgment stems from a stereotypical misrepresentation of Puritan preaching.[16] Like Luther, Puritan preachers strove to convey God's will through God's commands in Scripture and through biblical examples. They too strove to avoid diluting the significance of these ancient models of God's people for providing a general pattern and specific instruction for people of any age. But it is true that Luther tried to steer clear of forcing current events into rigid models from Bible times. Instead, he used models of human behavior from one time to explain the other, without squeezing either into the other, even though he did sometimes fall into this trap, as have biblical interpreters in all times.

This meant that he faced the temptation to impose his own conception of life on the biblical reports and also to impose a literal reading of the text as precise prescription for his hearers. His writings indicate that he tried to

---

12. WA 43:96.36–97.6; *LW* 3:309–10.

13. WA 42:304.28–32; *LW* 2:60.

14. WA 42:543.12–17; *LW* 2:391.

15. Bornkamm, *Old Testament*, 27.

16. Among many studies that give another assessment of "Puritan" preaching, which admittedly does cover a wide spectrum of treatments and approaches to Scripture, see Thomas H. Luxon, *Literal Figures: Puritan Allegory and the Reformation Crisis in Representation* (Chicago: University of Chicago Press, 1995).

avert both strategies when he believed them inappropriate. Certainly the latter seemed to him a danger, and he admonished his hearers of the necessity of sorting out which stories offered them models for their own actions and which provided warnings against courses of action that they should not follow. He also contended that some biblical stories reveal not God's exemplary actions but his extraordinary—Luther sometimes called them "miraculous"—interventions; for instance, in the lives of some Old Testament figures. These could not be used as excuses for breaking out of the framework that God's plan for usual, normal human life had set. Thomas Müntzer and other peasant leaders in the revolt of 1525 had used the examples of Abram's freeing Lot by the sword (Gen. 14) and David's battling the Syrians (2 Sam. 8:3–8; 10:6–19) in this manner.[17] Luther warned, "The examples of the saints and of the children of God must not be understood as something to imitate and as rule except when they follow the rule laid down in the Word."[18]

As with every Christian who has ever spoken the biblical message to others, Luther mixed his own predilections, prejudices, preoccupations, and problems with the message of the texts he treated in trying to connect his hearers and readers with the biblical world and its revelation of God and of what it means to be human. Thus as he strove to remain faithful to the story as it was told, he retold it within the framework of his own world. He recognized the discontinuities of human history on occasion, but usually he believed that human nature exhibited the same characteristics in his own day that it did in Abraham's or Peter's. His combination of this understanding of the biblical story and its stories with a lively and fertile theological imagination, an ear that caught the cadences and contours of the German language, and a sensitivity to the rhythms of daily life—all this made him a storyteller par excellence. Therefore his message in lecture and sermon, as well as in printed works of several genres, shaped elements in the thinking of generations in many parts of the world.

Some of the most influential voices in the development of narrative theology in the United States have found the Wittenberg reformer's employment of his metanarrative objectionable because it ignores the text's intended message and imposes on it his own—allegedly idiosyncratic—interpretive framework; but their suggestion is misleading.[19] Indeed, everyone who seeks to take ma-

---

17. WA 42:531.7–13; *LW* 2:374. WA 42:570.24–30; *LW* 3:30–31. WA 43:61.33–63.5; *LW* 3:260–62. WA 43:640.32–641.18; *LW* 5:307–8. WA 43:653.12–34; *LW* 5:325–26.

18. WA 43:322.39–41; *LW* 4:261.

19. Mark Ellingsen, "Luther as Narrative Exegete," *Journal of Religion* 63 (1983): 397–98; at least his citations seeming to support this interpretation do not confirm it. Brevard Childs, *Introduction to the Old Testament as Scripture* (Philadelphia: Fortress, 1979), 32, does discuss Luther at that point but does not address his use of narrative; nor does Hans Frei, *The Eclipse of Biblical Narrative* (New Haven: Yale University Press, 1974), 19, although on 20–21 Frei misrepresent Luther with his claim that Luther saw "only those portions of scripture as genuinely true and authoritative which proclaimed or clearly implied this awesome tension between

terial from the archive to the streets has to answer the "So what?" question, and Luther's readers and hearers were made aware that he was digressing, as in his sermon on the wise men in the Christmas Postil of 1522, "in order to reply to false teachers and human teachings and to preserve the Scriptures in their purity."[20] As Luther addressed human life and how human beings are constituted and function he tended to find the significance of all human activity within the framework of his distinctions that clarified what God is doing. Through the paradigmatic narratives of Scripture, Luther sought to reconstruct the worldview of his hearers and readers and to create for them a new identity as God's children and conversation partners.

Medieval Traditions of Preaching

The medieval modes of preaching that Luther had learned in the monastery had indeed featured narrative styles of preaching, based not only on biblical stories but also, prominently, on the stories of the saints.[21] Bishops and monks had borne the burden of preaching, so far as extant records indicate, since many parish priests could not. The founding of the preaching orders of the thirteenth century expanded the number and frequency of sermons available to the common people. By Luther's time manuals of preaching were circulating, particularly among the monks, especially mendicants who traveled with their sermons across the landscape. The fifteenth century witnessed the appearance of a number of postils, collections of sermons treating the appointed lessons for Sundays and festivals. The endowment of chairs for municipal preachers reflected the growth of a thirst for understanding the Christian faith that went beyond reliance on ritual performed, as it often seemed, for its own sake.[22] All these venues helped cultivate biblical knowledge but even more a familiarity with the miracles and martyrdoms of the saints. Many sermons

---

law and gospel," in contrast to Calvin's viewing "God's Word equally pervading all scriptural texts." Luther viewed the entire Bible as God's place of speaking but did distinguish passages that address hearers of his own time directly with law and gospel as more useful. See Robert Kolb, "The Relationship between Scripture and the Confession of the Faith in Luther's Thought," in *Kirkens bekejennelse in historisk og aktuelt perspektiv*, ed. Torliev Austand, Tormod Engelsviken, and Lars Østner (Trondheim: Tapir Akademisk Forlag, 2010), 53–62.

20. WA 10.1.1:592.14–16; CP 348.

21. For an excellent overview of the literature on medieval preaching and the current state of the discussion of the topic, see *The Sermon*, ed. Beverly Mayne Kienzle (Turnhout: Brepols, 2000). See also Alfred Niebergall, "Die Predigt des germanischen Mittelalters," in "Die Geschichte der christlichen Predigt," *Leiturgia: Handbuch des evangelischen Gottesdienstes*, ed. Karl Ferdinand Müller and Walter Blankenburg, vol. 2 (Kassel: Stauda, 1955), 236–56; and John W. Frymire, *The Primacy of the Postils: Catholics, Protestants, and the Dissemination of Ideas in Early Modern Germany* (Leiden: Brill, 2010), 10–25.

22. Elmer C. Kiessling, *The Early Sermons of Luther and Their Relation to the Pre-Reformation Sermon* (Grand Rapids: Zondervan, 1935), 13–41.

served to cultivate a faith at least partially focused on their intervention in heaven and their powers on earth.[23] Such stories served one of two purposes. Some directed the attention and the prayers of the people to those holy saints who exercised special power in providing for the welfare of common believers. Others served as models for good works, both sacred and everyday, that the common Christians were to perform. Luther rejected the theological basis of the former; he restricted the second kind of recounting the past largely to the biblical stories and placed them into the framework of his own understanding of Christian living, based in trust in Christ, expressed in love for others as well as devotion to God.[24]

To be sure, the medieval heritage of biblical interpretation, as variegated as it was, offered Luther good resources and examples of how to treat texts. Luther, like all exegetes, stood in the midst of a long conversation that "predisposed" his reading of individual passages of Scripture.[25] With the tradition he coupled the new humanistic methods that were clearing the way for a more serious historical look at the text.[26] One marked difference in Luther's expository technique lies in the relative decline in his use of "allegory" and "figural interpretation." Luther consciously referred to his use of the tradition of figural interpretation[27] and sometimes spoke critically of "allegorical" interpretations (but used them nonetheless). Although his "abandonment" of "allegory" is often heralded as his great exegetical breakthrough, his continued use of some allegorical flourishes in lecturing and preaching is often ignored or underestimated.[28] Also, his more important hermeneutical contribution is his development of his own formulation of the biblical metanarrative within the context of applying the distinction between law and gospel to everyday life.

Mark Ellingsen identifies the "allegorical" method as using biblical models to discover abstract truths that lie beyond historical experience in a "deeper,

23. See Michael Menzel, "Predigt und Predigtorganisation im Mittelalter," *Historisches Jahrbuch* 111 (1991): 342–84; Donald Weinstein and Rudolph M. Bell, *Saints and Society: The Two Worlds of Western Christendom, 1000–1700* (Chicago: University of Chicago Press, 1982); Peter Brown, *The Cult of the Saints: Its Rise and Function in Latin Christianity* (Chicago: University of Chicago Press, 1981); Kiessling, *Early Sermons*, 36–38.

24. Meuser, *Luther as Preacher*, 45–48.

25. Parsons, *Luther and Calvin*, vii; cf. Timothy J. Wengert, *Philip Melanchthon's "Annotationes in Johannem" in Relation to Its Predecessors and Contemporaries* (Geneva: Droz, 1987), 17–19.

26. See Niebergall, *Leiturgia* 2:257–75; and Albrecht Beutel, "Evangelische Predigt vom 16. bis 18. Jahrhundert," in *TRE* 27 (Berlin: de Gruyter, 1997), 296–98.

27. Sabine Hiebsch, *Figura ecclesiae: Lea und Rachel in Martin Luthers Genesispredigten* (Münster: Lit-Verlag, 2002), 73–91.

28. Compare, e.g., the *allegoria archae* of the 1527 publication of the sermons of 1523, WA 24:175–80; in his lectures on Gen. 6–8, almost two decades later, he uses allegory more sparingly, but he discusses the proper use of allegory in connection with the Noah accounts; see WA 42:367.3–377.24; *LW* 2:150–64.

fundamental, intuitive experience of God";[29] he distinguishes such allegorizing from narratives of the concrete course of human life. The latter do not always allow for neat application by imitation but nonetheless foster an attitude of person-to-person trust in God and a perception of his will that propels believers into the struggle against evil on their own behalf and on behalf of neighbors. In 1532, treating Christ's descent into hell on Easter eve, Luther rejected both an allegorizing of the descent and a literal interpretation that depicted locks and gates and a prison of wood or iron.[30] His literary sensitivity led him to try to sense the author's intent and sort out the precise use of language at hand in a text. He continued to use "figural" interpretations of the people who inhabited biblical narratives, particularly Old Testament individuals, such as Leah and Rachel, who could be used to point to a New Testament truth.[31]

The Wittenberg reformer's comments on the examples or models of the pious life that he found in the text fell in line with a tradition of literal interpretation stretching back to the early twelfth century, as Christopher Ocker has shown.[32] Ocker argues that at least some late medieval expositors of Scripture had departed from monastic predecessors who, following a Platonic model for interpreting language and reality, had tended to separate the literal reading of the text from the internal, divine truths that "cast their shadows on the reader's world, allowing the reader to move from shadow to image and from image to divine source." Alongside this allegorical approach, in the century or two before Luther, a developing attitude associated the spiritual meaning of the text with its literal sense based upon "the communion of (divine and human) writers with (past and present) readers, and a sense of continuity between all religious writers and readers. This attitude assumed a continuity of meaning that extended subjectively and inter-subjectively outside the Bible" and "a conviction of profound similarity, an aesthetic similarity of literatures, a shared biblical poetic." This poetic joined the external world and the literal text of the Bible to the inner experience of readers and hearers as they encountered there the truth of God.[33]

One possible source for Luther's viewing the text in this way may have been one of his predecessors in the Augustinian monastery in Erfurt, Hermann of Schildesche, who had inhabited his cloister briefly nearly two hundred years before Luther's arrival there. Hermann's *Compend on the Meanings of Sacred*

29. Mark Ellingsen, *The Integrity of Biblical Narrative: Story in Theology and Proclamation* (Minneapolis: Fortress, 1990), 10–14.

30. WA 37:63.5–64.2; *HP* 1:481.

31. Their prophetic representation of the church in Luther's sermons on Genesis has been analyzed by Hiebsch, *Figura*. See also David C. Steinmetz, "Luther and the Blessing of Judah," *LuJ* 71 (2004): 159–78, on Luther's figural treatment of Old Testament passages.

32. Christopher Ocker, *Biblical Poetics before Humanism and Reformation* (Cambridge: Cambridge University Press, 2002), 22.

33. Ibid., 216.

Scripture set forth an extensive analysis of the historical and nonhistorical divisions of the literal sense of Scripture and the use of persons or events as prefigurations of the future in each.[34] Whether Luther gained the resources to develop his approach to reading the biblical text from Hermann or from others, Ocker believes that late medieval interpreters, Hermann included, "lacked a literary method for handling the narrative construction of the Bible as a whole."[35] Luther found such a method in his understanding of God's conversation with his human creatures launched by God at creation and continued after the fall into sin, a conversation aimed at recultivating the vineyard of his people through the life of repentance. This conversation was taking place when he preached and lectured, Luther believed. He intended his preaching and teaching to be an instrument through which God grasped his hearers and engaged their entire lives.[36]

That he presumed this kind of communication would function in this effective way is attributed by Ocker, at least in part, to "changing religious and social expectations." Luther above all fits Ocker's profile of those who rejected the idea that divine knowledge belonged to the privileged few in the monastic estate. "Any well-intending reader could place himself into the conversation of God, prophets, apostles, and saintly commentators, inserting himself into a textual scene that encompassed sacred literature broadly conceived (the Bible and commentaries together), inserting himself like a patron figure at the foot of a painted cross or before a painted *pieta*."[37] Luther believed that the Holy Spirit was doing more than simply bringing hearers to observe what God was saying and doing. He believed that the Spirit was drawing all his hearers and readers into conversation with God by drawing them into the biblical story and making them hearers of the prophets and apostles, of the living voice of the Spirit.

Assessing Luther's retelling of the biblical stories reveals that he sometimes stood with the congregation, peering into the biblical world, and sometimes entered into the biblical world to speak out of its context to his own contemporaries or to draw his hearers or readers into the environment of ancient Israel and Hellenistic Palestine. Often he pointed out details as if he were standing outside the stage of biblical history. But his 1522 treatise on "receiving both kinds in the sacrament" also reveals his vision of the task before him and his

34. Ibid., 94–106.

35. Ibid., 21–22, 211.

36. Ulrich Nembach, *Predigt des Evangeliums: Luther als Prediger, Pädagoge und Rhetor* (Neukirchen-Vluyn: Neukirchener Verlag, 1972), 62. Unfortunately, Ulrich Asendorf's study of *Die Theologie Martin Luthers nach seinen Predigten* (Göttingen: Vandenhoeck & Ruprecht, 1988) does not discuss the role of narratives as a mode of presenting God's Word in Luther's sermons and mentions the Genesis sermons infrequently; indeed, these references, with but one exception, do not refer to the material treated in this chapter.

37. Ocker, *Biblical Poetics*, 217.

readers as a repetition of the pilgrimage that the ancient people of God had made as they retraced their steps from exile in Babylon to Jerusalem, with God as present for them as he had been on Sinai or in the pillar of fire and cloud. Yet Luther did recognize that his own contemporaries still had a long way to go in leaving behind their medieval religious habits on their way to a life faithful to God.[38] Thus Luther's preaching, including his use of biblical stories, did more than prepare hearers for the sacraments, where God bestowed grace. Preaching itself delivered grace sacramentally by cultivating trust in God, which constitutes the believer's new identity and new relationship with God.

Current Narrative Scholarship and Luther's Storytelling

The focus on narrative that has aided scholarly discussions of many kinds, in sociological and psychological research as well as history and literature, has enriched the discussion of Christian theology from several angles. This has happened in part because of scholarly fad and fashion. But what is more important, it has taken place because of the very nature of biblical revelation. As has been argued above, narrative permeates the biblical understanding of reality. Given Luther's rich use of stories, it is not surprising that the insights of those who have studied the several functions of narrative in Christian thought help illumine Luther's own way of practicing the discipline of theology and the art of preaching.

Historian of religions Ninian Smart places narratives or stories—he labels them "myths"—among the six fundamental dimensions of all religions, which also include experiential, doctrinal, ethical, ritual, and social elements. According to his analytical method, each dimension is interrelated with all the others, though each dimension assumes a different significance within each religion.[39] It is clear that for Christianity the narratives of God's actions as Creator, Redeemer, and Sanctifier form the basis of God's revelation of himself to his human creatures. Therefore Christian doctrinal content proceeds out of the actions of God in history and the interpretation of his actions given to the prophets and apostles. (Indeed, Kevin Vanhoozer cogently argues that Christian doctrine, reflecting the biblical view of reality in history, is best understood not merely as divinely revealed principles but also as direction or participation in the continuing conversation that God initiates in Scripture.[40]) Christian ritual arises from the stories of what God has done for his people. Christian ethics reflects the model of human behavior projected in the life of

---

38. WA 10.2:39.13–15; *LW* 36:264.

39. Ninian Smart, *Worldviews: Crosscultural Explorations of Human Beliefs* (New York: Scribner, 1983), esp. 79–95.

40. Kevin J. Vanhoozer, *The Drama of Doctrine: A Canonical-Linguistic Approach to Christian Theology* (Louisville: Westminster John Knox, 2005).

Jesus Christ and the faithful people of God even though the explicit statements of principles of behavior also become part of the biblical chronicle.
Christian community reflects the historic experience of God's people. The
narrative of God's saving Word in action as it reaches into individuals' daily
life to claim them for God functions as the "paradigmatic narrative" that
bestows a new identity as child of God and thus frames the experience of
every Christian.[41]

Within Christian theology, systematic theologian Hans Frei played a key role
among those at Yale University who laid the foundations of the exploration
of narrative's roles and functions. His analysis of the shift from precritical
to critical exegesis in the eighteenth and nineteenth centuries begins thus:
"Western Christian reading of the Bible in the days before the rise of historical
criticism . . . was usually strongly realistic, i.e. at once literal and historical,
and not only doctrinal or edifying,"[42] though for Luther it certainly was that
too. Like a stream of biblical preachers and commentators, above all Augustine, that had preceded him, the Wittenberg reformer "envisioned the real
world as formed by the sequence told by the biblical stories . . . from creation
to the final consummation to come."[43] Luther's practice in using Scripture
also reflected Frei's observation about the reformer's day and age: "Since the
world truly rendered by combining biblical narratives into one was indeed
the one and only real world, it must in principle embrace the experience of
any present age and reader."[44] Frei's colleague George Lindbeck said it this
way: the Yale school approach of intertextuality "redescribes reality with the
scriptural framework rather than translating scripture into extrascriptural
categories. It is the text, so to speak, which absorbs the world, rather than
the world [which absorbs] the text."[45] However, as Kevin Vanhoozer observes,
in practice Lindbeck renders the biblical text meaningless apart from its use
by the community. Vanhoozer depicts the relationship rather as reciprocal,
in which the text directs the church's life and determines its teaching even
as the community applies and delivers it in new times and places.[46] Luther's
understanding is closer to Vanhoozer's formulation than Lindbeck's. To be
sure, Luther moved from the sequence of biblical stories into the continuing
struggle between human sin and God's liberating mercy, but his interpretation of the biblical world viewed the lives of patriarchs, prophets, and contemporaries of Jesus and Paul within the context of his own experience of

41. See Charlotte Linde's theory of "paradigmatic narrative" at n. 22 in the introduction
above.
42. Frei, *Eclipse of Biblical Narrative*, 1.
43. Ibid.
44. Ibid., 3.
45. George A. Lindbeck, *The Nature of Doctrine: Religion and Theology in a Post-Liberal
Age* (Philadelphia: Westminster, 1984), 118.
46. Vanhoozer, *Drama of Doctrine*, 95–97.

human life and his own experience within the biblical writers' depiction of the world. Indeed, for Luther it was God who spoke in the biblical text and who determined its meaning.

Frei acknowledged his debt to the literary theory of German-Jewish émigré scholar Erich Auerbach.[47] Auerbach used the contrast between Greek epic ways of telling tales of human life and the biblical record as the basis for his observations about the representation of reality in Western literature. He classified biblical narratives as intrinsically historical in intent (even though he himself did not necessarily regard them as true in point of fact), contrasting them with those of Homer, and found a deep cleft separating the two literary traditions. Readers gain full benefit from the story of Odysseus, Penelope, and Euryclea, Auerbach argued, without being compelled to believe that these figures actually existed, "but the Biblical narrator . . . had to believe in the objective truth of the story of Abraham's sacrifice" of Isaac, and "had to believe in it passionately." Auerbach labeled this not as an orientation toward "realism" but toward truth. "The Bible's claim to truth is not only far more urgent than Homer's, it is tyrannical—it excludes all other claims. The world of the Scripture stories is not satisfied with claiming to be a historically true reality—it insists that it is the only real world, is destined for autocracy. . . . The Scripture stories do not, like Homer's, court our favor; . . . they seek to subject us, and if we refuse to be subjected we are rebels."[48] "The reality of the Old Testament presents itself as complete truth with a claim to sole authority."[49]

And yet the biblical text's hegemony over its readers is not exercised so simply as this might make it seem. Biblical narratives depict human life through stories full of "gaps," Auerbach emphasized. In addition, the entire Old Testament presents something less than one continuing story. It is episodic, and to harvest a unitary message requires an interpreter even though the message does emerge clearly from the texts.

> As a composition, the Old Testament is incomparably less unified than the Homeric poems, it is more obviously pieced together—but the various components all belong to one concept of universal history and its interpretation. . . . The greater the separateness and horizontal disconnection of the stories and groups of stories in relation to one another, compared with the *Iliad* and the *Odyssey*, the stronger is their general vertical connection, which holds them all together and which is entirely lacking in Homer. Each of the great figures of the Old Testament, from Adam to the prophets, embodies a moment of this vertical connection. God chose and formed these men to the end of embodying his essence and will.[50]

47. Frei, *Eclipse of Biblical Narrative*, vii.
48. Erich Auerbach, *Mimesis: The Representation of Reality in Western Literature*, trans. Willard R. Trask (Princeton: Princeton University Press, 1953), 14–15.
49. Ibid., 16.
50. Ibid., 17.

Auerbach therefore maintained that the biblical text demands an interpreter who will retell its stories for new hearers in new times and places, filling in the gaps on the basis of the claim of the text that it provides real experiences as a true account of authentic human life.

Luther slipped easily into this role. He accepted the challenge that Meir Sternberg later saw in this style of narrative: the "ubiquity of gaps about character and plot exposes to us our own ignorance: history unrolls as a continuum of discontinuities, a sequence of non sequiturs [for which Luther's understanding of sin and evil provided something of an account], which challenge us to repair the omissions by our native wit."[51] Luther filled the gaps in the biblical narrative with explanations of how God works in behalf of, and what he requires from, his human creatures while also illuminating the mysterious nature of the continuation of sin and evil in the lives of the baptized in the space provided by these gaps. He did so on the strength of his understanding of the biblical metanarrative. The hearer has no illusion of being able to take control of knowledge or direction in such situations: the children of God can only listen and hearken to the Word of the Lord.

Auerbach's comment alludes to two other significant claims he made that also illumine Luther's attitude toward and use of Scripture. First, the biblical narrative engages the reader in the midst of daily life as it really takes place. Auerbach notes the "domestic realism, the representation of daily life" in the Old Testament stories. Homer's stories remain "in the peaceful realm of the idyllic, whereas, from the very first, in the Old Testament stories, the sublime, tragic, and problematic take shape precisely in the domestic and commonplace."[52] "Far from seeking, like Homer, merely to make us forget our own reality for a few hours, it seems to overcome our reality; we are to fit our own life into its world, feel ourselves to be elements in its structure of universal history."[53] This engagement with reality takes place because "a part of the genius of these stories is that they depict neither simple heroes nor, consistently, upper class life, as Homer did. The Old Testament figures . . . can fall much lower in dignity."[54] To be sure, neither Abraham nor David was the chariot mechanic next door. But their situations, dilemmas, temptations, and trials resonate through the lives of the commoners of every age. Biblical people "are bearers of the divine will, and yet they are fallible, subject to misfortune and humiliation—and in the midst of misfortune and in their humiliation their acts and words reveal the transcendent majesty of God. There is hardly one of them who does not, like Adam, undergo the deepest humiliation—and hardly one who is not deemed worthy of God's personal intervention and personal inspiration."[55] Peter rep-

51. Sternberg, *Poetics*, 47.
52. Auerbach, *Mimesis*, 22.
53. Ibid., 15.
54. Ibid., 22.
55. Ibid., 18.

resents precisely this kind of person as well.[56] In addition, Abraham's reception of the promise of God, David's psalms of both lament and praise, and Peter's fear-filled denial and his confessions of faith are reflected in the experiences of the faithful through history.

Among the "gaps" that challenge modern readers of the Bible, the absence of insights into the inner workings of the minds of its figures looms large. The biblical narratives do offer verbal exchanges at points, particularly in the Abraham stories, and later biblical writers also interpreted the life of Abraham for their readers. Nehemiah began a summary of biblical history from the mouths of the Levites that recounted in prayer, "You are the LORD God, who chose Abram and brought him out of Ur of the Chaldeans and named him Abraham. You found his heart faithful to you, and you made a covenant with him" (Neh. 9:7–8 NIV). The exodus, the giving of the law, and the rebellions of Israel against God also won mention in this prayer. But Nehemiah did not feel compelled to fill in gaps in this instance, for the people of his time knew the stories well. Either they needed no further details, or they supplied them from their own memories or imaginations as they repeated the stories in their homes and synagogues. When Paul recounted the story of Abraham, he also presumed more extensive knowledge of the story than he related (Gal. 3:6–9; Rom. 4:1–25). Likewise, the writer to the Hebrews recapitulated the useful details of the Abraham accounts, but he also used his imagination to fill in one gap from Genesis 22 when he wrote that Abraham took Isaac to Mount Moriah because he believed that "God could even raise the dead, and so in a manner of speaking he did receive Isaac back from death" (Heb. 11:17–19 NIV). Luther could give a brief summary of a story, presuming that his hearers had some familiarity with its details, but he often felt the urge to read the minds of patriarchs and apostles alike and fill in the conversation or the events with his own imagination.

Auerbach's second significant claim is that "if the text of the Biblical narrative, then, is so greatly in need of interpretation on the basis of its own content, its claim to absolute authority forces it still further in the same direction."[57] Sternberg attributes the biblical text's authority and hold on its readers to two factors. First, he posits the omniscience of the biblical narrator, a view of his stories that is derived from the omniscience of God, whose servant and voice the narrator is.[58] This sets biblical writers "poles apart from the Homeric or

---

56. Ibid., 40–46.
57. Ibid., 15.
58. Sternberg, *Poetics*, 12–13. Sternberg (118) describes the connection between the biblical presentation of the person of God and the authors' art in depicting him and his actions: "The building of supernatural premises into the action, the preference of the dramatic method over commentary, the foreshadowing-fulfillment structure of repetition, the manifold patterning of redundancy, speech as creative act, the manipulation of sequence in units ranging from the entire Bible to a verse, similarly variable play of perspectives, forms of serialization, shifts between

Near Eastern" way of writing. Sternberg attributes this contrast to a disparity between different cultural ways of trying to define ontological reality: the
Greeks staked their success on human exploration or contemplation of the
Ultimate, and Israel's neighbors staked such success on human wit and wisdom,
but the Hebrew prophets listened for the word of the Lord.[59] This disparity
rested even more fundamentally on the absence in the thought of most Greek
thinkers of a Creator, a personal God, who functions as the Ultimate and
Absolute—and on the Hebrew consciousness of the overwhelming presence of
"the LORD," the God of Abraham, Isaac, and Jacob. Sternberg observes that
the Old Testament narratives are first and foremost the stories of this God,
his actions, and his address of his human creatures. Parsons agrees, noting
that for Luther, as for Calvin, "God is always the main and pivotal character
of Old Testament narrative," indeed of the entire Bible.[60] His actions form the
plot of its story. That plot reveals his character, his very essence.[61]

As the biblical writers bring together what Sternberg labels their three
functional principles of ideology, historiography, and aesthetics, the former
usually controls the latter two. The Old Testament narratives present a "history [that] unfolds a theology in action—one distinctively grounded in God's
control and providence; . . . history-writing doubles as a sacred contract,
uniquely explaining the processes of time by reference to a covenantal relation with divinity."[62] Luther treated biblical narration in this way, taking for
granted that readers of Scripture were engaging and engaged by the person of
the Almighty Father. He presumed that his hearers were real human creatures
who had interacted with God.[63] He trusted the biblical reports regarding
God's power and reliability and as reflecting the course of real human living.
Twentieth-century narrative theory allows for a separation of the viewpoint
of narrator and implied author,[64] but no such separation existed for Luther.
Whatever voice recited the story—Luther presumed that it was the voice of
the actual author—gave the point of view of the utterly reliable Creator.

Sternberg observes that in its narratives the Old Testament seldom tells the
moral or theological significance of the reported events. Though this is largely

---

overt and covert providence, spatiotemporal bounding, and so on: the strategy coordinating such
an array bespeaks an ideological crux of the first magnitude. Anchored in this composition,
moreover, the effect and the narrative stance of intermediacy from which it is generated afford
an equally powerful explanation for a set of other measures, great and small. Above all, their
ideological imperative accounts for the narrator's drastic self-effacement in the handling of a
plot that foregrounds God's omnipotence."

59. Ibid., 88–89; cf. 41–46.
60. Parsons, *Luther and Calvin*, 232.
61. Vanhoozer, *Drama of Doctrine*, 30—43.
62. Sternberg, *Poetics*, 44–45.
63. Heinrich Bornkamm makes this point in *Old Testament*, 6–7, 261.
64. Wayne C. Booth, *The Rhetoric of Fiction*, 2nd ed. (Chicago: University of Chicago
Press, 1981), 3–4, 151–65.

true, those narratives are set in the context of such elucidations of God and human life, in the covenants of the Torah and the prophetic interpretation and application that followed. Furthermore, Sternberg himself demonstrates that the Old Testament narratives carry with them the clear confession of the God of Abraham, Isaac, and Jacob as Lord of the universe and the clear presumption that human creatures are bound to hearken to his word. This does make the texts something other than ideologically neutral. Luther's application of the narratives did not simply retell the story and presume that sixteenth-century hearers would understand. His use of the narratives involved extensive interpretive comment at several levels.

Biblical narratives are continually revealing something of the nature of God and the nature of the human beings with whom he deals. The formulation of "doctrine" from narrative has certain challenges. It is not always clear when a story illustrates what is right and righteous and when it illustrates what is exceptional or wrong; more than apodictic statements or value-shaped pronouncements about God and humanity, stories leave much to the interpretive judgment of the one who retells them. James Voelz asserts that "we should not seek to put ourselves into the story" but instead "should attempt to see how we participate in the same underlying reality and attempt to determine what the story tells us about that reality and therefore about us, our situation, and our destiny."[65]

If narrative does not clearly set forth doctrine, ethical application—the focus of this study—can be even more ambiguous. Gordon Wenham observes, "In narrative it is often unclear whether the writer is making an ethical comment at all: he may be describing an action because it happened, or because it was a link in a chain of events, which led to something significant. Furthermore, in those cases where narratives appear more than descriptive and seem to be offering ethical advice, it is often very difficult to be sure where the writer and his 'implied reader' stand ethically."[66] Often the biblical context of the stories—above all, the fact that Genesis was inseparably linked as "Torah" with the law codes of the other four books of Moses—made it clear who was performing righteously and who was not. But some stories depict actions by heroic figures that are not at all heroic in a particular account, perhaps not even acting in accord with God's law, while in other stories exceptional rather than regular commands from God govern decision making. Such ambiguities have plagued interpreters of the text for centuries. Luther found his way through such swampy ground with a self-confident sure-footedness for the most part as he guided hearers to listen to the Word of the Lord. Above all, readers of the reformer should recognize that Luther agreed with Wenham's judgment that

65. James W. Voelz, *What Does This Mean? Principles of Biblical Interpretation in the Post-Modern World*, 2nd ed. (Saint Louis: Concordia, 1997), 331–32.
66. Gordon J. Wenham, *Story as Torah: Reading Old Testament Narrative Ethically* (Grand Rapids: Baker Academic, 2004), 1–2.

links trust in God's revelation of himself to the obedience that naturally is to flow from knowing God as Lord. After noting that "the law merely punished extreme forms of disloyalty to God, i.e., religious apostasy and idolatry," Wenham further observes that "fearing, loving, cleaving to the LORD was not fulfilled just by avoiding the worship of other gods. The ethico-religious goal was far deeper and more embracing: it involved both loyalty to God and an enjoyment of his presence."[67] Thus the personal relationship of God with his human creatures envelops both doctrinal and ethical instruction as well as all other aspects of human life in the telling of the biblical narratives. Luther's preaching and lecturing quite consistently followed this paradigm.

Luther's Literary Sensitivity

Luther's medieval education had given the raconteur of Wittenberg good grounding in dealing with texts and had made him sensitive to the literary construction of the biblical stories.[68] He appreciated the biblical texts as well-wrought works of art.[69] He displayed sensitivity to questions not only of grammar and syntax but also of genre, structure, and style. For instance, he pointed out to the Wittenberg congregation that Genesis 4 was written in the genre of "narrative and example."[70] His *Summary of the Psalms* (1531) provides readers with a synopsis of each psalm in a few lines, and almost all begin with an identification of the genre: a "psalm of comfort," a "prophecy of Christ," a "prayer psalm," a "psalm of thanksgiving," a "doctrinal psalm," and so forth.[71] Moses won Luther's admiration for his literary adeptness at relating stories in few words but gracefully constructed turns of phrase.[72] He explained the course of the story of Joseph's encounters when it approached its denouement in Genesis 44 as reaching its epitasis, or climax, meaning that catastrophe was near.[73] In Andreas Poach's edition of a sermon from 1532 on

67. Ibid., 82.
68. Eberhard Winkler, "Luther als Seelsorger und Prediger," in *Leben und Werk Martin Luthers von 1526 bis 1546*, ed. Helmar Junghans (Göttingen: Vandenhoeck/Ruprecht, 1983), 1:236. According to Nembach (*Predigt des Evangeliums*, 131–71), Luther's style of preaching took the form of Quintilian's genre of public admonition, but Gerhard Krause and Helmar Junghans place the reformer's rhetoric in a broader stream of rhetorical tradition. See Krause's review in *Theologische Literaturzeitung* 99 (1974): 274–75; and Helmar Junghans's review in *LuJ* 41 (1974): 149–50; plus Junghans's article "Rhetorische Bemerkungen Luthers in seinen Dictata super Psalterium," *Theologische Versuche* 8 (1977): 97–128.
69. Bornkamm (*Old Testament*, 35–44) details some of Luther's literary treatment of Old Testament texts.
70. WA 24:121.21.
71. WA 38:8–69.
72. WA 42:194.30–31; *LW* 1:263. WA 42:206.6–10; 42:206.39–207.2; *LW* 1:279–80. WA 42:208.30–32; *LW* 1:282. WA 42:239.3–5; *LW* 1:324.
73. WA 44:572.14–29; *LW* 7:366.

John 3:1–15, the story of Nicodemus's conversation with Jesus, Luther states that "more than the other gospel writers, John keeps tossing in sprightly and enlightening comments and little sermonettes, so that, as you read along, your heart keeps leaping with joy."[74] Different genres served different purposes: miracle stories highlighted God's power and love; accounts of the lives of the patriarchs, like many Gospel accounts of Jesus's ministry, provided examples of God's gracious action and examples for human conduct.

More than education grounded Luther in such literary sensitivities. In addition his colleagues, above all Philipp Melanchthon but also Justus Jonas and others, reinforced and steeped Luther in a way of thinking sensitive to language and literature. The Wittenberg collegium shared and used each other's literary insights. In a sermon of 1534, against the background of medieval dramatic enactments of Christ's suffering and death, Luther anticipates the dramatic analysis of Christ's passion that appeared in the 1546 commentary on John published by his younger colleague Caspar Cruciger.[75] Cruciger suggests structuring the sermon program on the drama of Christ's suffering and death in five acts: first, the Garden of Gethsamane; then two acts presenting the judicial process against Christ and his confession; fourth, Pilate's condemnation of Christ and his torture, crucifixion, death, and placement in the grave; and the fifth act celebrated the resurrection on Easter morning. Luther's analysis of how to stage the passion in homiletical form presumes a division into six acts, beginning with the Lord's Supper on Maundy Thursday, proceeding through Gethsamane in act 2, the hearing at Caiaphas's home in act 3, the events at Pilate's palace in act 4, the crucifixion in act 5, and concluding, in act 6, with his burial. Luther separates the resurrection from Christ's suffering and death.[76]

Luther's occasional comments on the literary composition of a text sometimes served to solve a problem that the hearer or reader might encounter. If the course of Abraham's life seems unclear at some points, the students were to remember that Moses had given little thought to the arrangement of his account of the patriarch's activities.[77] If some Wittenberg citizens had compared the evangelists' accounts of Andrew's calling to be Jesus's disciple and found contradictions, their preacher had also compared how each evangelist had exercised his own literary hand in presenting his particular perspective in telling the story. Luther's sermon for Saint Andrew's Day in the House Postil

---

74. EA² 5:239–40; *HP* 2:210.

75. Corpus reformatorum [CR] 15:393–421. See Robert Kolb, "Passionsmeditation: Luthers und Melanchthons Schüler predigen und beten die Passion," *Humanismus und Wittenberger Reformation: Festgabe des 500. Geburtstages des Praeceptor Germaniae Philipp Melanchthon am 16. Februar 1997, Helmar Junghans gewidmet*, ed. Michael Beyer and Günther Wartenberg (Leipzig: Evangelische Verlagsanstalt, 1996), 272.

76. EA² 4:393–94; *HP* 1:373; cf. original text, WA 37:322.27–30, where only the first five acts are posited.

77. WA 42:550.11–16; *LW* 3:3.

begins with the observation that Matthew (4:18–20), Luke (5:1–11), and John (1:35–42) seem to diverge in their versions of Andrew's call to be a disciple.

> Matthew says that Peter and Andrew had been fishing with each other as they were called. Luke reports nothing about Andrew and speaks only of Peter and how he had fished and through the great catch of fish had come to know Christ and that James and John were with him. But John says that Andrew had been a disciple of John the Baptist and had stood near John when John saw Christ, pointed to him, and called him the Lamb of God. That proclamation so moved Andrew that he left John and followed Christ and asked him where he was staying, so that he could come to him. He heard him preach, wanted to be his disciple, and stayed the entire day with Christ.

But, Luther informs the congregation, there is no inconsistency there. For from John it is certain that Andrew came to Christ before Peter did. From Luke it is certain that Christ accepted Peter as his disciple after the catch of fish. And it is probable that Andrew was also there, Luther concludes. "Because Simon and Andrew were brothers and had the same trade, and both came to Christ, Matthew places them together since he does not want to go into all the details so precisely as Luke and John do."[78]

Similarly, in treating the charges against Jesus before Pilate, Luther notes that Luke combines two charges that John counts separately (Luke 23:2; John 18:28–40) and then observes, "It is not at all surprising that the evangelists do not give all details in the same or identical words, for no narrative is so fixed that it cannot be told or described differently by another person."[79] Luther's literary imagination provided a solution to what seemed to undermine the credibility of the evangelists; it reveals a bit of his understanding of how human beings observe and tell their stories.

Luther regarded the stories of Genesis and the Gospels as historically true, but he recognized that pious fiction served the proclamation of God's Word as well. His preface to the book of Judith rules that book out of the canon because it "hardly squares with the historical accounts of Holy Scriptures." It is not "an account of historical events but rather a beautiful religious fiction by a holy and ingenious man who wanted to sketch and depict therein the fortunes of the whole Jewish people and the victory that God always miraculously granted them over all their enemies." He compares the book to Solomon's use of poetry in Song of Solomon and to the fictional depictions in Revelation and Daniel. Luther could even imagine that the author had inserted the errors of time and name to give readers the hint that this book is a fictional kind of sacred, religious work.[80]

78. WA 52:563.33–564.21.
79. EA² 4:435–36; HP 1:409.
80. WA, Die deutsche Bibel [WA DB] 12:4–7; LW 35:337–38.

Luther is often said to have been a very narrowly focused theologian, using Paul to the practical exclusion of any other biblical authors. It is true that he found in Romans "the chief part of the New Testament and truly the purest gospel,"[81] but he regarded the Psalms as better than all the books of the legends of the saints and other pious literature. "Here we find not only what one or two saints have done, but also what he has done who is the very head of all saints. We also find what all the saints still do, such as the attitude they take toward God, toward friends and enemies, and the way in which they conduct themselves in the midst of all dangers and sufferings."[82] For the most part, Luther's lectures to students examined Old Testament books. His decade-long journey through the narratives of Genesis equaled his frequent return to the poetry of Psalms texts in terms of length and importance. The Minor Prophets and portions of Isaiah also commanded his attention, while the story-rich historical accounts in Joshua, Judges, Samuel, Kings, and Chronicles as well as Ezra and Nehemiah attracted his attention neither in lecture hall nor pulpit. In the New Testament the Epistle to the Galatians twice served as the subject of formal university lectures, but more importantly his sermons for the Wittenberg congregation led him through the standard lessons, Gospel and Epistle. The Gospel pericopes often supplied him stories, as did special series of sermons on Matthew and John. His preaching on the Epistles produced fewer stories.

Luther's Techniques of Storytelling

Sometimes Luther presumed that his hearers knew a biblical story and therefore proceeded to comment on aspects of the story or make applications based on it without any retelling or rereading of its contents. In other instances, he interlaced a lengthier recounting of a biblical account with such comments or applications, often constructing elaborations out of his speculations about what must have been going through the minds of the characters of the story. In still other cases he concentrated on a few salient aspects of the story that aided or illustrated the concern he was expressing.

Storytelling requires imagination to bridge the breach between the hearer and various aspects of the story. According to recent narrative theory, stories contain three elements: events, characters, and settings.[83] A breach may emerge between the original story and the current hearers that makes any of these three difficult to understand. Such breaches may consist of elements of time, culture, and in the case of most biblical stories, the absence of certain

---

81. WA DB 7:2/3.3–4; *LW* 35:365.
82. WA DB 10.1:99.17–20; *LW* 35:253.
83. Seymour Chatman, *Story and Discourse: Narrative Structure in Fiction and Film* (Ithaca, NY: Cornell University Press, 1978), 19–27, 43–145.

specifics, including psychological reflections, that later receivers of the story expect. The preacher faces the challenge of Auerbach's and Sternberg's gaps, the details that are not given in the accounts, the untold details that hearers and readers long to know.[84] As lecturer and as preacher, Luther took a good deal of freedom in imaginatively reconstructing the stories, adding details of description or circumstance and even reassigning voices in the text. For instance, the text of Genesis 4:6 has the Lord addressing Cain, but Luther thought that Adam had spoken these words, and "Moses says that these words were spoken by the Lord because Adam had now been accounted righteous and endowed with the Holy Spirit."[85] More typically, he mastered the art of filling the gaps by adding details, extending the text's account. He notes the spareness of the conversation when the three men come to the oaks of Mamre with the Lord's promise of an heir for Sarah and Abraham (Gen. 18), but this preacher knew how to come to his hearers' aid.[86] Later he observes that Moses "left it to the reader to imagine all the things that could not be expressed or described in words."[87] Indeed, at Genesis 18 Luther fulfills Moses's expectations. Though the three men who come to Abraham in this chapter are not described in the text, the professor informs his students that they "appeared in a lowly and wretched form: naked, hungry, tired from the journey, and as exiles, so to speak, who had just recently been released from a disagreeable prison."[88] At Genesis 45:4–15 the text does not record his brothers' reaction to Joseph's revelation of his identity, but Luther is certain that "they are stunned and do not dare utter a sound."[89]

Luther not only inserted his own narrative elaborations into his exposition of a text. He also used the biblical accounts as the framework for his own catechesis, repeating the text's story and then making clear its significance for his hearers or readers with a down-to-earth elucidation of the words and concepts, making the point that the story seemed to him to illuminate. In his 1526 sermon on the baptism of Christ, the story provides that kind of framework for his synthesis of other Bible verses and thoughts to drive home the points he believed his hearers needed to digest.[90]

Frequently Luther did little more than expand the text's recital of an event. For instance, in the early 1520s, preaching on Nicodemus's encounter with Jesus in John 3, Luther wove narrative from the Gospel's first fifteen verses into his own reflections, which explored the Jewish leader's thoughts and

84. See pp. 41–42 in chap. 2 above.

85. WA 42:194.16–18; *LW* 1:262. Luther advances this interpretation in his sermon of 1523; see WA 14:15; 24:135.13–16.

86. WA 42:21.19–20; *LW* 3:205.

87. WA 44:289.1–5; *LW* 6:386.

88. WA 43:3.10–12; *LW* 3:178–79.

89. WA 44:595.33; *LW* 8:23.

90. WA 20:217–31; CP 210–13.

Jesus's revelation of God's plan for his new creation.[91] In 1534 his sermon for the festival of John the Baptist recounts the sordid tale of John's death, attributing the request for John's head to a carefully schemed plot between Herod, Herodias, and Salome. "Herod and Herodias hit on a plan. Herod would celebrate his birthday, host a banquet, and put on a dance act. So, let his little girl come in and dance; and when the good humor of the guests is at its peak, Herod would swear to give her whatever she wanted, up to the half of his kingdom, and this to exhibit his fatherly heart toward his daughter. He says half of the kingdom: he means John's head." The story unfolds. Luther comments, "She has some nerve, this daughter of an adulteress, who does not even tremble at the words, to say nothing of the deed, in bearing about his severed head in full view of everyone." Luther's indignation boils over with what scholars call a rhetoric of irony:[92] "What a fair assembly of saints are these! Herod swore an oath and intends to keep it. God forbid he should provoke the Almighty by breaking his oath. The guests at the table must have been gratified." Luther's sarcasm drips from the pulpit. "And the king is so dejected. My, my, how did such an idea come into her heart? He does it with a heavy heart. Just like the farmer sidling up to a pig with a knife behind his back."[93] In 1541 he treated the slaughter of the children of Bethlehem (Matt. 2:13–23) in a similar way, with some detail on what was happening on the streets and in the minds of the participants.[94]

For the past three decades scholars have distinguished "story" as content of what is told from "discourse" as the art of how the content is conveyed. Luther's "stories" aimed at conveying the story of God and his people into the lives of hearers and readers in order to reshape their lives as children of God. His "discourse" displayed several means of making that happen.[95] Some scholars have emphasized the power of the reader or the hearer in relationship to the text and to the storyteller. Luther read the biblical text with his audiences, or rather invited his audiences to read the text with him. Together they entered into the world of text, where the figures on the biblical page came alive through the preacher's or professor's creating a conversation between ancients and contemporaries. The biblical page—perhaps better, the specific concretizations of the metanarrative that Luther found on the biblical pages—provided the topics of conversation. Luther posed the questions and led the biblical characters—whether God or Abraham or Mary—to address his sixteenth-century German conversation partners' concerns. He wanted to create an exchange between the biblical writers and his hearers and readers. In John Maxfield's words, Luther was making it possible for "professor and

91. WA 20:414–32; CP 3:422–54.
92. Wayne C. Booth, *A Rhetoric of Irony* (Chicago: University of Chicago Press, 1974).
93. WA 37:467.22–468.8; *HP* 3:338–39.
94. WA 52:598–604; *HP* 3:255–64.
95. See above all Chatman, *Story and Discourse*, passim.

students alike to hear the word of God speaking in the historical narrative, unveiling and interpreting universal Christian experience and thus their own experiences. Prophets and apostles sat on the lectern as professor and students sat below at their feet to hear."[96] Narratives personalize observations and principles of life, teaching them more effectively than can simple recitation of the tenet that the storyteller wishes to impress upon hearers. Yet often stories also give the hearers more discretion over the lesson to be learned than the storyteller wishes to give them. Luther apparently sometimes saw that danger, so he usually employed biblical narratives as the starting point for a catechetical explanation of the applications he drew from the stories, which he wanted hearers to integrate in their own thinking and acting.

David Steinmetz likens Luther's handling of Old Testament narratives to the techniques of modern authors who combine fictional elaboration with biographical or historical description. He compares the reformer to André Maurois and Gamaliel Bradford, who "used the techniques of the novelist to re-create as a three-dimensional human event a moment of history at which they were not personally present and for which the remaining evidence is maddeningly incomplete." Luther's "narrative imagination," "his intuitive response to the Bible as a work of art," "grasps his readers not only at the level of their discursive reason but also at the level of their imaginative participation in their common humanity."[97] Bornkamm comments on how "very unusual" was "the precision in his interpretation of individual passages and at the same time the power with which he drew his hearers into the situation of the biblical persons and translated their experiences into the lives of these hearers."[98] Retelling the biblical narratives often demands the introduction of motivation, extenuating circumstances, and some clue to the process of attaining their godly or ungodly goal. In filling the gaps in the story Luther pays some attention to all three elements of narrative—events, characters and their character, and setting—but most prominent are his additions about the characters, especially regarding their moral character, and what they actually were doing.

Several of Frei's disciples have pointed out the importance of character over plot in the use of narrative in modern preaching.[99] Some character sketches simply heighten the drama of the account being rehearsed. Luther's postil sermon for Epiphany comments on Matthew 2:3: "When Herod the king

96. Maxfield, *Luther's Lectures*, 72.

97. David C. Steinmetz, "Luther and the Drunkenness of Noah," *Luther in Context* (Bloomington: Indiana University Press, 1986), 110–11.

98. Heinrich Bornkamm, "Erneuerung der Frömmigkeit: Luthers Predigten, 1522–1524," in *Wahrheit und Glaube: Festschrift für Emanuel Hirsch zu seinem 75. Geburtstag*, ed. Hayo Gerdes (Itzehoe: Die Spur, Dorbandt, 1963), 52.

99. See the summary of this position in Charles L. Campbell, *Preaching Jesus: New Directions for Homiletics in Hans Frei's Postliberal Theology* (Grand Rapids: Eerdmans, 1997), 167–73.

heard [the question "Where is he who is born king of the Jews?"], he was terrified, and all Jerusalem with him"; Luther gives brief portrayals of the state of mind that he imagines Herod and the residents of Jerusalem to have. Herod "feared for his kingdom because he knew all too well that he was a foreigner and had earned the opprobrium of the Jewish religious leaders, and he knew well that the Jews were waiting for Christ, who was supposed to liberate them, as Moses had once done. So he had to worry that he could face a revolt that would take away his realm. And the Jews were afraid of Herod and the Romans. They feared it could cost much blood if they would get a new king, for they had put up resistance to the Romans and Herod with bad results." Luther concludes that they placed more trust in human power than God's power.[100] Later in the sermon Luther suggests that Herod stood in fear of being deposed by this new king whom the wise men were seeking. He and his advisers feared for their own "billfold and belly," while the Jewish religious leaders were unsettled from seeing that foreigners would come to faith in the Messiah and diminish their standing.[101]

In comments on John 14, Luther focuses on another "villain," with whom he in this instance displays some sympathy, recognizing the viewpoint that causes Judas to ask Jesus what he meant when he said that he would hide himself from the world (14:22) as an expression of the piety of the time. Judas, along with the other disciples, the preacher explains, was trapped in the Jewish conception of the Messiah as an earthly king. So Judas mused, as Luther reads his mind, "What kind of a king is that supposed to be that does not let anyone see him, who goes around so far only as a servant, but openly preaches and does miracles? And now he wants his kingdom to be so secret and hidden and so narrowly conceived that no one is supposed to see him or recognize him?"[102] This rumination places all human perceptions of God's power and modus operandi in question, in line with Luther's theology of the cross, which saw God as working through that which appears weak and foolish to human reason (1 Cor. 1:17–2:16).

What the preacher does not repeat from the story delivered by the text is also part of the oral event. Luther selected the stories he wished to expand and employ for his purposes, and he selected the details from them. Arguments based on omissions are obviously arguments from silence and therefore worth little, so scholars largely avoid the guessing game necessary in trying to analyze what is not there, but the process of selection of both story and detail constitutes an important part of the art of storytelling. Luther sometimes omitted details that would have complicated his execution of his purpose, as in the faultless picture of King David in his commentary on Psalm 101, in which he

100. WA 10.1.1:574.15–575.15; CP 1:336.
101. WA 10.1.1:630.17–632.5; CP 1:375–76.
102. WA 21:451.9–19; CP 3:307.

uses David as an exemplary ruler; this depiction stands in sharp contrast to the reformer's dwelling on his sins in other places.[103]

Good storytellers draw their audiences into the story and create some feeling of presence, their own presence within the story as well as the presence of the figures in the story in the midst of the hearers or readers. Luther often provided his readers or hearers with an "on-the-ground" or "you-are-there" frontline perspective. He suggests that John the Baptist's disciples had not paid much attention to Jesus (Matt. 11:2–10) not only because of John's reputation but also because "Christ went around very simply and modestly, son of a poor carpenter and a poor widow. He was not from the priestly class or a learned man, but a layman and common journeyman. He had never studied, had been trained in carpentry, like any other layman, and so this simple layman and journeyman Jesus did not correspond to the lofty and splendid description John had told." John's disciples expected "someone who could put on airs, a learned, highly placed priest or a mighty king." He should "saddle a steed and put on fancy spurs and strut about as a lord and king of Israel."[104]

Dialogue was among the techniques that Luther frequently employed to enliven stories, to cultivate this two-sided sense of presence, or to enrich texts without a story line. In his *Prayer Book* of 1522 a dialogue between the sinner and God depicts the reformer's own struggles with his conscience and teaches persistence in grasping God's mercy against the voice of accusation that presses the sinner. This exchange between Creator and rebellious creature also drives home both the seriousness of sin and, at its conclusion, the immensity of God's mercy. The drama of this dialogue is heightened because it follows on the author's concluding comments in a commentary on the Lord's Prayer, specifically on the "amen." Luther tells readers that believers may have firm confidence and trust that God will hear their prayers even when they think that the object of their petitioning seems insignificant. Not their own zeal but the Word of God, his reliable pledge and promise, sanctifies their praying.[105] Luther's dialogue between the sinful soul and God follows.

The soul piously begins, "O our Father, who are in heaven, we your children dwell here on earth in misery, far removed from you. Such a great gulf lies between you and us. How are we to find our way home to you in our fatherland?" God gruffly replies that sinners have not honored him as Father but rather dishonored his name, with words echoing Malachi 1:6 and Isaiah 52:5. The soul persists, acknowledging the truth of what God says and its own guilt, then pleads for mercy so that "we may enhance your name and honor it above everything else," and finally asks for help in hallowing God's name. God rebuffs the petition, asking how sinful hearts and minds can hallow his

103. The commentary on Ps. 101 is found in WA 51:200–264; *LW* 13:145–224; cf. the contrast in David's depiction in the commentary on Ps. 51, in WA 40.2:315–470; *LW* 12:303–410.
    104. WA 10.1.2:150.1–22; CP 1:90.
    105. WA 2:126.28–128.2; *LW* 42:77.

name and sing his praise. Not put off by God's rejection, the soul again affirms the truth of what the Father has just said, issuing its plea for the coming of God's kingdom to drive out sin and to make sinners righteous and acceptable in God's sight. God will not be appeased. He describes his own modus operandi in the language of Luther's description of God's justifying action in law and gospel throughout his ministry:[106] "Him whom I am to help, I destroy. Him whom I want to quicken, save, enrich, and make pious, I mortify, reject, impoverish, and reduce to nothing," citing Deuteronomy 32:39. The soul perseveres, deploring its refusal to accept God's aid, surrendering to his will, to his punishment. God reminds the soul that its lips voice love, but its heart is often distant and unresponsive to chastisement.

The exchange continues in this manner through four more petitions, with the soul uttering the final word in response to God's promise to punish those who fall to temptation: "Since trials flow from these adversities and tempt us to sin, deliver us, dear Father, from these, so that freed from all sin and adversity according to your divine will we may be your kingdom and laud and praise and hallow you forever." Luther rather curtly addresses the question "What am I to do if I cannot believe that I am heard?" by directing readers to Mark 9:23–24. As Luther closes the treatise, he commends to them the prayer "Lord, I believe; help me in my unbelief."[107] The dialogue conveys Luther's own experience of wrestling with God. It taught those who read it that their own works could never be sufficiently pure to please God. But the sinful soul did not give up in the face of God's condemnation of sin. Like Luther, this soul trusted God in spite of what it heard him saying. The reformer wanted to cultivate that kind of faith in others.

The soliloquy also served several purposes for Luther. For example, preaching on Easter 1538, he calls on Saint Paul to elaborate what he meant when he wrote that "whatever was to my profit [in keeping the Old Testament law] I now consider harmful!" (Phil. 3:7). Paul tells Luther's hearers in the castle church and then the readers of the Church Postil,

> I was a pious man above reproach, not measured by my own human standard, but by the law of Moses. But since I know Christ, I regard all the righteousness I have under the law as harmful, not merely harmful. It is all rubbish and filth. I thought I was a great holy man because I kept the law strictly and very diligently, and I regarded that as my highest treasure, of the greatest benefit for me. But when I heard that Christ wanted to make me his brother and heir, O, how my arrogance and my confidence in my own righteousness vanished. I recoil from it and do not want to think about it any longer.[108]

106. See Robert Kolb, "God Kills to Make Alive: Romans 6 and Luther's Understanding of Justification (1535)," *LQ* 12 (1998): 33–56.

107. WA 2:128.3–130.19; *LW* 42:78–81.

108. WA 46:351.3–26; *CP* 2:264–65.

Allegory displeased Luther even when he was still a young lecturer on the Bible whenever it dominated what he regarded as the native meaning of a biblical text and was employed as the primary method of biblical interpretation. Nevertheless Luther never ceased to garnish the application of some truths he drew from the text with figural or allegorical elaboration. On the one hand, in 1535 he labels the allegorical sense that might be derived from a text as an inappropriate interpretation in comparison to the text's "historical sense." Allegorical ideas about Satan, based on Genesis 3:15, do not "bring out Moses's meaning," which can be obtained from other biblical descriptions of the devil.[109] Likewise, in his Church Postil he warns his priest-readers that they should not "look at every part of the parable [of the workers in the vineyard; Matt. 20:1–16] but rather the chief point, what Christ wanted to say, and not focus on what the penny or quarter means, not what the first or last hour might be, but that the owner of the vineyard had his intention and wanted his goodness to be regarded above all their work and effort. . . . The point of this parable is not the penny, what it is, nor the difference of the hours, but the effort to acquire and earn, how a person can acquire what is being offered."[110]

On the other hand, Luther did pursue allegorical augmentation of some narratives, both parables and reports of events, in order to teach and admonish his hearers and readers. After treating Mary's faith and God's institution of marriage in connection with the wedding at Cana (John 2:1–11) in the postil of 1525, Luther digresses into "the spiritual significance of the text. This and every marriage signify Christ as the true bridegroom, and the Christian church as the bride." Cana, which means zeal, represents the zeal for works demonstrated by Jews and by the contemporary church. The invitation of Christ and his disciples to the wedding represents the ancient promises of Christ and the apostles and disciples who would serve him. The waterpots are the books of the Old Testament, the law, and the purification by works without faith, made of stone like Moses's tablets. Jesus's changing the water into wine teaches that the gospel places the law in the proper setting, so that the law drives sinners to Christ, with his consoling gospel.[111]

In treating the story of Christ's calming the storm (Matt. 8:23–27) in 1525, Luther suggests that it pictures the Christian life, especially the office of preaching. "The ship signifies the Christian church, the sea the world, the wind the devil. The disciples are the preachers and pious Christians. Christ is the truth, the gospel, and faith." Christ's coming to the boat arouses the sea and wind since he has come to bring a sword (Matt. 10:34).[112] Luther's embellishment and application adds details to call the people to faith in the midst of the

109. WA 42:141.8–31; *LW* 1:188–89.
110. WA 17.2:137.4–8, 27–29; CP 2:106–7.
111. WA 17.2:68.8–71.15; CP 2:65–69.
112. WA 17.2:107.16–109.7; CP 2:96–99.

eschatological battle they were experiencing in their lives. Another instance came in the story of the devil-possessed man in Luke 11:14–23, as his postil of 1525 records Luther's sermon on the text. For Luther this man represents all who are possessed by Satan through original sin; Luther makes him deaf and blind in addition to being mute in order to heighten the imagery. The strong man who ousts the devil, according to Luther, is Jesus himself and the gospel of salvation in him.[113] The second edition of his Church Postil replaces a sermon for the thirteenth Sunday after Trinity, preached originally in 1523, that allegorizes the parable of the good Samaritan; he substitutes a sermon on the same text, Luke 10:23–37, that presents a straightforward exposition of the text.[114] Ancient teachers had devised allegory to move from narrative to abstract truth, and Luther found the genre of narrative more apt for driving home the essentials of faith and life through the catchy hooks of the stories themselves. The allegorical genre only reluctantly permits the development of parallel stories. Luther could spin details for the stories of parables, but his allegorical applications almost never retold the details in story form. They simply related the details of the story to Luther's ethical or doctrinal purpose in his exposition.

Apart from allegory, Luther could focus on the typological relevance of the text for later episodes in the history of God's people. Preaching on Trinity Sunday on the appointed Gospel from John 3 gave Luther the opportunity, in verse 14, to retell the story of the lifting up of the bronze serpent from Numbers 21. He rehearses the original account for the congregation. The people complained in the desert over their lack of food and water.

> God took away his helping hand and turned the evil loose on them. He attacked them with poisonous snakes. They bit the people. The people became feverish from the poison, and they died of fever, just as you die from a great big boil or carbuncle. From the moment the snakes hissed on them, their skin turned red as fire. They fell down to the ground and burned as if they were in hell. And even though they chased the snakes away, they kept on coming back. So when they were bitten by the poisonous snakes and were burning up with fever, one here, another there, and they were dying in great numbers, then the people cried to Moses, and Moses cried out to God.[115]

Luther then draws the typological parallel to Jesus: The bronze serpent and Jesus both had to be lifted up on a pole. The bronze serpent was not poisonous but looked like the poisonous snakes; Jesus was sinless but had the appearance of a human sinner. Focusing only on the serpent and on Jesus could provide salvation. From the history of salvation the preacher proceeds to apply this

113. WA 17.2:219.26–221.2; CP 2:162–64.
114. WA 10.1.2:355–67; 22:237–55; CP 5:17–35, 37–59.
115. EA² 5:240; *HP* 2:210.

story to individual hearers. Bitten by "that old snake, the devil," they must look alone to Christ on his cross.[116]

Preaching in the first generation of the Reformation involved some basic instruction in the biblical world as well as comment on the theological message of the text. In many cases the preacher could combine the two quite easily. In explaining the significance of being a tax collector in first-century Palestine as he preached on the parable of the Pharisee and the tax collector (Luke 18:9–14) in 1532, he describes the latter:

> Tax collectors were under contract with the Romans, somewhat like today the Venetians or Turks exact taxes from the mines or rural districts every year. They were called *publicans*, or tax collectors, because they exacted tribute and tax every year from the country's citizens in behalf of the Roman government. If they were to deliver a certain amount each year, they needed to get their share too. When they got a rich, affluent burgher or farmer in their clutches, they quickly took him by the head and put the squeeze on him, in order to strip him of his little stake. Whatever they could extract by this pressure, they kept a percentage for themselves.

Turning from text to hearers, Luther adds, "Just as corrupt public officials and tax collectors do today." But not only the bureaucrats could be compared to the tax collectors of Jesus's time. Luther begins this explanation by placing a general reflection on the temper of humankind in the mouth of the Pharisee as he recites what kind of person he was not: "I know how much defrauding and stealing goes on among people. Merchants sell bad merchandise; farmers overcharge people for their barley, grain, chickens, eggs, wood, and so on. The whole world is full of nothing but robbing and stealing."[117] Tax collectors, or rather their counterparts, were frequenting the Wittenberg market and hearing sermons in the town church. Luther was presenting a paradigmatic narrative that called for repentance and pointed the way to faithful living.

The variety of biblical stories invited the use of a variety of methods, but in Luther's hand all these methods pursued one goal: to integrate in his hearers the biblical writers' paradigmatic narrative and the sense of identity as child of God that it created and cultivated. The retelling of biblical stories nurtured the life of repentance that battled temptation, trusted God, and made his presence known in the world through the love of the neighbor.

Luther's Stories from Nonbiblical Sources

This volume marshals its evidence for Luther's use of narrative in the cultivation of the Christian life largely from his use of biblical stories. As rich as his

116. EA² 5:241; *HP* 2:211–12.
117. WA 36:233.12–17; *HP* 381.

recounting of personal experiences was at the supper table, in his sermons and lectures he largely avoided recitations of the personal type apart from an occasional reference to monastic experiences.[118] In treating Luke 11:14–28 in the sermon for Oculi Sunday 1534, he does employ a personal recollection to address the natural question raised by the text: "Why would Beelzebul drive out his own devils?" As a young man, either a student or a monk, he had witnessed an exorcism, probably in the Benedictine monastery at Wimmelburg, near Eisleben.[119] "I myself," he tells the congregation, "saw a man full of devils. But the priest who exorcised him was so confident that he placed his hand in the mouth of the possessed man. How can that be anything else but the devil driving out another devil? The answer: Saint Paul says that the devil will in the last times do signs. But they are false signs."[120] Luther continues with stories from the tradition of tales of the saints, in this case in order to criticize the use of material objects to work a kind of magical providence that encourages a false faith, a faith directed toward ritual that functions ex opere operato. Saints Cyriacus and Leonhard had also exorcised possessed people. "But the devil did not leave them because he could no longer remain, but he left willingly and gladly in order to strengthen their superstition. He made it look as though he had tremendous fear of consecrated candles, salt, water, and other things. He did it only to strengthen the people in their superstition and weaken their proper faith and trust in God's Word and grace. Paul calls these things deceiving signs, fabricated and deceptive miracles, nothing more than a specter."[121] For the most part, other personal memories, insofar as he brought them into public utterances at all, served his criticism of the papacy or the monastic way of life and his rejection of ritualistic religion of the sort in which he had grown up.

But with fondness Luther did recall certain stories from his wider environment as a young man. Although he never personally met Elector Frederick the Wise, he obviously admired the wisdom of his protector and benefactor. He actually told more stories in lectures and sermons about Frederick than about Electors John and John Frederick, with whom he had close relationships. In a sermon on Matthew 7:15–23, preached in July 1533, he recalls a report from the barber Peter Beskendorf, which confirms the reformer's insistence on the importance of diligence in the exercise of personal responsibilities. This characteristic did not belong to every ruler, he notes, but Frederick had his record book read to him as he was dressing in the mornings and again at evening. As Andreas Poach presents the text, "He watched his officials and administrators very carefully and trusted no one farther than he could see him. He was a prince who knew how to manage his household." Such a ruler,

118. WA 33:574.30–575.7.
119. Cf. WA 38:543n1.
120. WA 52:191.3–9.
121. WA 52:191.10–20 (House Postil); cf. Rörer's notes, in WA 37:321.22–28.

Luther concludes, is "a rare bird."[122] As the professor lectures on Joseph's policy designed to secure food supplies for Egypt in the face of famine (Gen. 41:33–36), he remembers the report that Frederick had faced criticism from some of his counselors and from Johannes von Staupitz that his storage policies reflected his greed and acquisitiveness. The elector had replied, Luther tells the students, that his motives were quite different: the townspeople and peasants were not thinking of the future but living only for the day and not preparing themselves for possible famine.[123] Frederick had also once said, Luther had heard, that the responsibilities of the ruler were a burden: he had been reported to say that peasants are happier than princes because they can live with wife and children without worries, under the protection of someone else, but princes have to struggle each day with worries of every kind.[124] Luther seems unaware that while *his* peasant relatives may have been relatively well-off, many other peasants were not.

The reformer also mentions to his students that his mentor, von Staupitz, had borne the burdens of his office, conscious of their weight. Luther relates that during Staupitz's first three years as vicar general of the Augustinian order in Germany, he had resolved to rule with strict justice, but then lacked success in fulfilling that goal. During the next three years he had followed the procedures of his predecessors and elders, again with no success. In the third period of his rule of the province, he had decided to rule according to God's will and with prayer, but it did not produce success either. Staupitz had said, Luther remembers, that he could do what he could do and no more since he despaired of the usefulness of all advice. According to Staupitz, God wants us to pray but does not listen to our desires and ideas even when we give him the wisest and best suggestions. Luther tells the students that believers must have patience and, like Staupitz, "let the heavy stone lie if you cannot lift it."[125] In these cases the personal recollections supported points the professor wished to impress on his students in—sometimes somewhat remote—connection with a text.

In addition to personal recollections, Luther could cite stories from ancient myths, ancient history, historical traditions of the church, and when it served his purposes, even from the *legenda* of the saints. What better example of greed than King Midas when attacking the worship of Mammon. He regales the Wittenberg congregation with the story: The "rich and greedy" King Midas "wished that everything he touched would become gold. The Lord God granted him his wish. He touched his clothing, the table, the bed, a pillar—everything turned to gold, the knife on the table, the bread, and so forth. Everything was gold. He had prayed that it would be gold and not bread. Whoever can curse

---

122. WA 37:125.20–26; EA² 5:388; *HP* 3:345.
123. WA 44:416.37–417.6.
124. WA 44:442.14–22.
125. WA 44:441.33–442.2.

greed, let him do it. Even if a person has all the gold in the world, you still have to have grain and be able to eat."[126] Wittenberg citizens, take warning!

Ancient history formed part of the medieval student's learning. Luther marshals material for his exposition of New Testament texts from Josephus, for example, in his sermon on Luke 19:41–48 and its prophecy of the destruction of Jerusalem. Luther urges hearers and readers of his Church Postil to read further themselves but gives some details from Josephus regarding the great numbers trapped in the city and their desperation, finally being reduced to eat leather and butcher their children and use dove's dung for salt.[127] In expanding on David's instructions for good rulers in Psalm 101, Luther warns against being too clever for one's own good from the story of Phormio: without experience in warfare, he tried to lecture Hannibal on how to conduct a war. "This kind of instructor is indeed no match for such a pupil."[128] In the commentary on 2 Samuel 23 published in 1543 under the title *The Last Words of David*, Luther briefly recalls two stories from ancient writers that, in Luther's opinion, illustrate the kind of joy that David had over the glory that his family received from having a descendent that would sit at God's right hand (1 Chron. 17:17). Diogenes Laertius had told the story of a father named Chilo, "who died for joy when told that his son had won the victory in the Olympic games." From Aulus Gellius comes the story of a Roman mother who dropped dead from the excitement of pure joy when she saw her son, who had been reported dead in the war against Hannibal but who returned home in good health.[129]

The ancient church had also placed narratives into the quiver of the sixteenth-century storyteller. Among the stories Luther loved were those about Augustine's mother, Monica. Her lifestyle in relation to her unbelieving husband, with its humility and wisdom, had brought her spouse to faith, a model for other Christian wives of her own time and Luther's as well, the preacher concluded.[130] She had wept "nine long years" for her son because she wanted him to marry a Christian woman who would turn him into a Christian husband. "She did not dare to hope or expect him to become the man he did later, although that would have pleased her."[131]

The *Legenda aurea* and other collections of the lives of the saints earned Luther's sharp criticism for their tales of magical miracles and emphasis on righteousness merited through good works,[132] but their stories of martyrdom

---

126. WA 37:532.13–19; *HP* 3:19–20.

127. WA 17.1:384.25–386.20; CP 4:319–20.

128. WA 51:208.1–34; *LW* 13:155–56.

129. WA 54:52.24–31; *LW* 15:296. The stories are found in Diogenes Laertius, *De vitis, dogmatibus et apophthegmatibus clarorum virorum* 1.72; and Aulus Gellius, *Noctes atticae* 3.15.

130. WA 41:321.6–28; CP 4:114.

131. WA 12:502.9–16; CP 2:277.

132. As in a sermon on November 18, 1537, in WA 45:261.22–264.15; see Robert Kolb, *For All the Saints: Changing Perceptions of Martyrdom and Sainthood in the Lutheran Reformation* (Macon, GA: Mercer University Press, 1987), 11–18.

or of virtue provided him with confirmation for his own concerns. He occasionally repeated the stories of the deaths of Saint Agatha and Saint Vincent.
Agatha went to her death with a joyful heart, saying, "They played me a dance
tune so that I may dance [my way to the grave]." Vincent looked forward to
his death with joy and laughed at the threats made to execute him by sword
or fire. He mocked his executioner and confessed his faith in the resurrection,
a model for all Christians facing death, Luther concluded.[133]

Luther could spin a tale out of his own imagination in order to depict God's
action, particularly in the setting of the eschatological conflict with death. In
his Large Catechism he succinctly sketches Christ's own battle against Satan
and death in his resurrection. There Luther confesses that he had lain captive
to the power of the devil, condemned to death, entangled in sin and blindness,
without resources, help, or comfort. But Christ came to rout "those tyrants and
jailers." "He has snatched us, poor lost creatures, from the jaws of hell, won
us, made us free, and restored us to the Father's favor and grace."[134] Preaching on 1 Corinthians 15:54 a year before his death, Luther depicted this duel
between God and Satan, between life and death. Poach elaborates on Georg
Rörer's notes, in the fashion he remembers hearing while Luther's student,
as Luther sketched the battle scene between God and death: "Who can list all
the ways by which death slays us human beings? Death lives, rules, dominates,
triumphs, and sings, 'I have won, I have won. I, death, am king and victor over
all the world. I have power and dominion over everything living on earth. I
spread death and slay all human beings, young, old, rich, poor, high class, low
class, noble, commoner. I defy anyone to try to defend himself against me.'"
God has the last laugh, in Luther's depiction: "Death will soon sing himself
hoarse; will sing himself to death. His cantata will soon be laid to rest. 'Christ
is arisen from the grave's dark prison. So let our song exulting rise. Christ
with comfort lights our eyes.'[135] Death, where is your victory? Where are you
keeping the one who lay in the grave, whom you killed on the cross?"[136] Such
an eschatological narrative is rare in Luther's writings, but it demonstrates
the imagination that he brought to the biblical text.

Luther's imagination could sketch a scene from everyday life as well. His
sermon on John 20 portrays the human situation by creating a picture of
the heart harder than steel, committed to ignoring God, that then loses self-
confidence and hope. The heart becomes softer than water, and such a person,
with fear gripping the heart, is afraid of the sound of a rustling leaf. Every
faint creak of the rafters, joists, or pillars seems to resound like thunder and
lightning. Luther comments that such people find no peace and quiet, and
"even countless words of comfort are too few to give them assurance." People

133. E.g., WA 36:163.16–23.
134. Large Catechism, Creed 29; *BSLK* 651–52; *BoC* 434.
135. From the twelfth-century hymn, translated for the hymnal issued in Wittenberg in 1524.
136. A longer passage from this sermon is found on p. 175; WA 49:769.19–32.

go from one extreme to another, he observes, and are either so hard of heart that they do not seek God at all, or they tumble into deepest despair, so that they are no longer receptive to any comfort at all.[137]

Once Luther had the congregation in Wittenberg cast itself in the role of the birds. God places their example before his people and says,

> Birds have not a care in the world, for they know they have an excellent kitchen chef and generous butler whose name is the heavenly Father. That is the reason they say, "Not to worry! Have you not heard what kind of cuisine and cellar we have, namely, as wide as the world? Therefore we fly wherever we wish and always find our food and our table well prepared."

Then the birds addressed the hearers,

> "The same heavenly Father wants gladly to be your kitchen chef and butler, if you would only believe it and want to have him. He proves it by what he does. He gives you land, storage bins, cellar, and barns, and he gives you in abundance much more than he gives the birds."

Indeed, Luther thought that the birds

> put us to shame, and we might well take off our hats to them and say, "My dear teacher, I have to admit that I do not have the skill you do. You sleep all night in your little nest with not a care in the world. In the morning you leave the nest. You are happy and bright. You sit on the limb of a tree and sing, praise, and give thanks to God. Then you go looking for your little kernel of grain and find it. For shame! Why have I, old fool that I am, not learned to do the same, I, who have so much reason to do so? If a bird can live without a care in the world and look after itself, deporting itself like a saint—it sings, praises God, is happy and in good spirits, for it knows that its granary is already built, even as promised, 'Your heavenly Father feeds them' [Matt. 6:26 NIV]—why do we not do the same, we who have the advantage and can cultivate the field, gather in the harvest, and lay in store for a time of need?"[138]

Such a story encouraged faith and built trust, in this case in God's providing care.

Luther viewed God as the ultimate storyteller, for he was the author and designer of the story and the events of world history—and its chief actor as well. God desires to continue his re-creative work by repeating the story of his action in behalf of sinners to create trust—that is, to restore their original

137. WA 49:136.16–21.
138. WA 37:531.33–532.7; EA² 6:43–45; *HP* 3:18–19.

relationship with himself—in the hearers and readers of his Word in every age. Luther believed that he and all other baptized believers were called to go on repeating the story, the message that executes his plan for salvation, not necessarily and not only through recital of biblical stories, although they obviously played a vital role in the formulation of every aspect of God's message of salvation. His linguistic skills and creative imagination enabled him to effectively engage hearers and readers in the narrative and bring it into their daily lives. He did so not only to give them a sense of a biblical paradigmatic narrative for their own thinking and acting as God's children but also to fill in details of how that sense of identity as the chosen people of God is to be fleshed out in everyday perceptions of reality and of the tasks of human life.

3

ABOVE ALL, FEARING, LOVING, AND TRUSTING IN GOD

Defining the Core of What It Means to Be Human

The central importance of scripture for Luther was its place at the heart of the Christian life—the practical life of faith and action."[1] William Graham's comment calls attention to Luther's way of making an intimate connection between daily living and God's speaking in Scripture and in each form of his communication with his people that arises out of its pages. Graham also correctly captures Luther's understanding of "the practical life" of the everyday routine of human existence by describing it as a combination of trust in God or some substitute for him and the actions that this fundamental trust produce.

Communal Faithfulness between God and His Human Creatures

In the final analysis the full essence of what it means to be human remained a mystery for Luther. He abandoned any attempt to assign measures of responsibility for what happens in the world to Creator and human creature and to allocate relative values and roles in God's interaction with human

---

1. William A. Graham, *Beyond the Written Word: Oral Aspects of Scripture in the History of Religion* (Cambridge: Cambridge University Press, 1987), 146.

beings to one party or the other. The mystery of being God's human creature, responsible for caring for neighbor and the earth, within the context of
God's total responsibility as Creator for everything—these human and divine
responsibilities remained in tension in Luther's thought.[2] But the Wittenberg
reformer was certain of some things; most important among them was God's
bestowing the fundamental orientation for human life in the gift he expects
his children to exercise, trust in God's person, as he has revealed himself in
Jesus Christ. Eilert Herms noticed the importance of the "personal being"
of the human creature for Luther. Herms equated it with the human "heart"
or "conscience,"[3] but it would better be equated with the faith or trust that
determines the entire person or being of an individual, as Luther taught.

Luther defined what it means to be human fundamentally in terms of the
identity of the human person as one whom God regards as righteous and
as his child rather than in terms of the human actions that Luther counted
as derivative from and secondary to the person. That reflected his intensely
personal understanding of God, in whose image human beings are created.

As stated above,[4] Luther summarizes the core of what it means to be human
in his explanation of the first commandment: "We are to fear, love, and trust
in God above all things." Each of the other commandments, according to
Luther's Small Catechism, speaks of proper and improper human actions
that proceed out of the simple fact that "we are to fear and love God."[5] The
Wittenberg professor's surprisingly anthropocentric-seeming explication of
what it means to fear, love, and trust in God in his Large Catechism centers
on the word "trust." "To have a god is nothing else than to trust and believe
in that one with your whole heart. . . . It is trust and faith of the heart alone
that make both God and an idol."[6] This expression of what it means to be
human links humanity inescapably to the Creator: it understands being human
as proceeding from the Creator's word and centering on trust in him as the
ultimate source of "all good" and the "refuge in all need"[7] that human action
presupposes. God's design for humanity, Luther continues, begins with his
command that his human creatures place their "true faith and confidence of
the heart" in their Maker and that their faith and confidence "fly straight to
the one true God and cling to him alone." That means that God is saying to
his people, "See to it that you let me alone be your God, and never search for
another. . . . Whatever good thing you lack, look to me for it and seek it from

2. Bengt Hägglund, "Luthers Anthropologie," in *Leben und Werk Martin Luthers von
1526 bis 1546*, ed. Helmar Junghans (Göttingen: Vandenhoeck & Ruprecht, 1983), 1:63–76.

3. Eilert Herms, "Das Evangelium für das Volk: Praxis und Theorie der Predigt bei Luther,"
LuJ 57 (1990): 25; cf. 32–37 on the concept of faith.

4. See "The Creator and His Human Creatures," on pp. 5–6.

5. *BSLK* 508–10; *BoC* 352–54.

6. *BSLK* 560; *BoC* 386.

7. *BSLK* 560; *BoC* 386.

me, and whenever you suffer misfortune and distress, crawl to me and cling to me. I myself will give you what you need and help you out of every danger. Only do not let your heart cling to or rest in anyone else."[8]

Wilfried Härle has explained this relationship between Creator and human creature, as Luther defined it, against the background of the Old Testament concept of "communal faithfulness" or "faithfulness within a communal relationship." For Luther, God's godness first of all expresses itself in relationship to the human creature in God's creation of all things through his Word simply because he desires to create. His godness also expresses itself in his establishing himself as a God of conversation and community. Luther further believed that God's godness or righteousness consists above all in his mercy, which fulfills his faithfulness to be the Creator of his human creatures, to whom he has promised life and well-being. Likewise, Härle maintains, the human creature's humanness consists first of all in faithfulness to the Creator, in the trust and confidence of heart that clings to God and flies straight to him.[9]

Even modern psychologists who place the concept of trust in a key role in their anthropologies do not have an explanation for how trust works. But following the lead of Erik Erikson, many emphasize that the ability to trust is a key to human personality and to personality development. Erikson defines trust as "the first and basic wholeness; . . . it seems to imply that the inside and the outside can be experienced as an interrelated goodness."[10] Mothers' reliability and love cultivate a sense of trust and thereby a sense of personal identity, Erikson argues. He further maintains that religion serves "the ritual restoration of a sense of trust in the form of faith while offering a tangible formula for a sense of evil against which it promises to arm and defend man. . . . All religious practice includes periodical childlike surrender to the Power that creates and re-creates, dispensing earthly fortune as well as spiritual well-being."[11] Luther's understanding of humanity embraced a "Person," rather than an impersonal "Power," from whom human life proceeds. He held that, by very definition, human life can be whole only when lived in and on the basis of trust in the Creator of life. Likewise, his understanding of sin centers on the breakdown of trust that marked the fall into sin,[12] and he believed that God restores the trust in himself that constitutes the heart of humanity on the basis of Christ's death and resurrection.

Luther did not try to explain how trust works. He had neither the tools nor the inclination to formulate a psychological explanation for it. He did insist, nonetheless, that God alone creates his human creatures' trust in him

8. *BSLK* 560–61; *BoC* 386–87.

9. Wilfried Härle, "Die Entfaltung der Rechtfertigungslehre Luthers in den Disputationen von 1535 bis 1537," *LuJ* 71 (2004): 228.

10. Erik H. Erikson, *Identity, Youth, and Crisis* (New York: Norton, 1968), 82.

11. Ibid., 103, 106.

12. See Luther's treatment of the fall in WA 42:105–65; *LW* 1:141–221.

and that their trust arises in response to God's promise of this restored relationship of communal faithfulness between himself and his rebellious human creatures.[13] The Holy Spirit creates this communal faithfulness in a manner as mysterious and beyond human grasp as God's saying "let there be" in Genesis 1. He creates this new reality of the human relationship to God on the basis of what Jesus did in dealing with sin through his crucifixion and in restoring the righteousness, the very humanity, of human creatures through his rising from the dead (Rom. 4:25). God restores this relationship through his promise of salvation and everlasting well-being through Christ, but he also promises his presence in every need, and the Christian's faith responds to, and rejoices in, these promises of his providing care as well. An important part of Luther's understanding of this faith was found in spite of human experience: despite experiencing the seeming absence of God, faith clings to God and to his promise. Finally, faith flows into the fruits that demonstrate God's love, through praise and prayer to him in the vertical dimension of humanity; and in love and care for the neighbor, in its horizontal dimension. Luther's treatment of John 4:46–54 includes encouragement for trusting in God's promise as the royal official does when he comes to Jesus to request healing for his son. That reminds the preacher of Paul's praise for Abraham in Romans 4:20–21: Abraham "did not waver at God's promise because of unbelief but was strong in faith" in God's ability to carry through on his promises.[14]

Trust Breached and Betrayed

For the definition and constitution of the human person, the centrality of trust became clear as Luther preached and lectured on creation and Adam and Eve's fall into sin in the first three chapters of Genesis. In chapter 2 Luther expounds on original righteousness as Adam and Eve's love for God and adherence to his Word, without moving from doctrinal discussion to narrative.[15] Genesis 3, however, provides the story of temptation and fall; for his students in 1535, Luther spins out his reconstruction of the thinking that drove the events. The story is the recital of "the will that is good and righteous, that pleases God, obeys God, trusts in the Creator, and makes use of his creation with an expression of thanks"—that goodwill being lost "to such an extent that our will makes a devil out of God and shudders at the mention of his name, especially when it is troubled by God's judgment. . . . From the image of God and knowledge of God, from the knowledge of all other creatures and a very honorable nakedness, the human creature has fallen into blasphemies,

---

13. Oswald Bayer, *Promissio: Geschichte der reformatorischen Wende in Luthers Theologie* (Göttingen: Vandenhoeck & Ruprecht, 1971).

14. EA² 6:156; *HP* 3:120.

15. WA 42:86.11–87.8; *LW* 1:113–15.

into hatred and contempt of God, indeed, what is more, into hostility toward God."[16] Luther affirms that the human will can execute the management of cattle, the construction of buildings, the cultivation of the soil quite well after the fall into sin; but humans have broken their relationship with the Creator.[17] The reformer refuses to indulge in the slightest speculation about how evil could invade what the perfectly good and fully powerful Creator had made, but he had no doubt about the fact of that matter.[18]

Luther's commentary on the story of Adam and Eve's desertion of God begins by sketching the character and strategy of the serpent and explaining it within the context of Luther's Word-centered and trust-centered theology. The snake attacks God's Word with its own word, a question designed to deceive, for "unbelief is the source of all sins."[19] "Satan imitates God. Just as God had preached to Adam, so Satan preaches to Eve."[20] His message, delivered with an "awful boldness," "invented a new god and denied the true and eternal God with such unconcern and assurance. It is as if he were to say, 'Surely you are silly if you believe that God has given such a command, for it is not God's nature to be so deeply concerned whether you eat or not.'"[21] Luther was depicting the scene in Eden with the goal of helping his students understand the nature of the continuing eschatological battle with the Deceiver. "At first Eve resists the tempter admirably. For she is still being led by that Spirit, who is lighting her path." But Satan is clever and wages his attack by reasoning theologically. It works. She reaches the conclusion that God did not give the command not to eat of the tree even though she struggles with her argument by distinguishing among trees (3:2). But Satan's "You will not die" is powerful in its rhetoric and overpowers Eve (3:4). So Eve agrees with Satan when he charges God with deception and, as it were, strikes God in the face with his fists. Eve joins Satan in despising God and denying his Word. She believes the father of lies rather than God's Word.[22]

The professor sharpens the edges of the story. He drifts in and out of the narrative, using it as the occasion for expanding his treatment of the human condition as people of all times resist and flee God's Word, its promise, and its commands. The retelling of the story resumes at Genesis 3:10, with Adam's answer to God's "Where are you?" "Just as Adam stupidly began to flee, so he answers most stupidly. So thoroughly had sin deprived him of all discernment and good sense!" His desire to let God know that he is naked reveals his confusion and betrays and condemns him. It is not as if God has never

16. WA 42:106.32–107.9; LW 1:142.
17. WA 42:107.29–32; LW 1:143.
18. WA 42:108.33–109.32; LW 1:144–45.
19. WA 42:110.32–111.33; LW 1:147; cf. WA 42:112.20–22; LW 1:149.
20. WA 42:111.12–13; LW 1:147.
21. WA 42:112.22–26, 33–37; LW 1:149.
22. WA 42:113.18–117.33; LW 1:150–56.

seen him naked before, Luther tells the students. But now he is "no longer the same as previously. He had undergone a change and become a different person, as he tried to make up an excuse." All sinners end in such actions that show their own guilt, Luther's listeners are reminded. The entire life of the sinner becomes a flight from God.[23]

The professor's gaze bore in upon Adam. The law of God was stinging Adam's conscience. The dialogue continued, as Luther spins it out: God said (3:11), "You know that you are naked, and for this reason you hid. But your nakedness is my creation. You are not condemning it as something shameful, are you? So it was not the nakedness that confused you. It was not my voice that terrified you. Your conscience convicted you of sin because you ate the fruit from the forbidden tree." Luther suggests that, as God approaches, Adam has been thinking to himself, "I have eaten the fruit, but I will not tell him that I am fleeing for that reason. I shall not mention the sin. I will say that I am frightened because I am naked, and his voice scared me." But God goes to the deed itself. Adam refuses to admit his guilt, as Luther maintains he should have, but blames Eve and puts a positive construction on his own action. Luther's Adam continues, "I did not listen to the serpent. I did not take pleasure in gazing at the tree. I did not reach out to pick the forbidden fruit. The woman whom you gave me did all this." Luther concludes that this kind of attempt at self-justification is the only way the sinner can find to escape if no offer of forgiveness is given. So he had to express his resentment and anger against God and argue, "You placed this burden of trouble upon me. If you had given her her own garden and not put the burden of living with her on me, I would not have sinned. It is your fault." Adam exemplifies all sinners, Luther asserts.[24]

In great detail he intensifies the story's message for his students' future hearers with such penetrating elaboration and adds his observations about the nature of the sinful person in order to help these future pastors understand how to bring both law and gospel to their parishioners.[25] For in the midst of expounding the rest of the conversation in Genesis 3, Luther reminds his students that God's curse fell upon the serpent, which the professor views as a consolation for Adam and Eve since the curse did not fall upon them. This "revealed the depths of God's goodness. . . . Adam and Eve had their hope aroused by this promise. With their whole hearts they grasped the hope of their restoration, and filled with faith, they saw that God was concerned about their salvation."[26] Brian Brock states that in comments on the Psalms Luther

23. WA 42:130.10–131.14; *LW* 1:174–75.
24. WA 42:130.10–133.23; *LW* 1:174–78.
25. WA 42:133.26–176.17; *LW* 1:178–236.
26. WA 42:142.1–143.3; 42:144.8–10; *LW* 1:190, 193. In a somewhat parallel homiletical exegesis shortly before his death, Luther briefly mentions stories of God's wrath—his punishment of Egypt under Pharaoh in Exodus, the conflagration of Sodom and Gomorrah, the flood—to

defined sin as "concrete but aberrant responses to God's gifts, a filled-out and personified antidoxology."[27] Here the reformer saw God as turning that antidoxology back into praise and trust.

In this exposition of Genesis 3, Luther's definition of the gospel centers on the forgiveness of sins, on the restoration of the life of hope and the hope of life, rather than on an act of newly creating the relationship between God and his human creatures. But the reformer often did specify that forgiveness and restoration are parallel with the act of creation in Genesis 1. In telling stories from the Old Testament, Luther repeatedly made it clear that God alone initiates human life, that his Word of promise is his instrument for restoring fallen humanity to a proper relationship of trust with him. God created by speaking, and he re-creates by speaking. What he re-creates when he forgives sin is a justified person. Then as God's child, this justified believer fulfills God's expectations in demonstrating his love and carrying out his will in the world.

His study of Genesis gave Luther several good examples of faith, including that of the builder of the ark. Nonetheless, as great as Noah's faith was, Luther proclaimed to the Wittenberger hearers in 1523, even greater is the example of Abraham's trust in the Lord and the love it produced.[28] Abraham served as Luther's favorite example of faith and of God's responsibility for that faith, of God's initiating human faith with his promise and creating trust in his chosen patriarch.[29] In 1535 he told his students, "God speaks, and Abraham believes what God is saying. Moreover, the Holy Spirit comes as a trustworthy witness and declares that this very believing or this very faith is righteousness or is imputed by God himself as righteousness. . . . When the Divine Majesty thinks about me that I am righteous, that my sins have been forgiven, that I am free from eternal death, and when I gratefully grasp the way God thinks

---

highlight the trust that God's people could have in the kindness and love of God for his people; see WA 51:119.25–120.21.

27. Brian Brock, *Singing the Ethos of God: On the Place of Christian Ethics in Scripture* (Grand Rapids: Eerdmans, 2007), 174.

28. WA 14:219.1/28–221.24/35; 24:243.18–248.19.

29. See Juhani Forsberg, *Das Abrahambild in der Theologie Luthers: Pater fidei sanctissimus* (Stuttgart: Steiner, 1984), 26–31. Because he does not consistently follow his own recognition of the significance of Luther's understanding of God's Word as the instrument of his power, Forsberg repeatedly invents a false differentiation between the reformer's "forensic-juridical" understanding of justification and his own definition of justification as a change of the "being" of the believer. As Gerhard Forde says, "The absolutely forensic character of justification renders it effective—justification actually kills and makes alive. It is, to be sure, 'not only' forensic, but that is the case only because the more forensic it is the more effective it is!" See *Justification by Faith: A Matter of Death and Life* (Philadelphia: Fortress, 1982), 36. Forsberg rightly understands the reality-creating power of God's "regard" for or "thinking" of the sinner as righteous, but he somehow fails to see that this is a vital part of Luther's reality-creating "forensic" view of justification; see Forsberg, *Abrahambild*, 65–66. More helpful on this point is Ulrich Asendorf, *Lectura in Biblia: Luthers Genesisvorlesung, 1535–1545* (Göttingen: Vandenhoeck & Ruprecht, 1998), 82–102.

of me in faith, then I am truly righteous not through my works but through faith, with which I grasp the way God thinks about me."[30]

Luther presumed that his hearers knew Abraham's biography so well that he could refer to it as an example of God's initiative in creating the relationship between himself and his human creatures and an example of the trust that responds. In depicting Nicodemus's struggle to understand and believe what Jesus was telling him in John 3—and this as early as 1522—the Wittenberg preacher explains what the term "born again" or "new birth" means with reference to Abraham. Luther mentions Abraham's trust that his son would inherit the world and his descendents would be numbered like the stars when God subsequently commands him to sacrifice Isaac (Gen. 22:1–19). The patriarch demonstrates his confidence in the person and promise of God by proceeding to do what God has said he should. "If Abraham had proceeded on the basis of reason, he would have concluded, 'Well, God promised me descendents through whom my tribe is to be increased. Now he comes and tells me to sacrifice this son. Well, this must be the devil, not God.' Abraham put his reason to death and gave God honor and thought, 'Well, God is so powerful that he can awake my son from death and increase my tribe through him, or he can indeed give me another son or in some other manner find a way, unknown to me. Go, and put it in God's hands.' Behold, Abraham crawls out of his old skin and surrenders to God, believes him, and becomes a new person." Luther concludes his use of Abraham's example with the reminder of the angel's intervention and the comment regarding the angel's giving him a substitute, the ram for sacrifice: "Abraham could not have imagined that God would do something like that. He had already killed his son in his heart."[31] Reality existed fundamentally for Luther in that relationship between God's creative Word and human response to it, in Abraham's case with a trusting heart.

That God reckoned Abram to be righteous because of his faith in Genesis 15:6 opened the door for Luther to tell about God's way of working with his human creatures. He did so already in the Scholia of 1521, creating a dialogue between the promising God and trusting Abram. In this dialogue Abram responds to the promise by assuring God that he will not doubt the Lord's protection and he will act in such a way that does not cause his enemies to hear evil regarding the Lord's name.[32] Other examples confirmed Abraham's model for trust. Esau's kindly attitude toward Jacob when he returns from serving Laban (Gen. 33) depicts how God, and God alone, can change hearts.

---

30. WA 42:563.17–20; 42:563.38–564.2. David Steinmetz notes the importance of the correlation of God's Word and human trust in "Abraham and the Reformation," in *Luther in Context* (Bloomington: Indiana University Press, 1986), 33, 38–41.

31. WA 10.2:300.21–37; CP 3:414–15.

32. WA 9:355.3–5; cf. similar comments on Gen. 12 in WA 9:428.33–429.32; on Gen. 16 in WA 9:356.28–357.21; and on Gen. 22 in WA 9:1–22.

"This is the work of the power and majesty of God alone to change an angry and offended heart and mind into a quiet and kind one. For otherwise the human heart is so ungovernable that it cannot be changed by any power."[33]

In the New Testament era this trust arises out of hearing of God's love in Jesus Christ, who fulfills the hopes of the Old Testament believers who looked forward to his coming. Luther also tried to cultivate trust in his hearers and readers by retelling accounts of faith from all parts of the Bible. Both Old Testament stories and many from the New Testament provided him with models able to induce the trust that rests in God alone and the service that trust creates. He used such stories to demonstrate God's faithfulness and the sometimes steadfast yet sometimes wavering trust of biblical figures.

Trust in Christ Delivers Sinners from False Faith and Disobedience

The trust that constitutes the core of human life was not, for Luther, simply a human sentiment or an effort of will, mind, and emotion. It was a relationship with God, with the person of God in human flesh, Jesus Christ. Therefore Luther concentrated his preaching on the creation and strengthening of the love and confidence that bound his hearers and readers to this person. He did so, above all, by preaching of Christ's death and resurrection. An analysis of his proclamation of Christ's atoning work for sinners would fill a book itself and will not be investigated here. But alongside this proclamation his sermons featured many models or examples of human beings who had received the gift of trusting Christ from the Holy Spirit.

In the parable of the rich man and Lazarus (Luke 16:19–31), Luther found a good example of the nature of faith, specifically faith's focus on God alone. This story demonstrates the significance of having the correct object of trust. The problem of the rich man lies not in his outward conduct: he has lived an upright life, Luther presumes. His life has not caused offense. But "the gospel has sharp eyes and looks deep into the heart's foundation, and it reproves even the works that reason cannot reprove. It looks not at the sheep's clothing but at the true fruit of the tree, whether it is good or not good, as the Lord said in Matthew 7 [vv. 16–20]." However, reason looks at the costly clothing and rich food that the rich man has been able to enjoy and reckons that such people have earned these things because they have performed good works. Reason cannot see that sin is rooted in a failure to trust God. The rich man's desire for the pleasures of this life reveals the result of "the sin hidden in his heart, the failure to trust. For where faith exists, a person does not worry about clothing and rich food and knows no blessing, honor, desire, power, or anything else apart from God himself, and seeks, longs for, clings to nothing other than to

33. WA 44:117.31–35; LW 6:157–58.

God as the only highest good." Luther added brief recollections of the stories of Esther and David to confirm that godly people do not place their confidence in riches and pleasures but rather in God alone.[34]

The Gospel lesson for the twenty-fourth Sunday after Trinity, Matthew 9:18–26, presents two sterling examples of trust placed in the person of Christ. In this passage the leader of the synagogue whose daughter has died and the woman suffering from continuing hemorrhages direct their trust and their pleas to Jesus. Luther's sermon of 1525 was incorporated into the Church Postil; Dietrich edited that of 1533 for the House Postil. In the 1525 sermon Luther describes the psychological setting in which the leader of the synagogue comes to Jesus:

> No one could hope or believe that any help or support was possible, but he did not despair. While the others at his house had given up all hope for her, were wailing and crying and thinking of nothing else than laying out the corpse and arranging for the pipers and others, this leader of the synagogue went to Christ. He had firm confidence that if he could bring Jesus to the little girl, she would live again. He believed that Jesus was the man who could not only restore people to health who were still alive, and preserve their health, but also he could restore life itself when the soul had left the body. Faith had propelled him to seek Christ's help, for he knew that he was the true Messiah.[35]

Wittenberg hearers found his story to be a paradigmatic narrative for themselves. The woman who suffered hemorrhages for twelve years also demonstrates this confidence focused on the person of Christ. The 1533 sermon identifies her problem as dysentery and notes that this most extraordinary case had gone on for twelve years, although "in these lands anyone who contracts this disease [usually] does not survive very long."[36]

In the 1525 sermon Luther comments that as soon as she heard of Christ—in this case Luther resists the temptation to remind his hearers of Romans 10:17, "Faith comes by hearing"—she came to him, "with a resolute trust that doubted not in the least that he could help her in her distress, and with this confidence in her heart, that he was reliable and kind, that he would help her and not let her down. She is so certain and assured of this that her heart has no worry or anxiety at all, although this was a matter of great ritual significance for her, and without doubt she felt strong nudges in the direction of doubt." Luther presumes that he and his hearers would find themselves in similar situations. He recounts how the woman hopes that merely touching Jesus's clothing's hem would heal her. Despite the pressing masses, "her faith and desire" propels her through the crowds, and she touches him. "Notice how her faith overcomes

---

34. WA 10.3:178.19–181.25; CP 4:18–20.
35. WA 22:392.35–394.3; CP 5:347–48.
36. WA 52:537.27–538.5; *HP* 3:184–85.

two great obstacles. First, her faith is so strong and can believe that he will help if she just touches his clothing. She does not think it necessary that she should come and bother him about her distress with a lot of words for him to have mercy on her and help, or that others should pray for her, but if she could just reach him and touch him. When that happened, she would certainly receive help. She did not doubt either his power or his will [that she would not remain any more in distress], and so she did not think it necessary to talk with him." She did not regard herself as worthy of talking with Jesus, but her heart was so full of firm confidence in him that she simply went on with her plan. "That must have been a tremendous overpowering enlightenment from the Spirit and a recognition of faith that a poor, simple woman should see that help and power from this man was of such that it was not necessary to have a long talk with him. . . . That means that she believed that in this man there had to be divine almighty power and might so that he could see and understand the secret thoughts and desires of her heart." Luther goes on to conclude that "what faith is and does is dependent on the person of Christ, that is, this kind of heart, which regards him as Lord and Savior, God's Son, through whom God revealed himself and promises his grace, that for his sake and through him God wants to hear us and help us." That is true worship and the proper honoring of God, the preacher tells his hearers and readers.[37]

The 1533 sermon on the text reflects what Luther had written in his Large Catechism: Jesus's praise for the woman's faith makes it clear what shape this trust in him takes.

> That is the reaction he regards as most precious, the highest kind of service, that pleases him most. What a great desire he has for you to expect all good things from him and seek his help. . . . It is as if he wanted to say, "Look, learn to believe with confidence in whatever distress it may be. For my desire to help is much greater than your desire for help. I want to rescue you from death more than let you continue in the life you now have," and he proved it by healing her. . . . We should learn from this example that we too believe and expect all good things from Christ in every distress and concern.[38]

In addition to the obstacle of not being able to believe that such a great blessing lay within the realm of the possible, this woman also overcame a second obstacle: "She overcame her own unworthiness and cast the huge stone from her heart that had lain heavily on her. It had made her afraid that she should not approach Christ publicly, as others did." The judgment of the law on her, according to which she was "an impure woman, forbidden community with other people" (Lev. 15:19–31), had become a great burden on her and, along with the disease itself, weighed heavily upon her. "Thus she could not

37. WA 22:394.15–396.5; CP 5:348–53.
38. WA 52:538.6–34; *HP* 3:185–86.

hold on to her faith without battle and conflict." However, "her faith, which clearly focused on the kind and gracious heart of Christ, broke through the obstacles. . . . This Savior must be grasped, despite the law, her own heart, the world, and indeed even what Jesus himself might say. 'He is the one who could help and who is also an upright, kind, faithful Savior; and I am a poor, miserable woman who needs his help. He will not change into some other kind of person and deprive me of his grace and help.'" Luther praises her faith, which acknowledged its own unworthiness but continued to trust and did not doubt Christ's grace and help. Her faith also had confidence that Christ wants to display his power to help his people.[39] She faced problems not unlike the inhabitants of Wittenberg faced, and they shared her doubts and inner conflicts. With her faith embodied in a paradigmatic narrative, Luther intended to strengthen the faith of his hearers.

Zacchaeus also provided a model for a kind of reckless trust that is seeking a haven and is finally found by Christ. Mixing metaphor with the report of this tax collector's encounter with Christ, Luther depicts the scene. Zacchaeus merely wanted a glimpse of the celebrity because "when a poor naked debtor hears that salvation comes only from Christ, he runs to him, chased there by his fraudulent, misled heart." Yet climbing a fig tree is, metaphorically, the wrong move. "This wild fig tree has abundant full leaves, strong branches, lovely boughs. Everyone who sees it considers it lovely in every way. But when you seek fruit among its leaves, you will never find any. Therefore it is correctly called a wild or counterfeit fig tree because it looks good but has no fruit. . . . This wild fig tree represents those who look good and teach according to human wisdom. They stand out from the crowd, and people marvel at them. People are attracted to them. It does no good." Therefore, when Christ comes near, he calls Zacchaeus away from the tree. "What can a poor, thirsty, parched soul do? It quickly climbs down and joyfully receives the Lord Jesus so that it becomes a sanctified temple of the Lord for eternity."[40]

Encouragement to trust Christ came not only from presentations of the power of the gospel to change the orientation of the sinner. Luther also compared his hearers' and readers' faith with examples of faith that should put them to shame. From 1533 and 1534 his sermons on John 4:47–54, the healing of the royal official's son, illustrate how Luther, within the space of one year, could retell a story with somewhat different accents. In each case the preacher sketches something of the thinking of the official, as Luther speculated. The second sermon makes the father an official of King Herod, possibly a Jew, who knows nothing more about Christ than what he has heard from others. In Luther's earlier sermon the father shows slightly more familiarity with Jesus's recent activities. In the first sermon, Luther sketches the story in more

---

39. WA 22:396.6–397.34; CP 5:353–54.
40. WA 17.2:501.2–3; FS 2:214–15.

detail and in it provides a model of the admonition of the law as a call to faith. When a potentially fatal illness strikes the boy, the official remembers that "a prophet had arisen whose powerful teaching was being supported by mighty deeds. It is even possible that he had personally heard Christ preach. . . . He may have heard how Jesus made water into wine at the Cana wedding feast. All of this may have so moved him that he had become a believer, and now, in the desperate situation of his boy's illness, he hurries to Christ and pleads for help." Luther sets the example in place: "What a receptive heart! After just one sermon and one miracle he had faith enough to go immediately to Christ in his time of need." This faith was to teach the Wittenberg hearers two things: first, "that we have God's Word in richest measure, yes, the Holy Scripture itself, and that it was written a long time ago for our learning and comfort; and second, that this Word is preached to us every day."

Luther acknowledges that the official's request that he "come down and heal" the son seems to be a weakness of faith because Christ replies, with a tone of impatience, "if you do not see signs and wonders!" But the preacher provides a short glance into the official's struggle with his doubt. Despite this inner conflict, on the strength of knowing about the miracle of Cana, Luther speculates, he has confidence in Jesus's ability to heal his son. With his imagination impelling him ever more deeply into the story, Luther contends that this meant he had advanced much further in faith than the Wittenberg hearers. John presents this example "both to make us blush with shame and then to stimulate our faith. Indeed, on the last day the royal official will step before all false believers and judge them: 'Shame on you, you despicable people!' I heard only one sermon and saw only one solitary sign, namely, that the Lord made wine out of water, and yet I learned enough so that I believed he had power to do all things." For many years the residents of Wittenberg had heard the gospel and had seen God's mighty acts, "and yet your life does not show it, and you make little progress in spiritual growth." Luther returns to the official's faith as a pattern for his hearers' trust: "The officer possessed a very wonderful, outstanding faith. He trusted Christ completely at his word, never doubting that when he reached home, he would find his son alert and well. The hope in his heart was as certain as if he had already experienced the reality. He clung to the mere word in true faith, and the miracle took place."[41]

Luther not only scolded and admonished; he also preached to console and encourage. His House Postil contains still another sermon on the royal official's faith. It retells less of the story recorded in John's Gospel than had the first sermon, but it holds up the example as one "recorded for our sakes, so that we too might summon up courage to come to God. For faith is nothing else than sincere trust in God. Whoever has deliberate trust in God and comes to him with courageous heart possesses a true faith. . . . Here the official has a

41. WA 37:189.5–190.33; EA² 6:152–58; *HP* 3:118–20; cf. WA 37:561.4–31; *HP* 122–23.

beautiful faith in Christ, that is, he is very confident that Christ will grant him mercy and help." Luther portrays the royal official as a model of Wittenberg repentance. He had thought to himself, "Even though I am a wicked scoundrel, he still allows his loving-kindness to govern over the evil and the good, and therefore he will help me just as he has helped them.[42]

Luther used the story of Jonah to comfort those whose faith becomes weak and who are angry with God. In front of his hearers he depicts Jonah as struggling with "unreasonable anger" over the conversion of Nineveh, begrudging the Ninevites their salvation, and wishing them every evil. He was angry without cause and just plain wrong. "Yet he has enough faith at the same time to ask God to let him die; he does not care to live any longer. He could not have prayed thus if he had not trusted God completely." "He remained in the faith and was acceptable to God since God conversed so affably with him and granted him a sign, acting like someone who chats and deals in a friendly way with others."[43] Luther intertwined Jonah's story (chap. 4) with the account of Peter's mission to Cornelius (Acts 10): both of them had zealously protected the Hebrew heritage against the threat they perceived in extending God's graciousness to those outside the chosen people. Both Jonah and Peter had to learn that God wants all people to be saved and come to the knowledge of his truth (1 Tim. 2:4).[44] Luther concludes that, in the end, in spite of the sinful rebellion of Jonah's anger over God's blessing Nineveh, he remains "God's dear child. Jonah chats so uninhibitedly with God as though he were not in the least afraid of him—as indeed he is not. He confides in him as in a father." From this, Luther points out to his students that "God permits his children to blunder and err greatly and grossly," as Christ did with his disciples. This consoles believers who "sin and stray occasionally." For they can trust in the God who deals "kindly, paternally, and amiably with them."[45] Like the royal official's story, the narrative of Jonah provided a pattern for the exercise of the Wittenberg hearers' identity as the children of God.

Luther's consolation of those who were struggling with doubts about God's mercy or who were despairing because the sin they were striving to defeat was persisting in their lives may seem to contradict his scolding the hearers for their weakness of faith and indifference to Christ. However, the two contrary messages reveal his delivery of both law and gospel, each to a different kind of hearer: the law calls those defying or ignoring the gospel to repentance; the gospel builds up the trust of those plagued by doubt or guilt. Both messages were intended to create the new way of living for which the scolding of the law prepared the way, a style of living that proceeds from the gospel's action of creating and strengthening faith in Christ.

42. WA 37:561.20–562.3; EA² 6:159–60, 165–66; *HP* 123–24.
43. WA 19:239.20–241.3; *LW* 19:91–92.
44. WA 19:241.6–243.15; *LW* 19:93–96.
45. WA 19:240.30–33; *LW* 19:92.

Ultimately, this trust brings believers to life eternal in heaven after they die. The cultivation of faith directed against the terrors of death will be discussed in chapter 7 (below). Yet for Luther the story of human salvation offers more than deliverance from earthly miseries through exiting to the blessedness of heaven. Trust in God produces peace and joy amid the struggle against evil of all kinds during daily life on earth. The reformer's affirmation of trust in God despite and in defiance of temporal misfortune reflected his trust in God's love in Christ and the Creator's power over his creation.

Trust in God's Providence during Earthly Life

God's provision for both the spiritual and the physical needs of his people unfolded before the eyes of Luther's hearers as he sketched the scenario that Christ suggested in Matthew 23:37, the protections of the chicks by the hen. Fred Meuser suggests that Luther may have been watching a hen with chicks in the Wartburg courtyard as he composed his sermon for the festival of Saint Stephen in 1521.[46] He defines the characters in the story: the mother hen is Christ, the chicks play as his faithful people, and the hawks are the devils and evil spirits that wish to make believers their prey. The chicks are none too clever but know enough to rely on Christ's righteousness as their shelter and shield. They creep, snuggle, crouch in the protective love of Christ, trusting that he will protect them. The mother hen searches and scratches for food and tries to coax her chicks into eating. Christ, like this mother hen, with concern showing in his voice, spreads wings of his merit over his people, warms them with his natural heat, that is, the Holy Spirit, and defends them against the devil. The hawks—Luther enriched the story by adding boars to their throng—devour and pursue the chicks and tear apart their victims, but God indeed protects and provides.[47]

Luther turned not only to his own stories to confirm that the Creator exercises providential control over his entire universe. Scripture also offers many comforting examples of God's care for his people. That God sustained Jacob as he went to meet Esau (Gen. 32) reminded Luther that the whole course of nature and human life reveals more good than evil, demonstrates that "a very small part of life is subjected to the devil's power."[48] God rules. Even when the ungodly forget God and their obligations to him, he is leading and governing them as well as the godly in all their actions.[49] Believers persist in trust even when evil seems to triumph. It had become so bad in Noah's day that God regretted creating human beings (Gen. 6:6), and Noah, Luther speculates

---

46. Fred Meuser, *Luther as Preacher* (Minneapolis: Augsburg, 1983), 62.
47. WA 10.1.1:280.5–282.3; LW 52:96–97.
48. WA 44:67.9–10; LW 6:90.
49. WA 44:68.1–27; LW 6:92.

before the congregation in Wittenberg, must have sensed that divine disgust with fear and trepidation. Noah knew that God had planned everything in human history, but he also realized that God can change and turn. God conveys that sense of imminent change to the pious.[50] They remain confident that ultimately God loves them and works in their behalf, protecting them and providing for them. Yet in the face of evils of various sorts, God's presence does not always mean victory against them in terms desirable to natural human inclinations and judgment.

When preaching on Jesus's revivifying the official's child and his healing of the hemorrhaging woman (Mark 5:24–34) in 1533, Luther pointed out to his audience that these two examples remind them that "the Lord showed himself no less powerful against other afflictions and infirmities as well." But his theology of the cross involved the recognition that God sometimes works "under the appearance of opposites." Thus Luther strove to cultivate in the congregation a faith that rested in confidence on God's presence and promise even when his strength was being perfected in their weakness, as God had told Paul he was doing in the apostle's life (2 Cor. 12:9). In this sermon on Mark 5 Luther, in both temporal and spiritual dimensions of life, poses the contrast of what human beings see in the world and what Christ sees. David had seen himself as a poor shepherd, and so had the world, but Christ viewed him as a king. "All of you who have faith in me regard yourselves as poor sinners, but I regard you as precious saints; I regard you as like the angels. I simply speak not more than a single word, and sin, death, sickness have to yield, and righteousness, life, and health come in their place. The way I speak determines how things are; they cannot be otherwise."[51]

Luther went on to comment that the eyes of human reason see the world differently than do the eyes of Christ. "Such eyes, when they see death, sin, and hell, say, 'I see no death, I feel no sin, I am not condemned, but I see through Christ nothing but holiness, life, and salvation.'" Such eyes have a different vision of the world as well:

> Therefore, even if I am poor, I feel no poverty. Even if I am emaciated, I have enough. For I have Christ, who can give me what I need every hour even if I have nothing. Whoever has this kind of eyes will gladly boast that he has Christ's eyes and would see more deeply into what is the case in times of famine or epidemic than we usually do. Everybody looks to what he has in the cellar and in the storage space. Whatever he finds there determines his disposition. If he finds a lot, he is happy. If he finds too little, he is sad and wants to despair. So in deadly epidemics those who can flee, flee, and they think they will be safe in another place. But Christians, when it is possible that they might have a thousand deadly diseases in their bodies, think, "I have Christ. If it is his will, this epidemic will

50. WA 24:168.31–169.23.
51. WA 52:540.15–27; *HP* 3:188–89.

harm me as little as a flea under the arm that bites me a bit but cannot take my life away." And it is certain that whoever has such a heart will remain assured and will without fear have a hopeful disposition.

However, Luther warns, we are more likely to be troubled and despairing.[52]

Therefore his sermons aimed at cultivating the bold yet humble trust displayed particularly in the New Testament accounts of Jesus's healings. The lesson for the third Sunday after Epiphany, Matthew 8:1–13, presented Luther with the opportunity to comment on the faith of the leper who told Jesus, "You can heal me if you want to do it." The Church Postil of 1525 presents Luther's praise of this faith: "The leper would not have been so bold as to go to the Lord and ask to be cleansed if he had not trusted him with his whole heart and expected that Christ would be so kind and gracious and would cleanse him. Since he was a leper, he had reason to hold back since the law commanded lepers not to associate with people. Nonetheless he ignored the law and the people and the purity and holiness of Christ." However, the leper did not have anything else in mind but seeking and receiving the simple kindness and grace of Christ, given apart from all merit.[53] Luther uses the precise wording of the leper's plea in Matthew to expand on the nature of faith. That the leper here tempers his prayer with the clause "if it is your will," which he addresses to Jesus, is no indication that he had doubts about Christ's kindness and grace, his almighty power and knowledge. "That is a living faith that does not doubt that God does what we ask out of his kind and gracious will." But the leper's faith models a humility recognizing that God knows what is truly good for his children. For that reason they place their petitions in God's hands, trusting his wisdom as well as his power.[54]

As Luther traces the short narrative of the text, he depicts two brief scenarios that permit him to address the false piety with which he and many hearers had grown up. First, with a polemical thrust against the medieval works righteousness he wanted to root out of their minds, he points out to his hearers and readers that the leper had a repentant spirit, recognizing and feeling his own uncleanness and unworthiness. "That is a true faith, a living confidence in the kindness of God." If the leper had said to Jesus, "Look, Lord, I have prayed or fasted so much and the like that you will want to take this into consideration and for that reason make me clean," Christ would not have healed him, Luther ventures. That would have robbed God of his honor. Luther adds that the leper's reasoning had not produced his faith but rather his faith sprang from all that was being noised about concerning Christ: faith comes by hearing and hearing from God's Word (Rom. 10:17).[55] In this case the preacher fashions for his

52. WA 52:541.22–542.24; *HP* 3:188–89.
53. WA 17.2:73.19–74.19; CP 2:71–72.
54. WA 17.2:75.36–76.14; CP 2:75–76.
55. WA 17.2:73.19–74.19; CP 2:72.

narrative a counterimage reflecting the medieval paradigm of pious life so that he can reject it and urge his hearers to discard this attitude of dependence on their own works. Deconstruction of the old paradigm could take place through the presentation and construction of a new one.

Trust against Reason and Doubt

Trusting is not always an easy task since it is counterintuitive to sinners' desire to manage and preserve their own lives through their own way of doing things. Luther's theology of the cross presumes the necessity of crucifying such reasoning and its claim to dominance over human reflection on God and humanity. This reliance on rational argument extended to the common sense that kept the world in order, thought the people of Wittenberg and their contemporaries. Luther's sketch of what was going on in Nicodemus's mind during his conversation with Jesus in John 3, particularly Jesus's dictum "You must be born again," led the reformer to explore the way in which the Creator's approach to the restoration of fallen sinners offends common sense. In an aside intended probably for students among the hearers (perhaps mostly students since this sermon was delivered in Luther's home), Luther explains that "to be born again" was a contradiction in terms (*fallacia*). But also being reborn spiritually could not have appealed to the hypocritical Pharisee, who says to himself, "It would be the fires of hell if I had done all these good works, all this fasting and praying, for nothing!" But that is what Jesus said. "This confuses Nicodemus, and he does not understand, just as it is impossible for human reason ever to comprehend the fact that salvation cannot be achieved by keeping the law. It is part of the nature with which we were born that we all desperately want God to consider us as pious people who have done many good things. . . . The whole person must become new and different. A tree must become a good tree before it can produce good fruit." As Luther traces the conversation recorded in John 3:2–13 between the two, he hazards the observation that it seems Nicodemus intended to trap Jesus in his own words. Nicodemus presumed that he understood what Jesus was saying, and he knew he could not reenter his mother's body. He knew he could not ascend into the air and be born again by the wind. Jesus explained that he was talking about baptism and the Holy Spirit, and he said simply to Nicodemus, "If you are not willing to believe that, you most certainly will never understand [how to enter into the kingdom of God]."[56] Jesus went on to make clear what he was saying about God's initiative and control in the salvation that the Creator effects for sinners through retelling the story from Numbers 21 of Moses's raising the bronze serpent in the wilderness to heal Israelites bitten by snakes.

56. WA 36:185.2–187.16; EA² 5:236–39; *HP* 2:207–10.

Often, however, either reason or experience causes faith to stumble and cower. Peter provided several pictures of faith that cannot quite believe. Luther had had such experiences himself, and he anticipated that his hearers in Wittenberg would have the same problem from time to time. "Peter was too timid when the Lord wished to wash his feet and said, 'Do you think you are to wash my feet?' He did not understand how much he needed Christ, but finally his heart propelled him to grasp that it was necessary for Christ to wash his feet" (John 13:2–11). Luther observes that "our heart is in the same condition: we wish to see the Lord Jesus present to help us, and yet we are so timid that we are afraid of him and do not think as much of his loving-kindness as we freely profess to do." Peter's confession after the great catch of fish (Luke 5:6–8), "Go away from me, Lord, for I am a sinful man!" (NRSV), indicates that "our timid nature is always afraid of Christ, in whom there is nothing but good, and who has come to help everyone. . . . We must not make Christ into a tyrant but let him be a loving Lord and Savior, who has no other desire than to help sinners and to invite and attract everyone by his words and example."[57]

This wavering of faith occurred throughout the Old Testament too. Luther marvels at Abram's steadfast trust in God when God keeps him on the road in Genesis 12, not bestowing the land of Canaan on him immediately after promising it. Luther expands on this issue for the readers of his German sermon:

> This is a marvelous story and a marvelous faith that God led this man from the temporal to the eternal. God mentioned and pointed him to a temporal blessing, the land, and did not deliver it. But this faith that was clinging to God's Word, even though it was speaking of something temporal, brought him eternal salvation. It depends on God's Word. If God speaks of a mere stalk of straw, it is nevertheless an eternal Word. Whoever believes this Word is justified and upright. For he has God and enough for eternity. . . . If the Word is present, you have enough, for it is the eternal truth and God himself, and there is faith and an eternal treasure.[58]

Of all the biblical figures, Mary provides the supreme example of trusting the word of the Lord. Medieval piety's veneration of the mother of Jesus had not rendered a realistic model for most laypeople at Luther's time, the reformers were convinced, so Luther strove to depict her as the girl next door. In his sermon of 1523 on the Magnificat, Luther writes: "Mary was a poor young lady, . . . perhaps a poor orphan, regarded with contempt, for she says that God looked upon the nothingness and rejectedness of his servant. Great things were announced to this poor young girl, that she should become the mother of the

---

57. The sermon on Easter Monday 1523, on Luke 24:13–35, published separately in 1524 and in the Church Postil of 1524; in WA 12:502.17–36; CP 2:277.
58. WA 24:253.34–254.14; cf. 14:223.17/35–224.13/31; 14:298.8–25; 24:379.18–380.19.

Highest, who would be called a son of God. That meant that he would be a king and his rule would have no end. That is a hard piece for faith to swallow. . . . She could just as well have said, 'Who am I, a poor worm, that I should give birth to a king,' and doubted. But she closed her eyes, trusted God, trusted that he was mighty and could bring that to pass even though it was contrary to reason and all creatures."[59] In his sermon of 1521 on the Magnificat, Luther states, "Where there is this experience [of God's revelation of himself] that he is a God who looks into the depths and helps only the poor, despised, afflicted, miserable, forsaken, and those who are nothing, there a hearty love for him is born. The heart overflows with gladness and goes leaping and dancing for the great pleasure it has found in God. There the Holy Spirit is present."[60] In his 1521 exposition of the Magnificat, alongside Mary's faith, Luther reminds the readers of David, Peter, Paul, and Mary Magdalene as models of trust in God, presuming that readers would remember the stories of their clinging to God in times of desperation over their sinfulness.[61]

Mary also epitomizes the faith that clings to God even when he—in this case, Jesus—seems to be turning his back. Luther sees a moment of high drama in John 2:4, when Jesus deflects his mother's request to aid the poor wedding manager who had run out of wine. "What have I to do with you?" Luther depicts a Mary so confident in the ability and desire of Jesus to help that she did not need to say, "Supply some wine!" She merely says, "They have no wine!" Jesus had not acted earlier, Luther explains, because people whose needs have been filled do not appreciate grace. At the point of the Gospel lesson, the need had become pressing.

> But see in what an unkind manner he brushes aside the humble request of his mother, who speaks it with such confidence. See how faith is held at bay. What does it have to grasp hold of? Nothing but nothing, and darkness. It recognizes the need and sees no help, and in addition God seems distant and unmanageable. He seems not to recognize his own. All that is left is just plain nothing. That is the way it is in the conscience when we feel our own sin and lack of righteousness or are in death's grasp. We feel what is lacking in our lives or the terrors of hell, where eternal salvation is not present.

Luther continues his description of the desperation of the tortured sinner, again comparing it to Mary's situation at Cana. "Here faith is in a real battle. See how his mother acts. That is a lesson for us. How harsh his words sound. How unkind he acts. But in spite of everything, in her heart she attributes that not to anger or contrary to his kindness. She remained convinced that he was kind and did not let his humiliating her take her off track." She did not

59. WA 12:458.34–459.9.
60. WA 7:548.5–11; *LW* 21:300.
61. WA 7:569.27–31; *LW* 21:323.

act without reasoning, as Psalm 32 (v. 9) says the horse and mule do, Luther observes. Again, he compares giving up on God to the despair over sin that overtakes a person who thinks that God is totally repudiating him and saying, "What have I to do with you?" "A blow from hell!" Luther exclaims. So, he concludes, on the basis of Mary's example,

> We give God the honor, as one who is kind and gracious, whether he seems to be the opposite or not. . . . By doing that, this feeling will be put to death and the old Adam will perish and pure faith in God's goodness will remain in us, not just some mere emotion. For here you see how his mother held to her faith with abandon. She is a model for us! She is certain that he will demonstrate his grace even though it is also certain that she feels the opposite. Thus she commends the situation to his kindness with abandon and does not prescribe the way he should act or limits of time or place to him. Let him do it when he wishes.[62]

Such a faith Luther commends to his hearers and readers.

Faith Restored through Repentance Generates and Elicits Trust

God remains ever faithful to his promise. His claim on the sinner never expires. However, the believer's capability to run away from God and fall into rebellion against him again formed, for Luther, a significant part of the mystery of the continuation of sin and evil in the lives of the baptized. His conviction that the whole life of the believer is a life of repentance[63] informed his proclamation of God's Word in almost every sermon. He addressed repentance and the kind of trust that turns to God through the retelling of biblical stories as well as in catechetical and expository preaching. Among the best examples is his retelling of the parable of the Pharisee and the tax collector in the temple. This parable (Luke 18:9–14) portrays two ways of approaching God. It offered Luther rich material for transforming the way in which his hearers and readers viewed their own identity, worth, and dignity.

The preacher sketches two kinds of character. The Pharisee embodies the person who has lived an outwardly pious life. He boasts first of his worship and praise of God and thanks God for preserving him from sin and shame of the kind that obviously has marked the life of the tax collector praying within his sight. Then he boasts of his keeping the commandments regarding other people. "He has strictly kept the sixth commandment and has not committed adultery or led an unchaste life, but kept his body in subjection and discipline, and also fasted every week—not a false fasting . . . but a real fasting such as the Jews observed from morning till evening." He has not extorted from his

---

62. WA 17.2:64.30–67.4; CP 2:62–64.
63. See p. 16.

neighbors; he tithes and is in general quite obedient to God. The tax collector, part of a corrupt system that inevitably carries its agents into exploiting people, is by contrast a public sinner who has failed to give any of his material blessings to serve God and the neighbor.

Obviously, Luther observes, the Pharisee does not earn God's condemnation because he keeps the divine commandments. But God's judgment differs from the world's judgment, he explains. The Pharisee's beautiful and praiseworthy gifts do not alter the fact that he has not kept the first commandment. He has made an idol out of his own gifts and works. "This is the great sin and vice. Here he opposes God himself, of course, blind and hardened, like an unbelieving pagan or Turk who knows nothing of God and is without repentance. The Pharisee, on account of his own [presumed] great holiness, wants to acknowledge nothing of his own sin and does not fear God's wrath. He is presumptuously standing upon his own works and does not see that he and all others, even the true saints themselves with their own righteousness and life, cannot stand before God but are guilty and deserving of his wrath." Luther hammers home his deep concern for faith directed toward God alone: the Pharisee "sins so horribly against the first and highest commandment, in shameful and horrible idolatry, presumption, and defiance. He depends on his own holiness because he does not fear God, nor does he trust or love him, but seeks only his own honor and praise." Luther concludes, "He does not honestly, from the heart, observe any of the other commandments. Everything is false and lies that he pretends with his prayers and worship, and therefore he abuses and disgraces God's name in the highest degree when he adorns his lies with it and thus brings down upon himself God's wrath and sharp condemnation."[64] According to the reformer's interpretation, this parable presents the heart of humanity: trust in the Creator, letting God be God, along with a realistic assessment of human life caught in a sinful world.

The true slaying of the old self is what Luther depicts through the tax collector, who

> had the advantage of confessing himself a poor sinner, convinced by his own conscience and condemned, and therefore has nothing of which he can boast or be proud before God or the world. He must be ashamed of himself, for the law has so smitten his heart that he feels his misery and distress and is terrified and filled with anguish at God's judgment and anger. He sighs from his heart to be delivered but finds no comfort anywhere for his evil plight. He can bring nothing before God but only sin and shame. This burdens and oppresses him so much that he cannot even lift up his eyes. He senses and feels that he has deserved nothing else than hell and eternal death and must condemn himself before God.

He cannot trust in himself for comfort and has to flee to God's mercy.[65]

64. WA 22:197.13–198.17; 22:199.1–200.32; CP 4:352–54.
65. WA 22:207.35–211.13; CP 4:358–61.

Luther explains that such repentant honesty is possible not through rational assessment of the sinner's situation but only through the Word of God and its promise. The gospel of forgiveness and life in Christ is a necessary presupposition, the necessary agent, for building this desire to slay the old self and trust in God. Luther contrasts the attitude of the tax collector with others beyond the gross, public sinners Paul describes in 1 Corinthians 6:9. "Some rascals try to imitate the tax collector and use the Lord's Prayer. They have heard the words that God will be merciful to poor sinners and have learned to repeat the words and smite their breasts and can present themselves so humble and penitent in words and questions that you could swear, and they would swear, that they are just like this tax collector, and yet this is a false delusion." Luther knew that such false Christians sat before him in Wittenberg's town church and would be reading his printed works. He cultivated their slaying of the old self by holding this mirror before their eyes.

The preacher also addresses those who would hear this admonition and be in doubt about their own sincerity in confessing their sins. "When the tax collector must come before God with only sin and shame, stripped of all his praise and full of nothing but corruption, here is anxiety and worry, so that he grasps hold of and appropriates the words to himself, 'Be merciful to me!' Here his own modesty and all human wisdom stand in his way and obstruct him even more. The devil himself uses the law of God and insists on it and enforces it, which he has no right to do, to bring human beings into distress and despair." This led Luther to the key element in his recultivation of the piety of his people:

> Therefore it is indeed a skill above all human skills, yea, the most wonderful thing on earth, that a person has the grace to know himself truly as a sinner, and yet again turn and cast away all thoughts of God's wrath and cling to grace alone. For the heart that truly feels sin cannot otherwise think or conclude that God is unmerciful and angry at him. Therefore let those with ability learn from this lofty wisdom and become a student of this tax collector, so that you may be able to distinguish these two parts from each other, so that wrath may not remain and cling to the sin, but you may lay hold of reconciliation and forgiveness.[66]

Here both the paradigm and the counterparadigm are aimed at the deconstruction of the old image of piety and the construction of the new.

Trust Produces Love

The reconstruction of the new paradigm of piety based on trust in Christ embraced also the fruits of that faith. As discussed above, Luther defined what

66. WA 22:204.34–209.4; CP 4:360–65.

it means to be human in terms of two modes of human relationship: (1) the "passive" mode, or "the righteousness that has its origin outside the self" (*iustitia aliena*); and (2) the "active" mode, or "the righteousness that has its origin from the self" (*iustitia propria*). Brian Brock is conscious of Luther's insistence that, despite a natural ethical sense in fallen human creatures, Scripture exercises ultimate authority also in determining the shape of human life. Brock observes that for Luther, the biblical presenter of the stories of God's people "as narrator must assume a God's-eye view of events in order to tell us about the deeds of the saints. But Christian ethics cannot be a mimicking of the saints' deeds. What is required is a renewal of the heart."[67] That is true because wrong deeds that hurt other people stem from the failure to fear, love, and trust in God above all things: "Idolatry is a gangrene that destroys by projecting itself outward through teaching into the social matrix."[68] The restoration of peace on earth depends on human creatures being able to trust that God is holding their lives secure and in order.

God is ultimately responsible for the creation of both human trust, the human side of passive righteousness, and human performance, the human side of active righteousness.[69] Through the action of the Holy Spirit, Luther believed, sinners are brought to trust in God and, on the basis of that trust, to love other human beings and care for God's entire creation. The two modes of being human cannot be separated, even though they must be sharply distinguished to prevent people from thinking that their performance can somehow create or contribute to their identity as children of God. This identity remains solely a gift, which expresses itself in following in Christ's footsteps and displaying love. God's command to Abram to be blameless in Genesis 17:1 provided occasion for Luther to observe that there is "a twofold righteousness: the perfect righteousness through which we are righteous before God through faith, and the imperfect righteousness through which we are righteous before God and other human beings insofar as our conduct and reputation are concerned."[70]

The suggestion that Luther—or even more prominently Melanchthon—taught a "forensic" doctrine of justification is often greeted with horror; Luther is excused of this doctrine more often than Melanchthon. The misunderstanding of their forensic—and common—understanding of justification rests on the refusal of scholars to recognize how the forensic (that is, the Word-driven) teaching on justification functions for both of them. The Wittenberg theologians may have expressed their fundamental view of justification with different language at times, but they agreed that just as God created the world through

---

67. Brock, *Singing the Ethos*, 170.
68. Ibid., 182.
69. See pp. 22–24.
70. WA 42:604.29–32; *LW* 3:79; among many other passages in the Genesis commentary with the same analysis of what it means to be human is WA 42:608.20–36; *LW* 3:84–85.

speaking, so also his word of forgiveness in Christ to sinners creates a new reality, not a legal fiction: as if this sinner were righteous. This new reality exists in God's sight and in God's regard, and for Luther and Melanchthon alike, nothing could be more real. Such forgiveness becomes the chief identity of the sinner through trust in Christ. This view of faith and of the power of God's Word of absolution confirms Bengt Hägglund's insight that Luther always viewed the change wrought in God's forgiveness as genuine change. Luther held this view because divine forgiveness awakens faith and brings into being a relationship with God on the strength of God's Word. In this relationship God does not take sin into account, even though the believer encounters it because of the mystery of sin and evil's continuation in the lives of the baptized.[71] But Luther also believed that the word of forgiveness changes the disposition of the sinner and creates genuine improvement, even if not steady progress, in the way believers conduct themselves in their worship of God and their love for the neighbor.

Luther taught that because faith in God, the fundamental characteristic of the Christian, shapes the entire disposition of the believer, God-pleasing works arise from faith's way of viewing life. In contrasting Hagar's arrogance to the simple trust in God that Abraham and Sarah were displaying, Luther explained to his students that this faith recognizes God's gifts of learning, wisdom, and riches but avoids the devilish arrogance that original sin produces. When the Holy Spirit rules in people's lives, they strive to use their gifts properly in faith toward the one who has given.[72] Rebekah's difficult decision to send Jacob off to her brother Laban reflects her belief and hope in God (Gen. 27:43–45).

The rich man who had ignored Lazarus in Jesus's parable in Luke 16 provides insight into the nature of faith and why it produces love for the neighbor. In 1522 Luther told the Wittenberg congregation: "It is the nature of faith that it looks to God for all good and relies on him alone. This faith enables the human being to recognize God, how kind and gracious he is, and out of this recognition the heart becomes so soft and merciful that it wants to do to others as God has done to it." Unbelief, however, expects nothing from God, and therefore the rich man had no place for love toward Lazarus in his life.

> Love is impossible where there is no faith, and faith is impossible where love does not exist. The two want to be together; they must be together. All believers love everyone, serve everyone, but a false believer is at heart the enemy of everyone else and wants to be served by others. The false believer, however, covers such terrible, perverted sin with some small appearance of hypocritical work, with the sheep's skin, like that large bird the ostrich. It is so foolish that when it hides its head in a bush, [it thinks that] its entire body is covered. But here you see that nothing is more blind and unmerciful than unbelief. The dogs, which are

71. Hägglund, "Luthers Anthropologie," 73–74.
72. WA 42:588.31–38; *LW* 3:56.

easily provoked to attack, are more merciful to poor Lazarus than is the rich man. They recognize his need and lick his wounds, but the hard-hearted, blind hypocrite is so callous that he cannot favor him with a crumb from his table.

This model of unbelieving conduct reminds Luther of contemporary clergy who say, "Quick! fast! into my purse! The other guy for better or worse" and cover their unbelief with acts of piety and religiosity.[73]

Luther clearly states the distinction in speaking of the works that he attributes to the tax collector, whose humble confession of sins and of faith Jesus contrasts with the self-righteous Pharisee (Luke 18:9–14). The tax collector "is taking the right path and is righteous in two ways, once through faith in relationship to God, in the second instance in relationship to me through works. He gives God his honor and responds to him through faith in his praise, but in relationship to me he carries out his duty with love, and he puts words in my mouth and shows me how to pray. He had paid everything he owed, to me and to God, as his faith has brought him to do this. He is one person,"[74] but in two modes, one receiving, one giving. In this way Luther demonstrates that the re-created child of God lives by God's gift of life and a new identity in Christ but also lives by acting out God's expectations. He interprets the sentence "The tax collector went to his house justified" as a reference to the fruit produced by the justifying faith he displayed in his confession of sin in the temple. On the basis of Matthew 7:16–20, Luther sketches the way the produce of a fruit tree comes to be good and then concludes, on the basis of the tax collector's good works that he is reading into the parable: "Faith is alive, something that takes on substance, that makes people completely new, changes their orientation toward life, completely converts them. It penetrates to the very foundations and renews the entire person. Where I have previously seen a sinner, now I see another way of conduct, another essence, another life. Thereby I recognize that this person believes, so lofty a thing is a true faith. Therefore the Holy Spirit moves so vigorously to good works for they are a result of faith and a witness to faith."[75]

Brian Brock explores the relationship between Luther's understanding of God's gift of new life and living out that gift on one hand, and the role that God's active, living Word plays in producing that new life in word and deed on the other. "Luther correctly observes that the psalmists explain the genesis of their praise as the experience of rescue." But that genesis does not take place because of human digestion of the information that God has rescued sinners. God's Word has re-creative power. "Luther goes far beyond Wittgenstein and the communitarians, who do not have the resources to describe how God generates the Christian ethos: praise as an epiphenomenon of human

73. WA 10.3:182.23–184.24; CP 4:20–22.
74. WA 10.3:299.15–21; CP 4:343.
75. WA 10.3:296.13–298.1; CP 4:340–41.

experience is inadequate to explain the texts themselves, which demand to be understood as emerging from the *experience* of God's work."[76] That experience embraces both God's action in his re-creating Word and the trust it generates. That experience enables the one who trusts God to serve both him and his other creatures.

The relationship between these two modes of being human becomes clear for Luther in many biblical accounts, which serve him as paradigmatic narratives. In both the sermons of the 1520s and the lectures of 1535–45, Luther appropriates examples from Genesis of the two modes of being human, or as he calls it in describing Jacob, "two kinds of saintliness."[77] In introducing his printed sermons on Genesis in 1527, he reminds readers that God has given many examples and sayings in which he makes it clear that faith alone lies at the basis of human living.[78] The first mode or dimension of human righteousness is focused on the first commandment and what God does for his human creatures by creating them and giving them their identity as his child; the second mode is focused on the last nine commandments and what human creatures are made to do for God and others. Both become clear at many points in the unfolding of Abraham's story.[79]

Even before Abraham, however, the story of Cain and Abel reveals how human righteousness in God's sight depends simply and alone on God's favorable disposition toward his people. In 1521 God's regard for Abel serves for Luther as a summary of God's merciful beneficence toward his people, who can console themselves with this story of God's holding his own in his hand.[80] In 1535 the professor tells his students, "This is the chief point [*summa*] of our teaching, . . . that a person rather than his work is acceptable to God and that a person does not become righteous as a result of a righteous work, but that a work becomes righteous and good as a result of a person's being righteous and good. . . . Abel rather than his work was righteous, and that work pleases because of the person, not the person because of his work."[81] Also Noah, "a righteous man, blameless among his contemporaries" (Gen. 6:9), illustrates this definition of humanity: "He is declared righteous through his faith in God because he believed the universal promise. . . . He is declared perfect because he walked in the fear of God and carefully avoided murder and other sins."[82]

---

76. Brock, *Singing the Ethos*, 176.

77. "Duplex sanctitas," that which the Word establishes in relationship to God and that which human creatures perform; see WA 43:575.22–576.35; *LW* 5:213–14; cf. WA 43:588.37–589.37; *LW* 5:232–33.

78. WA 24:17.14–19. Luther repeats this theme throughout the sermons, among many examples, cf. WA 24:296.19–37; 303.14–28; 318.30–319.18.

79. WA 43:484.6–17; *LW* 5:79–80.

80. WA 9:338.24–30.

81. WA 42:190.37–191.5; *LW* 1:257; cf. WA 42:191.5–192.13; *LW* 1:257–59.

82. WA 42:301.7–14; *LW* 2:55; cf. WA 24:183.17–33.

Again and again Luther emphasized for the Wittenberg congregation that "Abram was a man of the gospel" and therefore "proceeded in pure faith, and his entire life was based on God's Word." For the Wittenberg congregation, Luther was cultivating a new understanding of what it means to live in God's Word, and so he expanded on this point: Abram's example proves that "a Christian is the kind of person who bases life completely on God's will and does everything that he knows will please God. On the other hand, he also lives in such a way that he closes the eyes to his own works and does not look at how large or small, short or long, clever or foolish it seems to be according to reason, which always differentiates works and says, 'That one is worth something, that one much less.' Faith looks only at God's will. If it is God's command, faith performs it."[83]

Abraham served as Luther's prime instance of a life that clearly differentiates and unites the two dimensions of what it means to be human. "We do not deny that works must be performed. . . . Faith and works indeed fit together well and are inseparably joined, but it is faith alone that obtains salvation; . . . faith alone justifies. . . . Works do not save; they do not have this glory. No, they are the fruits of the person who has been saved. Our righteousness comes through faith."[84] Abraham thus provided Luther with the classic paradigm for the way the Creator, who brought the world out of nothing in Genesis 1, re-creates sinners. Commenting on the call of Abram in Genesis 12, Luther tells his students, "God chooses as patriarch an idolater, who is estranged from God and a prisoner of Satan." "Abram is merely the material that the Divine Majesty seizes through the Word and forms into a new human being and into a patriarch. And so this rule is universally true, that of himself the human creature is nothing, is capable of nothing, and has nothing but sin, death, and condemnation. However, through his mercy Almighty God brings it about that he is something and is freed from sin, death, and condemnation through Christ, the blessed seed."[85]

Again and again Abraham's story revealed for Luther that the relationship between all believers and their Lord was created alone by God through his Word.[86] Abram's profile in Genesis 15:6 provided Luther with the template for explaining the two kinds of righteousness. This distinction between two dimensions of being human enabled him to give attention to the performative righteousness of the obedient child of God without losing his emphasis on human life and core identity as God's gift, apart from any human performance.

Even though God demands our virtues and does not want us to be addicted to the lusts of the flesh but earnestly charges us not only to hold them in check but also to slay them completely, yet our virtues cannot help us before God's

83. WA 24:271.10–12, 18.25 cf. WA 14:231.10/32–16/37.
84. WA 43:256.36–42; LW 4:166.
85. WA 42:437.42–438.2; 42:437.31–36; LW 2:247.
86. WA 42:439.9–13; LW 2:249.

judgment. . . . If faith is formed by love, then works are the main thing for which God has regard. But if it is works [that form the basis of God's regard and establishes human identity as children of God], then it is we ourselves. . . . The chief and most important part of teaching is the promise . . . , a gift, a divine plan, by which he offers us something. It is not our work. . . . Afterward there is the law also. For God does not only promise but also gives orders and commands. The law covers your accommodating your will to what God commands.[87]

Trusting in Christ produces more than the disposition to love God, neighbor, and the world in a general way; Luther could also connect faith with specific actions or virtues. In a sermon preached on Easter eve 1531, he presents the courage of Nicodemus and Joseph of Arimathea alongside the hatred and rage of the Jerusalem leaders against Jesus. The leaders wanted to break his legs to add to his misery. "Or if that was not their intent, perhaps they just could not wait until he was dead." "It seems that nothing satisfied their grim hatred—not that he was condemned to death and that judgment was meted out to nail him to the cross. Eagerly they awaited the moment he would die." To the leaders of Jerusalem, "how his body would be cared for and how it would be buried was of no concern. Their only concern was that he be dead. His body could be devoured by birds and wolves, as far as they were concerned." Luther made it clear to his Wittenberg hearers that the atmosphere around the cross was fraught with danger for Christ's followers. Amid the danger a challenging opportunity opened up for two men, Joseph and Nicodemus, who loved Jesus. Luther portrays the situation of the two to further sharpen the profile of the character that the Holy Spirit was shaping in them. "Joseph came from Arimathea and was wealthy, a respected official in Jerusalem. Nicodemus was a Pharisee and member of the Sanhedrin. Thus in that very hostile crowd of high priests, scribes, Pharisees, elders, and people in general, Christ at his death finds two brave men to claim his body, . . . discounting all risk to life and limb, to earthly possessions and reputation." The leaders of the people "are not worthy to take his body from the cross to bury it. . . . The Holy Spirit had called others for this, namely, Joseph and Nicodemus. They were inspired with courage and bravery. . . . They were disciples empowered by Christ's suffering. Before they had been anxious and frightened; now they are confident and courageous because of their faith. Christ's sacrifice and prayers on the cross penetrate and bear fruit. The thief at Christ's right hand was the firstfruit of Christ's death; Joseph and Nicodemus the second. They, like the thief, became courageous," Luther concludes, implying that meditation on Christ's passion should produce similar results in Wittenberg: "Now they have greater faith, confidence, and courage than when the Lord was alive, so great is the fruit and power of the suffering and death of Christ."[88]

87. WA 42:564.27–29; 42:565.5–8, 12–18, 21–23; *LW* 3:22–23.
88. WA 34.1:259.15–260.23; *HP* 1:437–38.

God's Dominion and Responsibility, Human Dominion and Responsibility

However, two fundamental axioms in Luther's reading of Scripture could give rise to either excessive human dependence on human decision and performance (that must be called to repentance by the law) or a fatalism that in a false way takes seriously the power of the Creator (and needs to be dissolved by the gospel). Luther found narratives in which it becomes apparent that the Holy Spirit not only governs the universe but within the Spirit's governance also creates faith and moves faith to the obedience of love. Yet he also recognized the biblical writers' calls and commands designed to elicit human action. Did Abram rescue Lot or did God? Did Joseph and Nicodemus find the courage to seek Christ's body for burial, or did the Holy Spirit give them the courage?

Such stories provided good illustrations of the tension that Luther perceived between Scripture's proclamation of God as almighty Creator—Lord of all creation, responsible in every way for it and its continued functioning—and Scripture's insistence on human beings' full responsibility in their own sphere of responsibility as it is created for them by God. The distinction between two kinds of righteousness made it easy to interpret and understand the distinction between the relationships that parallel in limited fashion parental responsibility and the responsibility of siblings (though Luther did not use this analogy directly). Clearer is the contrasting of the Creator's power with the power of the creatures to whom he has given responsibility. No description, however, captures the mystery of the relationship of Creator and human creature, in view of the total responsibility within their respective and contrasting spheres, which Scripture asserts but never explains.

At least twice in his Genesis lectures, without attempting to harmonize and homogenize human and divine responsibility, Luther cites Augustine's observation that "God governs the things he has created so that he nevertheless allows them to function with their distinctive impulses. . . . God makes use of definite means and tempers his exercise of his miraculous powers so that he makes use of the service of nature and of natural means."[89] In his sermon on Genesis 6 in 1523, Luther speaks of Noah's exercising his own responsibility for saving his family. If you say, "God will sustain me," and get lazy and do no work, it will not happen. "It is true that he gives all things; he sustains and preserves everyone. But if you do not want to use what you are able to put to use, that is tempting God. It is his will that you put to use what you have at hand, that which he has given you and placed at your disposal, not that you

---

89. WA 42:316.21–25; *LW* 2:76. WA 42:512.19–20; *LW* 2:350; cf. Augustine, *De Trinitate* 3.4. See also Martin Seils, *Der Gedanke vom Zusammenwirken Gottes und des Menschen in Luthers Theologie* (Gütersloh: Mohn, 1962).

close your mouth and let his creation go. He has given it to you. He will not perform a miracle for you when it is not necessary."[90]

God's threat of destruction for Sodom (Gen. 19:12–14) sets Luther out on another path for exploring how God executes his will through the agency of his creatures. Sodom's destruction was an exception. Luther confesses that "God governs this visible world" through human beings and angels. "He could kill thieves without the services of an executioner and without the verdict of an officer of the state, as he sometimes does, especially in the case of murderers. He could also create human beings without the union of a male and female, just as he created Adam and Eve. But it has pleased the Divine Majesty to make use of the help and services of human beings, evidently in order to reveal his marvelous divine power in his creatures, whom he did not want to be idle. Therefore Paul calls us all God's fellow workers" (1 Cor. 3:9).[91] In trying to unravel the story of Rebekah's deceit in obtaining the blessing for Jacob, Luther comments that "in the management of the household, father and mother are the instruments through which the house and household affairs are governed. But they themselves should also acknowledge that by their own power, diligence, or effort they can never bring up their children properly and successfully." Rulers too need to recognize the same as they carry out God's commands responsibly while remaining no more than instruments of the Almighty's hand.[92]

The story of Joseph's serving in Potiphar's house illustrates for Luther how God blesses his human creatures and at the same time exercises his self-imposed responsibility to provide for his human creatures as he leads them to serve one another. "It is not human effort that accomplishes what God's blessing bestows, yet God wants us to fulfill our responsibility and to work diligently," as Joseph was doing in Potiphar's household, "so that the flesh may be exercised and may not snore and become listless from inactivity."[93] Luther declares that the Holy Spirit was guiding Joseph in interpreting Pharaoh's dream (Gen. 41), but at the same time he cautions his hearers: "God did not create us and put us into this world that we should abandon ourselves to ease and pleasures and cast every care upon him as if there were nothing whatever for us to do. When a person has carried out his own responsibility in his own position, then indeed the success and outcome of all activities must be entrusted to God."[94] Jacob's decision to send his sons for grain in Egypt (Gen. 42:1–4) illustrates this point again for Luther. No one should use the fact that God provides for his people as an excuse for not seeking sustenance "with toil and zeal."

90. WA 24: 181.6/19–9/26.
91. WA 43:68.17–24; *LW* 3:270.
92. WA 43:513.34–514.19; *LW* 5:124.
93. WA 44:348.32–34; *LW* 7:65.
94. WA 44:384.5–10; *LW* 7:115.

Luther recognizes the danger that his emphasis on God's providential power might be falsely understood and lead the faithful to wish to tempt God. Rebekah might have dared God to protect Jacob by keeping him within Esau's reach, but "this godly and sensible woman makes use of the means that are at hand and have been provided by God." She took reasonable precautions. Luther makes application to two situations in his own day. A person dare not say, "I do not want to eat or drink. If I am to live, I shall live. If I am not to live, food or drink will not help me." Second, a person should not think he can become a parent without marrying. "Who would not regard someone with such thoughts as crazy? You must make use of the gifts of God that have been put at your disposal. You dare not leave such things to predestination or promise." Where God has promised, simple faith suffices. Where God has not promised some miraculous means, believers are to use the normal, created order as God has put it at their disposal.[95] In a lecture the professor warns his students against saying, "I am the pastor of a church about which I know that God is concerned. Therefore I shall do nothing and shall not be concerned about my ministry." "The head of a household should not be lazy and slothful; but everyone must be vigilant and toil in the station in which God has placed him or her. For God does not forbid toil and does not want us to be idle, even though he governs everything by his presence and will. . . . Faith must come first and at the same time prayer, and the works that one's calling requires must be practiced. Though works contribute nothing to the matter, still God wants us to eat our bread in the sweat of our faces."[96] Speaking of Jacob and his family settling into Goshen, Luther again comments on how God exercises his responsibility for all that happens but at the same time works through the exercise of human responsibility. Living on the basis of God's promise, Jacob's family turns to God when "their toil and knowledge did not suffice." However, they also recognize that

> God rules us in such a way that he does not want us to be idle. He gives us food and clothing, but in such a way that we should plow, sow, reap, and cook. In addition, he gives an offspring, who is born and grows because of the blessing of God and must nevertheless be provided for, cared for, brought up, and instructed by parents. . . . Thus God could rule the church through the Holy Spirit without the ministry, but he does not want to do this directly. . . . God could have made children without Adam, just as at the beginning Adam did nothing at all since he was formed from the mud of the earth. . . . But later God said, "Be fruitful and multiply," as if he were saying, "Now with your cooperation I will create children." This is true in all other actions of our common life.[97]

95. WA 43:551.1–29; *LW* 5:177–78; cf. the parallel treatment of Gen. 28:20–22 in WA 43:605.28–606.7; *LW* 5:256–57.
96. WA 44:461.37–462.5; and 44:463.22–32; *LW* 7:219.221–22.
97. WA 44:648.17–35; *LW* 8:94–95.

Nonetheless, in the last analysis God always remains in charge, as Luther sees in Joseph's finding success in prison. That was not the way the professor himself would have designed the patriarch's life at this point. "I too have often attempted to prescribe to God definite methods. . . . But the Lord undoubtedly laughed at this wisdom and said, 'Come now, I know that you are a wise and learned man; but it has never been my custom for Peter, Dr. Martin, or anyone else to teach, direct, govern, and lead me. I am not a passive God. No, I am an active God who is accustomed to doing the leading, ruling, and directing."[98]

Trust stands at the center of, and anchors, human personhood and personality, Luther believed. This reflects his conviction that no understanding of what it means to be human is complete that is not centered on our relationship with God, a relationship not of mere knowledge nor of slavish submission but of childlike dependence. Without this perception of humanity as grounded in trust in an ultimate source of good, one cannot understand the Wittenberg conception of what it means to be justified by faith or trust. Trust in Jesus Christ restores the fullness of humanity because trust in God determines the fundamental orientation of human life. Trusting in God and his Word of promise restores the Edenic relationship. Faith provides the total orientation and the motivation that moves all people to live as the children whom God in the first place fashioned for his family. That life, lived out in the midst of the struggle against Satan's lies and attempts to take away true human life from God's human creatures, exhibits itself in devotion to God and love for others, and it comes to its earthly end in trusting God's promise of life in community and conversation with him forever.

Luther could quite vividly describe what trust is abstractly, as he did in the Large Catechism, coming as close to formal description of it as do modern psychologists from a different perspective. But concrete personifications— whether in reports of real people or in the fictional figures of Jesus's parables, sometimes as Luther's imagination elaborated both—enabled the reformer to make trust come alive. The stories aided the comprehension and absorption of this vital and fundamental building block of Christian living. Luther's views of both God and what it means to be human were so intensely personal that therefore, because trust determines human personhood and personality for him, narratives served him as effective tools for the mysterious cultivation of trusting people of God.

98. WA 44:376.20; *LW* 7:104.

4

SUFFERING BUILDS FAITH AND CALLS TO REPENTANCE

Affliction as Part of Daily Life

Wittenberg reform had taught people how to suffer, Luther claimed in 1531. Five hundred years after Luther's time that seems a strange thing to teach people, but the reformer and his contemporaries knew that human suffering is inevitable. The question was how to deal with suffering and what it might do to and for the sufferer. The school of anguished experience had taught Luther many lessons about suffering. He rejected any attempt to formulate a complete explanation of why suffering happens, just as he refused to solve the mystery of God's choice of his own people out of the mass of sinful humanity. In discussing Genesis 2 and 3, the professor comments, "We are not to try to define or investigate too curiously why God wanted to create the human creature in this middle condition, or why, once so created, all are propagated from the one."[1] Such questions lay beyond Luther's grasp, and he had learned that no answer would satisfy. In the midst of suffering and questions about the reasons for evil, he simply turned to his Creator.[2] His theodicy, his explanation of evil, began and ended by being still and recognizing God as God. Yet throughout his life Luther recognized that the suffering of

---

1. WA 42:85.6–13; *LW* 1:111–12.
2. *De servo arbitrio*, in WA 18:685.14–15; 689.18–25; 712.31–35; 717.25–39; 719.9–12; *LW* 33:135, 145, 181, 188, 190.

all human beings, and particularly those who trust in Christ, posed a severe problem for pastoral care.

Though he refused to formulate a definitive explanation for the origin of evil and therefore for suffering, he traced the roots of the latter (though not the former) to a threefold source. Melanchthon offers an apt summary of Luther's understanding of the sources of evil in the Augsburg Confession when he traces it to the perverted wills of Satan and human creatures.[3] But suffering is a three-edged sword, stemming from human sinfulness, from Satan, yet also from God's testing his faithful and calling them to repentance. This both complicated his treatment of human misfortune and made his address of its consequences more realistic and applicable to the Christian's life. His "theology of the cross" in part tried to cope with this problem. This hermeneutical scheme presented more than one key principle for his understanding of reality, but it included, particularly in later years,[4] the concept of God's working *sub contrario*, "under the appearance of the opposite of what his disposition toward his people truly is." Because God acts in this way, imposing or permitting suffering that seems to stand in contradiction to his omnipotence and his love, Luther usually avoided extensive analysis of individual instances of suffering or the phenomenon in general, believing that such analysis would be no more than vain speculation. He did, however, elucidate God's call to repentance through biblical stories of hardship and adversity, and he found consolation and encouragement for sufferers in accounts of the biblical saints whose troubles and tragedies had provided the Holy Spirit a theater for the display of God's merciful intervention in human history.

God's people often experience his intervention "under the appearance of opposites," making concrete God's promise to Paul that God was making his power perfect in the apostle's weakness, demonstrating the sufficiency of God's grace (2 Cor. 12:9). In fear and distress, Jacob was preparing to meet his brother, Esau, when he returned home after his years with his uncle Laban. He prays, and in the night "a man"—whom Luther, with the exegetical tradition, interprets as God himself on the basis of the text (Gen. 32:30)—comes to wrestle with him and wrenches his hip. Luther compares Jacob's distress, in the face of what he imagined would be a violent confrontation with his brother and his wrestling with God, to Christ's path to kingship. He had to die on the cross as a totally despairing scoundrel as he was fulfilling his role as eternal king, just as the children of Israel had to go through the sea, threatened by death at the hands of the Egyptians, in order to experience their liberation from Pharaoh. Luther brings Jacob's story together with Israel's and Christ's for his Wittenberg hearers so that they can be assured that their trials and

3. Augsburg Confession, Article 19, in *BSLK* 75; *BoC* 52/53; cf. Apology of the Augsburg Confession 19, in *BSLK* 313; *BoC* 235.

4. Robert Kolb, "Luther's Theology of the Cross Fifteen Years after Heidelberg: Luther's Lectures on the Psalms of Ascent," *Journal of Ecclesiastical History* 61 (2010): 69–85.

troubles, their own struggling with the Lord, indicate God's love and presence in their lives rather than his absence.[5] Michael Parsons observes, "Luther describes Jacob as an ordinary believer in that in his anxious and troubled state he manifests weakened faith. However, the Lord speaks to him. And he speaks to Jacob, not *despite* his weakness, but rather almost *because* of it. It is this seeming incongruity that causes Luther to consider Jacob as 'saintly.' His righteousness is alien to him, it comes from outside of Jacob, it is given by a gracious God."[6] Luther saw nothing incongruous about this at all. His "theology of the cross" presumes that God makes his own strength dramatically clear in the weakness of those who trust in him.

Luther took sin and evil very seriously and recognized that not all evil that befalls believers is a direct or even indirect response to their own sinful deeds, mistakes, and failures. Evil loomed much larger in Luther's experience. He believed that Satan exercises powers beyond the human ability to perceive them, comprehend them, or cope with them, and that sin so permeates the human person that these powers cannot be tamed apart from God's intervention. In the story of the rape of Dinah, we see the vulnerability of members of God's people facing Satan's trickery. While still a minor, Jacob's only daughter, Dinah, ventures into the territory of Shechem and is raped (Gen. 34). Jacob endures the agony of the deed itself and the thought that it was punishment for some sin he had committed. Dinah has Luther's sympathy; at the same time she offers him an example for warning the students how powerful sin and evil are in this world.

> Dinah wanted to see the daughters of this region, how they dressed up and made themselves pretty and how beautiful they were. The text seems to indicate just that—namely, that she was curious—since she really did go out without permission from her father or her mother, on her own, without anyone accompanying her. She was secure and confident. She was still a child and had no fear of any threat to her chastity. She sinned out of curiosity in going out without telling her parents. But that is the nature of young girls, who enjoy the company of others their age in the vicinity.

So the devil sets his traps for believers.[7]

In this story Luther also finds a classic illustration of the contrast between the way sinful reason looks at the world and its happenings and the way God views them. For Satan is not supreme. God rules his universe despite the mystery of evil that plagues his human creatures. In the eyes of the world, the judgment was justified that "Jacob is a beggar and a vagabond who is worn

---

5. WA 24:573.31–581.14.

6. Michael Parsons, *Luther and Calvin on Old Testament Narratives: Reformation Thought and Narrative Text* (Lewiston, NY: Edwin Mellen, 2004), 119.

7. WA 44:142.32–143.41; *LW* 6:192–93.

out by troubles, calamities, the cold and heat, with misfortune on all sides. He has children who are disobedient and criminals. Reuben went to bed with his mother.[8] Dinah was raped by Shechem. Jacob does not have any blessing at all." But God has the last laugh, Luther says, citing Psalm 2:4. He "allows these things to take place to exercise our faith so that we may learn to depend on his Word alone and not have to look for visible signs, perceptible to the senses. Instead we rely on that which cannot be seen," and this is the consolation of the faithful children of God.[9] For all the promises that God had made to Jacob remain. God continues to be his God and faithful to the patriarch.

Suffering as the Rod to Induce Repentance

God loves his chosen people so much, Luther contended, that he strives to turn them to himself not only through the proclamation of the law against their own transgressions but also through experiencing the pressure that the law's divine design for life exerts when human actions offend and oppose this plan for human conduct. Jonah's story constitutes an apt example of how sharp God's rod could become for inducing repentance. His experience offers believers comfort, for they recognize that God will not abandon them but rather pursue them when they sin against him.[10] Michael Parsons calls attention to the contrast between Calvin's treatment of Jonah's story, which "stresses the awfulness of Jonah's sin against the dignity of a sovereign God," with Luther's handling of this story. The Wittenberg professor assesses Jonah's flight before God's presence "from a pastoral perspective, exalting divine grace, stressing that no sin is unforgivable, moving from the negative (Jonah's rebellion) to a positive application. . . . It is Luther who clearly identifies and empathizes with Jonah and who marvels at the forgiving grace of God. . . . Luther repeatedly underlines God's initiative in igniting Jonah's faith, his grace in giving his Spirit in order for Jonah to look outside of himself and his situation."[11] Indeed, Luther points out to his students that Jonah resists the call to repentance; he remains silent as the storm rages around the boat. He watches the poor sailors, terrified for their lives, while they desperately try to save him, themselves, and the ship. Then to save them, he has to pronounce his own death sentence. But he is "blinded, obdurate, and submerged in sin, yes, dead, lying in the pit of his unrepentant heart." When the lot is cast and falls to him, remorse overcomes him; he confesses his sin and does pronounce his own death sentence for jeopardizing the lives of the sailors against their will. He then reveals the

8. Although Bilhah was Jacob's concubine, Luther viewed family relationships in a way that defined this relationship as incest.

9. WA 44:226.10–227.20; LW 6:304–5.

10. WA 19:198.11–200.25; LW 19:46–47.

11. Parsons, *Luther and Calvin*, 183.

"real art and skill of extricating ourselves from all distress and fear." Jonah confesses his sin, and he confesses his God, the Creator of the earth.[12] In this predicament Jonah demonstrates the necessity of enduring God's wrath and punishment in deep sorrow over sin so that sinners may recognize the need to die to that sin.[13] Jacob's wrestling with God (Gen. 32) also permitted Luther to give aid to those who had experienced their own struggles of conscience. He applied this example not only to those struggles in which God seems to be neglecting believers but also to the struggle against the just accusation of God's law. In these struggles God's promise of salvation through Christ aids the believer in the struggle against the condemnation.[14]

Yet for Luther, David most often embodied the believer who commits grievous sin and is brought to repentance by the Word of the Lord.[15] David's fall into the sins of adultery and murder, and his subsequent repentance when Nathan rebukes him (2 Sam. 11–12), provided Luther with a prime example of this theology of repentance. To be sure, early in his career the reformer could comment on Psalm 51 with hardly a mention of David's adultery and subsequent repentance under the admonition of Nathan.[16] But most often for Luther, David embodies the believer who commits grievous sin and whom God brings to repentance through his Word. Because Luther believed that David composed Psalm 51 in reaction to the events reported in 2 Samuel 11–12, he used this narrative to set forth the basis of his extensive explanation of the nature of sinfulness and repentance. David's wrongdoing also illustrated, for the Wittenberg reformer, the tyrannous power of sin. He used that point to remind his hearers and readers of the necessity of clinging to Christ and depending on the power of the Holy Spirit. Preaching on Matthew 24:15–28, in 1537, Luther reminded his hearers that David was a great man, but when God removed his support, he fell into sin. That demonstrated the power of Satan.[17]

In a sermon of 1522 he observes that in Psalm 51 David is saying as much as "Look, I am only flesh and blood, made in this way, which is in and of itself sin, and I cannot do anything else but sin. For even if you manage your hands

12. WA 19:208.19–216.7; *LW* 19:57–64.
13. WA 19:216.8–220.33; *LW* 19:64–68.
14. WA 44:103.36–108.17; *LW* 6:139–45.
15. Much of the following material was written for the article "David: King, Prophet, Repentant Sinner: Martin Luther's Image of the Son of Jesse," *Perichoresis* 8 (2010): 203–32.
16. In his treatment of Ps. 51 in 1517, before his theology focused on the action of law and gospel in producing daily repentance had fully matured, Luther only mentions his presumption of the association of David's own sin and repentance with the psalm; see WA 18:505.20–23; *LW* 14:173 (though note that the extant text reflects a revision made in 1525). His initial lectures on the psalms, in 1513–15, contain a similar mention of David's sin and repentance in connection with this psalm, without any development of the story from 2 Samuel; see WA 3:291.24–28; *LW* 10:240.
17. WA 45:262.19–23.

and feet or your tongue so they do not sin, the tendency and desire remain because blood and flesh is so, even if you go to Rome or Saint James."[18] He could also use David's sin as a reminder of the inevitability of sin in the lives of all and especially in the lives of those whom God places in positions of political power. In commenting on Psalm 45:6, "the scepter of your kingdom is a scepter of uprightness," Luther observes that

> David was a holy king, and he ruled by divine aid and favor. Peter declares in Acts [2:25] that he administered his kingdom according to God's will, and in [1] Kings [14:8] God says, "I have found the man who will carry out my every wish." Yet he was responsible for many injustices, as in the case of the miserable orphan Mephibosheth [2 Sam. 16 and 19] and the case of Uriah, whom he ordered killed so that he might have his wife [2 Sam. 11:15]. . . . It is impossible for people in power not to sin; neither are they able to administer justice to everyone. The reason is that the magnitude of affairs and Satan's artfulness exceed their strength. It is enough, however, if they do not sin willfully and intentionally, but have the will to administer their office faithfully. What takes place accidentally other than they intend is wiped out as though by a sponge and absorbed by the remission of sins.[19]

In his lectures on Psalm 51 in 1532, edited for publication in 1538, Luther makes a different and fuller use of the story of David's adultery, his arranging for Uriah's death, and his subsequent repentance under Nathan's rebuke. The story gave concrete meaning to the psalm for his hearers and readers. As he begins his exposition, Luther expresses his surprise that in interpreting the text, scholastic exegetes had concentrated their attention on David's actual sins of adultery and murder. He points out that the text presents the king's acknowledgment of his "external sins but also of his total sinful nature, the source and origin" of those sins. "The entire psalm speaks of his entire sinfulness or the root of his sin, not only about what he did, but both the fruit borne of the tree of sin and its root." The Wittenberg reformer often replaced the medieval Latin term "original sin" not only with the typical German translation "inherited sin" but also with "root sin." In addition, Luther explains that David not only stood guilty of adultery and Uriah's murder but also of wanting to appear in public as a holy man, lawful and just, while plotting for the killing of Uriah, "a good man without doubt, of outstanding trustworthiness in David's kingdom." In breaking the fifth and sixth commandments, David had defied and despised the Lord and thus had become guilty of blasphemy against the first commandment. David thus served as an excellent example of the interconnectedness of individual sinful acts and their root in the rejection of God and doubt of his Word.

18. WA 10.1.2:235.3–14; CP 2:370.
19. WA 40.2:524.40–525.23; *LW* 12:237.

Luther also emphasizes the importance of the call to repentance. "If Nathan had not come, David would soon have sinned against the Holy Spirit."[20] Luther directly applies David's experience with Uriah, Bathsheba, and Nathan to the lives of his hearers and readers: "It is our sin since we are born and conceived in sin. David speaks here of his own experience. Therefore, by definition, 'sin' signifies the corruption of all our powers, interior and exterior. . . . This psalm is a general teaching regarding all the people of God, from the beginning until this day, by which David, or rather the Holy Spirit in David, teaches us to recognize both God and ourselves."[21]

David recognized both his guilt in the case of Uriah and Bathsheba and, "in the mirror" of these sins, "the impurity of his entire nature, as he thought to himself, 'Look at me, I, who have governed the state and supported the church and the worship of God, I, who "have guided them with the skill of my hands" . . . [Ps. 78:72], how could I have fallen into this hideous situation, into so many and such terrible sins?' For from one sin comes the recognition of all sin, as if he would have said, 'If I, the kind of man I am, have fallen as if from heaven into hell, what a huge attestation this fall is to myself and others that nothing good exists in my flesh?'" Luther comments,

> Great is the wisdom that recognizes we are nothing else but sin, so that we do not deal lightly with sin, as the teachers of the pope do, who define sin as that which is said, done, or thought contrary to God's law. According to this psalm you must define sin in its totality, which is present when we are born from father and mother, before we reach the age where we are able to say, do, or think something. Out of this root nothing good in God's sight can arise from within us. This is the origin of the distinction of two kinds of sin. First of all, the whole nature is corrupt through sin and subject to eternal death. Then other kinds of sin exist, which a person who has the law can recognize, such as, for example, stealing, adultery, murder, and so forth.[22]

Throughout the rest of this commentary, Luther places the words of the psalm into David's situation as he repents of his adultery and murder, particularly the "Have mercy on me" of Psalm 51:1.[23]

In addressing David's confession in verse 8, "Let the bones you have broken rejoice," Luther returns to the scene in which Nathan rebukes David, and he places David's repentance there into the context of these words. He stresses the necessity of God's promise coming to the contrite heart, which believes that God is the father of mercy and all consolation (2 Cor. 1:3). "The reliable means of purging, the most effective medicine that is necessary to cleanse the bones and

20. WA 40.2:318.26–321.16.
21. WA 40.2:325.32–34; 40.2:326.29–33.
22. WA 40.2:321.33–322.27.
23. WA 40.2:330.22–350.28.

conscience of the sinner, came to David, as it came to Paul and Peter," when God brought them to repentance as evil sinners so that they might receive the mercy of God.[24] Luther notes in commenting on verse 7 that in 2 Samuel 12, the purging that the king experiences with Nathan's call to repentance leads to great joy at the words, "You shall not die."[25] David needed to be reduced to his own purgatory[26] in this life, weighed down by the sorrow over his own sin and God's wrath, to be able to cling to God's faithfulness in showing mercy. As he wrote the psalm, David knew that from his own experience he should bring other transgressors to repentance (v. 13).[27] Luther was able to confront the sins that he himself had committed and the permeating nature of evil in his own life and in the web of human society on the basis of his own ongoing battle against the unexplainable force of the mystery of evil. This led him to see daily repentance as the fundamental pattern that should lead the sinner and/or victim of evil to flee to God. David provided a paradigmatic narrative for living out this life of repentance as Luther recapitulated David's pattern of sin and repentance.

Judgment on Nations and Cities

Luther firmly believed that God's call to repentance not only addresses sinners individually but also that God sends his chastening rod upon cities and nations in order to move their populations to acknowledge their individual and collective sinfulness and return to trusting him alone. The Wittenberg reformer also believed that his fellow Germans had greeted the gospel of Jesus Christ too often with contempt, and so he did not hesitate to point out to his congregation and his students that God's judgment would someday fall on them. In 1532, as Emperor Charles's threat to eradicate the Lutherans with force seemed less serious than it had even a few months earlier, Luther nevertheless uses the parable of the king who visited his wrath on those who spurned his invitation to his son's wedding (Matt. 22:1–14) to warn the people of Wittenberg to live the repentant life. He explains the parable by reciting, probably from Josephus (though in this instance without mentioning his source), what had happened in fulfillment of Christ's prophecy of judgment on Jerusalem. Throughout its history, Luther points out, Jerusalem had executed God's prophets and finally God's Son himself.

> What happened? The king became angry and sent out his army—the Romans! He placed them in his service, and they put the murderers to death, burned the

---

24. WA 40.2:415.24–417.17.
25. WA 40.2:409.35–410.21.
26. Although Luther had abandoned belief in purgatory more than a decade earlier, he used the term metaphorically for the experience of purgation while a person was still alive.
27. WA 40.2:437.22–24.

city, and abused the Jews so horribly that they were sold more cheaply than sparrows, thirty Jews for a penny, when for a penny one could buy but one sparrow. Pitiful wailing and lament went up from the Jews. How great is the injustice to be so tormented by the pagans! But that is the way they had wanted it. They had caroused for a long time and let preaching fall on deaf ears. Then came the time of accounting for the bill. God was no longer willing to listen to them. He, the father of the house, dealt with them as with serpents and toads. Don't let this happen to you![28]

This historical recollection sharpened the focus on Luther's foretelling of what his contemporaries were earning for themselves:

When the precious gospel is expounded, the world plays its little game, becoming worse than it was before, as everyone gets busier and busier. Earlier, before the gospel's advent, they did not carry on like this. But now that they are invited through the word of the gospel, they have so many things to do that they cannot attend the wedding banquet. Peasants, burghers, and noblemen alike, with the gospel light beaming, become more avaricious, proud, and arrogant. They show more wantonness and wickedness than earlier under the darkness of the papacy. They give their parish pastors, who have invited them to this kind of supper, all manner of grief. They become ten times worse than they were under the papacy. Let no one grumble about the pride and cockiness of peasants, burghers, and nobles and their trampling on God's Word and their pastors. . . . Now they are secure, and they do not regard our Lord God as one to be feared. But watch out! Our God is indeed a gracious host who will dish out goodies for a time, but he does not go on being host to those who do not mend their ways. He is biding his time right now, letting burghers and peasants, despite the gospel and every bit of earnest admonition and teaching, pursue their wantonness, accumulate money, overcharge people for everything they need—wood, grain, butter, eggs— and yet he remains silent as if he did not see what was going on. But when the time comes, today or tomorrow, he will send pestilence—and people will fall in droves—or war—and Italian and Spanish mercenaries will invade your home, plunder what they find, and in addition beat you to a pulp, literally strangling you, violating your wife and children right in front of your own eyes, while you cry out, "Bloody murder! How could God deal so horribly with us?"[29]

Luther lists the sins he believed were besetting his hearers: "anger, impatience, greed, belly-serving, sexual voyeurism, evil lusts, fornication, hatred, and other vices . . . are nothing compared to the terrible disdain of the divine Word, disdain that is so deep and pervasive that in truth greed, stealing, adultery, whoremongering, and so forth cannot even compare." "Germany must also pay the piper."[30]

28. EA² 6:123–24; *HP* 3:93.
29. EA² 6:123–24; *HP* 3:92–93.
30. EA² 6:124–26; *HP* 3:93–94.

A year later Luther examined the same text and enriched his telling of the story with illustrations of those who do not prepare rightly for the wedding feast. Sitting among the guests, he says, is one who has little to do but ridicule the bridegroom. "At a wedding a person ought to dress up out of respect for the bridegroom and the bride. It is a great insult to both if he does not. If a blacksmith arrives from his forge dressed in his long overgarment and skullcap, with a coal-black beard and face covered with soot, and wants to mix with the wedding guests and be a part of the wedding procession, everyone, especially the bridegroom, would think that he was either crazy or that he wanted to spite the bridegroom." That is precisely what those are doing who attend worship, are baptized, receive the Lord's Supper, yet demonstrate no serious intent to live as Christians. So the king pulls this guest aside, as Luther tells the story, gliding from the biblical parable into the lives of his hearers. He says, "Is it that you are here because you have the name, because you are called a Christian, even though you do not believe what a Christian is supposed to believe? In all your born days, you never were serious about how to rid yourself of sin or how to become righteous and attain salvation. All you thought about were possessions, prestige, good days, and so on, and now you come as a guest covered with soot. Get out of here! You do not belong among those who have come properly dressed. Your filth may make them dirty."[31] Though this was shaped in the form of an address to the entire German people, Luther's hearers obviously were supposed to understand that their personal repentance was necessary for their own sake as well as the sake of the entire nation.

His lectures on Genesis, in this case chapter 37, illustrate how God's judgment has salutary effects. When God's rod of chastening brings repentance, he is demonstrating his love. Joseph's brothers experience this blessing, finally in their anguish, and so the Wittenberg students are encouraged to see the blessing of God's confronting his people with their sins through chastening blows and the suffering of crosses. Those who do wrong are unfortunate when they succeed with their evil plans. Joseph's brothers receive the gracious gift of such a call to repentance. Luther comments, "This is a holy, blessed, and well-protected kind of life when God does not close his eyes to our faults and forbidden pursuits but immediately corrects and chastises us with his rods, troubles, and crosses of every kind or through people who by their admonitions lead us back to the right path so that our foolish lusts are curbed. However, it is a very bad sign when all things succeed according to his heart's desire for a scoundrel who is plotting evil."[32] The further developments of the lives of Joseph's brothers prove his point and confirm his warning to his students.

31. EA² 6:137; *HP* 3:103–4.

32. WA 44:244.12–17; *LW* 6:327. On Luther's treatment of the somewhat parallel case of Lot's daughters, see Mickey Leland Mattox, *"Defender of the Most Holy Matriarchs": Martin Luther's Interpretation of the Women of Genesis in the "Enarrationes in Genesin," 1535–45* (Leiden: Brill, 2003), 171–85.

Genesis 37 also gave Luther the opportunity to speak to the situation in which his people suffer as victims of evil. He constructs a dialogue of sorts with the voices of God and the believer echoing across the lecture hall. As Joseph moves toward his brothers, who are going to sell him into slavery in Egypt and doom his father to years of mourning and misery, Luther steps back with his students to catch a glimpse of the way God works in hidden ways to bring his people through evil into good. God thinks, "I will first mortify [Jacob and Joseph] because I not only want to give benefits to them but I also want to care for all of Egypt through them." The reformer explains, "This was God's purpose and good pleasure at that time, however sad and troublesome the outward appearance of being disregarded by God was," as Jacob from one perspective and Joseph from another must have experienced the son's captivity and disappearance from his family. Luther then gives voice to his students' reactions to such hardships: "Why God neglects me in this way, I do not know, but I have no doubt about the excellent, wise, and most useful plan of the Father, although the flesh does not see but murmurs and struggles against the Spirit. Nevertheless the cross must be borne and overcome by faith and patience, for in the saintly fathers I see the wonderful plans of God by which they are ruled." Luther returns to comments on the story of Joseph and then raises the voice of the believer from the hearers in his lecture hall: "Well! God has loaded me down with this or that cross. So what? I shall bear it with equanimity." For, the professor concedes, the flesh is weak and complains. But God responds, in Luther's words, by saying, "You know nothing; you are a fool! Wisdom belongs to me, and from this cross of yours I will bring forth the greatest good." That is the comfort of believers, Luther is demonstrating to his students.[33] Before he leaves the passage, he juxtaposes the words that, because of the overwhelming flood of afflictions and evils, believers find so hard to say in the midst of tribulation—namely, "I have been baptized; I have God's promise"—alongside the admonition of the psalmist in Psalm 34:8, "O taste and see that the LORD is good!" (NRSV).[34]

Likewise, Luther believes that when Joseph is released from prison (Gen. 41:14) he must have been angry with himself for his impatience, and has him say, "Why did I murmur in the prison? I see that God in his great mercy stood by me when I was sad and murmured. I should rather have exulted, laughed, and been joyful in tribulation. Ah, Lord God, pardon my weakness! . . . You are a God who gives beyond what I could hope and comprehend." To that prayer, God in rather matter-of-fact manner replies, "That is my customary procedure. . . . My works are of such a nature that they surpass all understanding and human reason."[35]

33. WA 44:263.4–23; *LW* 6:352.
34. WA 44:266.37–267.10; *LW* 6:357.
35. WA 44:400.14–20; *LW* 7:137.

Mortifying the Flesh

Such warnings served to undergird one of the essential elements of Luther's understanding of Christian piety in a world of sin. To attain the practice of active righteousness and to abolish the false gods that continually lure believers, they must actively strive to kill their own desires to live life on their own terms; mortification of the flesh is the negative side of fulfilling God's commands in the context of God's callings. Luther often repeated his principle that killing off the sinful identity of God's people and bestowing or renewing their identity as his children is his natural way of doing things in a sinful world. He used this description of God's activities among sinner-saints in reference to both their core identities in relationship to him and the practice of their callings in his world. In his portrayal of the relationship of Abraham with Sarah and Hagar, Luther finds the patriarch mortified in regard to both the first and the second tables of the law.[36] God's command to Abraham to sacrifice Isaac constituted true mortification, "sitting in sackcloth and ashes."[37] In retelling the story of God's covenant with Abram in Genesis 15, Luther declares, "It is also the purpose of this passage to teach us what God's nature is. He is indeed the deliverer and liberator from death. But before he delivers, he destroys; before he makes alive, he plunges into death. He is accustomed to act in this way, 'so that out of nothing he may make everything.'"[38] Hagar herself exemplifies the trials of the believer and demonstrates how tribulations lead to repentance, in Luther's imagination. His portrayal of Hagar as moving from humiliation to faith leads John Thompson to comment, "One may truly say that Luther loves these characters deeply. He dwells at spectacular length on the sadness of the episode [as Abraham and Sarah send Hagar into the wilderness] and on the broken hearts of all."[39] Luther expands on the added suffering that thought of being rejected by God brings to physical hardship. But also Abraham suffered from these tensions within his family: "Abraham was not a log or a stone, but he had a heart filled to overflowing with compassion and love for those who were very close to him, and even more for the members of his household, of course for his wife and firstborn son. Where in this way trial follows trial and tears force out more tears, the mortification is real, and real are the struggles of faith that mortify even innate love."[40]

36. WA 43:167.22–34; *LW* 4:44–45.

37. WA 43:213.29–31; *LW* 4:109. See the treatment by Gerhard Heintze, *Luthers Predigt von Gesetz und Evangelium* (Munich: Kaiser, 1958), 277–78.

38. WA 42:572.21–23; *LW* 3:33; cf. the treatment of this concept in Luther's discussion of Joseph's mortification: WA 44:454.36–456.12; *LW* 7:210–11.

39. John L. Thompson, *Reading the Bible with the Dead: What You Can Learn from the History of Exegesis That You Cannot Learn from Exegesis Alone* (Grand Rapids: Eerdmans, 2007), 28.

40. WA 43:168.27–32; *LW* 4:46.

Luther also observes that in the case of Joseph, his students should see that God "not only makes everything out of nothing but first makes nothing out of everything."[41] Likewise, the promise of many descendents to Hagar reveals that "God alternates things in this way: comfort follows affliction, hope follows despair, and life follows death."[42] God does often inflict mortification on believers, as Luther notes in commenting on Joseph's afflictions at the hand of his brothers: "The entire Holy Scripture teaches this again and again, and it is God's will that we are mortified according to the flesh and made alive according to the spirit."[43] He takes no pleasure in afflicting us but uses powerful and bitter remedies to make the deformity and foulness of the depraved sinful nature clear to his people and to cleanse them, as the story of Joseph's leading his brothers to repentance shows.[44] Leah's having children while her more beloved sister and rival, Rachel, did not (Gen. 29:31) resulted from God's regard for her and also as his means of crucifying Jacob's love and attitude and breaking Rachel's pride. That is consolation for the Leahs of this world, who are disconsolate, and it is also an admonition for those believers who refuse to accept God's way of doing things.[45] The threat of Esau's revenge also mortified Jacob's desire to manage life and thereby strengthened his faith in God's mercy.[46] This struggle against sin must be conscious and active, Luther believes, seeking to diminish or eradicate sin at every turn, as Reuben did by diverting his brothers from murdering Joseph (Gen. 37:21–22). For, Luther concludes, departing from the story line, "old guilt does not rust," as a German proverb states: guilt holds its perpetrators tightly in its grip.[47]

Mortification takes place not only by God's design but also through Satan's attacks. Luther found no contradiction between the claim that God was putting human suffering to use as a call to repentance and attributing the evil of suffering to Satan. He felt no necessity of fully explaining the mystery of sin and evil, and therefore he could freely address situations with whatever partial explication might serve his pastoral purposes. Luther firmly believed, however, that the Holy Spirit actively intervenes in the battle of the faithful against the devil's deception. Satan and his minions are responsible for many of the attacks and afflictions, temporal and spiritual, from which Christians suffer, both from inside themselves and from others. Therefore, as Eberhard Winkler observes, the devil's use of suffering is part of the battle between

41. WA 44:593.33–34; *LW* 8:20.

42. WA 42:593.20–22; *LW* 3:63.

43. WA 44:265.33–34; *LW* 6:355. Luther describes Joseph's life in a similar way in his exposition of Gen. 45: WA 44:586.20–588.14; *LW* 8:10–12; cf. WA 44:637.40–638.28; *LW* 8:79–80; cf. comments on Jacob's mortification and consolation in WA 44:134.9–135.5; *LW* 6:179–80.

44. WA 44:468.22–469.42; *LW* 7:228–30; cf. WA 44:569.7–12; *LW* 7:362; and WA 44:582.37–585.38; *LW* 8:5–8.

45. WA 43:645.23–646.13; *LW* 5:314–15; cf. WA 43:654.9–40; *LW* 5:327.

46. WA 44:71.39–72.23; *LW* 6:97; cf. WA 44:90.20–22; *LW* 6:121.

47. WA 44:282.16–19; *LW* 6:377.

Satan and God, and this means that "comfort is often closely associated with admonition."[48]

The very presence of the faithful provokes the devil to visit catastrophe upon their surroundings. In commenting on the famine that broke out when Isaac lived in the land (Gen. 26:1), Luther points out to the Wittenberg congregation that the devil tries to disrupt lives of those who serve God, and he expands Isaac's story with two other anecdotes. One tells of a man who was accustomed to curse incessantly and taught his children to do the same. When a pious man visits this household and asks the man to stop cursing, he does, and the devil shakes the house to its foundations. To that Luther adds a similar story from Ambrose. He makes it clear to his hearers and readers that Satan uses many approaches to undermine God's rule on earth.[49] The death of Abel gave the preacher the opportunity to instruct the Wittenberg congregation regarding the persecution of God's people by evildoers.[50] Also in sermons not directly on the text of Genesis 4, Abel serves as an example of Satan's efforts to destroy proper worship of God, as do the stories of the prophets. The martyrdom of Stephen (Acts 7) gave occasion to recall not only Abel's death but also those of the prophets whom Kings Saul and Ahab killed, as well as Zechariah's.[51] Abraham's deception of Abimelech (Gen. 20:1–17) reminds Luther that "not only passive evils are inflicted upon us, bringing good upon us, but also the active ones, that is, the evils we ourselves do," producing the blessing of repentance.[52]

In addition to suffering persecution, believers face other kinds of temptations to fall from faith. Abimelech placed before Isaac the temptation to lie and to subject his wife to the king's advances. Luther comments, "If the devil notices that you have the Word and are confident that your life is pleasing and acceptable to God on account of the Word, he will not rest but will put in your way trials and afflictions of every kind even in the most trivial matters. . . . All these things will happen in order that your faith may be exercised."[53] Joseph's being mishandled by his brothers and his employer served to illustrate such suffering and give a basis for encouragement that God stands by his saints in the combat against the devil.[54] From Joseph, Luther's students learned to recognize that "the sons of this age . . . crucify me. I cannot escape or draw away

48. Eberhard Winkler, "Luther als Seelsorger und Prediger," in *Leben und Werk Martin Luthers von 1526 bis 1546: Festgabe zu seinem 500. Geburtstag*, ed. Helmar Junghans (Berlin: Evangelische Verlagsanstalt, 1983), 228.

49. WA 14:342.2/16/21–344.7/13/38; 24:454.29–458.18.

50. WA 24:135.28–136.23.

51. WA 10.1.1:271.18–278.9; 52:89–94.

52. WA 43:115.7–8; *LW* 3:334.

53. WA 43:432.5–9; *LW* 5:5.

54. WA 44:284.26–35; *LW* 6:380. WA 44:287.28–288.7; *LW* 6:384–85. WA 44:292.27–293.4; *LW* 6:391. WA 44:300.31–301.27; 44:354.18–34; *LW* 7:73; 44:37. WA 44:370.31–378.6; *LW* 7:96–106. WA 44:390.25–394.35; *LW* 7:124–29.

that horrible mask that hides the face of God, but I must stay in darkness and in very thick mist until a new light shines forth."[55] Outright persecution and unjust treatment also plague the righteous, such as the suffering that Esau's wives brought to Rebekah and Isaac (Gen. 26:35)[56] and that Laban brought to Jacob (Gen. 31).[57] Furthermore, Satan attacks believers with temptations to sin. Joseph's battle against the seduction of Potiphar's wife patterns resistance to such temptations, Luther explains to his students at some length.[58]

Perhaps the crowning example of the battle against Satan's lies presents itself in the temptation of Jesus (Matt. 4:1–11), the Gospel lesson for Invocavit, the first Sunday in Lent. In 1523 Luther used his own analytic tool in structuring his treatment of the text: this story was written both to teach us and to admonish us. "First, it teaches us what we should know—how Christ has served us and helped us through his fasting and starving—through the spiritual attacks on him and his victory. Those who believe in Christ will not suffer any want, nor shall any spiritual assault harm them. Instead, they shall have what they need in the midst of want and shall be secure in the midst of spiritual attack. For their Lord and head has conquered all this for our benefit." As admonition, this story encourages hearers to follow Christ's example and suffer want and personal attack gladly in service to God and for the benefit of the neighbor. "Thus this Gospel lesson is a great comfort and strength against our unbelieving, shameful belly. It will lift up our conscience and strengthen it so that we do not worry about our physical sustenance but are certain that God desires and is able to sustain us."[59]

Luther pursued the lessons the Wittenberg hearers could learn from the story of Christ's temptation. First, he was driven into the wilderness, where God, angels, human beings, and all other creatures abandoned him and left him all alone. What a temptation! "But it hurts when no one feels obliged to back us up, and I am supposed to support myself without a penny, without a piece of thread, without a twig, and feel that I have no help from other people and no resources. That is what it means to be led into the wilderness and left alone. Then I am in the real school of life and learn what I am, how weak my faith is, what a great and rare thing a true faith is, and how deeply shameful unbelief lies in the hearts of all people."[60] Luther recognizes that the company of other Christians aids the battle against temptations of all kinds.

Christ's temptation also came in the form of concern for the sustenance of the body. Luther explains the devil's appeal:

55. WA 44:603.41–604.3; *LW* 8:33.
56. WA 43:490.29–491.24; *LW* 5:89–90.
57. WA 9:579.1–581.32; 44:35.11–37; *LW* 6:48.
58. WA 44:355.35–365.7; *LW* 7:75–88. On Luther's treatment of Potiphar's wife, see Mattox, *Defender*, 225–43.
59. WA 17.2:188.35–189.15; CP 2:136.
60. WA 17.2:189.16–29; CP 2:137.

"If you are the Son of God, speak, so that these stones become bread." It is as if he said, "Well, just rely on God and do not bake a thing. Hang on until a roast chicken flies into your mouth. Just say that you have a God who is taking care of you. Where is your heavenly Father, who is taking care of you? I think he will forsake you. Eat and drink of your faith. See how satisfied you will get. Indeed, as if it were stones. How fine that you are the Son of God; how fatherly he acts toward you, that he does not send you a crust of bread but lets you be so poor and thirsty. Believe more that you are his Son and he is your Father." With such thoughts the devil attacks all the children of God. And Christ certainly felt the attack, for he was not a stick of wood or stone, although he was pure and without sin and remained so. We cannot remain so.

Indeed, Christ answered this attack with the weapons of concern for the body and greed. "The human being does not live by bread alone" means "You want to point me to nothing but bread and deal with me as if I am supposed to think only of physical nourishment." Luther points out that this kind of attack happens often, especially for those responsible for a family. Christ's example of struggle against this temptation for forty days is to be a comfort for the residents of Wittenberg. He held to God's Word and resisted by citing Deuteronomy 8:3, which described God's humbling the people by letting them go hungry and then supplying them with manna. If he had not done that, they could not have acknowledged that they lived not from bread alone but from the Word of God. "If you were going to live on bread alone and feed yourself, you would have to be continually gathering bread. The Word that feeds us, however, is the Word he has promised us and has proclaimed to us." The lesson that the Wittenberg hearers are to take with them is simple: "He is our God and wants to be our God."[61]

Satan's second temptation lured Jesus to test God's power and love by throwing himself down from the temple, "which was not necessary since there undoubtedly were good steps there." This temptation comes to people whom the devil brings to thinking that they are "full of faith and on a proper, holy path," who not only stand within the temple but also know the temple inch for inch and otherwise appear to have true faith. So the tempter quotes Scripture to them. Luther elaborates Matthew's account with a short story of two hermits who would not accept bread from others because they wanted to receive it directly from God. "One of them died and went to his father, the devil, who had taught him such a faith and told him to jump from the pinnacle of the temple."[62] Medieval piety had created a range of temptations out of its perception of how God and human beings relate. Most involved too much reliance on one's own performance, but Luther also recognized that pious people can fail to acknowledge the responsibilities that God has given them.

61. WA 17.2:189.30–191.3; CP 2:137–38.
62. WA 17.2:193.1–194.19; CP 2:141–42.

His own concept of God's providential love could have contributed to such an attitude, and he was aware of this.[63] This temptation could be combated through the story of Jesus's temptation.

The third temptation leads people away from God by offers of riches, favor, advantageous connections, honors, desires, power, and so forth, attacking from the physical side and the emotional side. This temptation receives no explanatory narrative, neither dialogue nor monologue, to apply it to the Wittenberg hearers' experience. Luther simply warns against the allure of fame and power. The preacher closes the story by repeating Matthew's report that the angels had come to minister to Jesus at the end of the forty days. "That was written for our comfort so that we know that the angels serve us when the devil attacks. When we fight valiantly and we remain faithful, God will not let us suffer want. Before that, he would have to send us angels from heaven and have them serve as our bakers, waiters, and cooks and take care of all our needs."[64]

Preaching on the end times on the basis of Matthew 24:15–28 in 1537, Luther briefly reminds his hearers of the stories of Job, "how the devil brought him to the point of cursing and blaming God for the day he was born" (Job 3:1–19), and of David, who "was a great and outstanding person, but when God withdrew his hand, David succumbed to adultery and murder." Both experiences demonstrate that "we have to be aware that in the face of the devil's tricks and power, no one is ever safe." But the Bible itself did not have as many dramatic stories of confrontation with Satan as did the tradition of the church and its contemporary life. So Luther expands his discussion of Satan's power to delude and seduce the godly with the story of a child in Hesse, whose breathing was stopped for a while by the devil, who also blinded the people in the village into thinking that the child was dead, so great is his power. The preacher fails to inform the congregation of the outcome of this event. He also relates another report from Hesse, in which Saint Anne had restored to life a child that had lain under water for three days. That was a lie, as are many stories of Saint Francis, he observes. But from German oral tradition, he repeats what was apparently a popular legend of a monk whom the devil dressed as a king. He and his brothers in the monastery believed he was wearing royal clothing, velvet and silk. They wanted him to go to the bishop of Saint Martino to show his kingly garments, but he refused, telling them that the angels who had given him this gift forbade it. When they tried to force him to go, the clothes vanished. Finally, from the *Lives of the Fathers*, a chief source of tales of the saints, Luther appropriates the legend of the pious parents whom the devil bewitched to believe their daughter had become a cow. They went to Saint Marcarius for help. Since he had not been bewitched, he

---

63. See pp. 22–24.
64. WA 17.2:195.23–197.13; CP 2:145–47.

told them that their daughter did not have the appearance of a cow, but they refused to believe him, so he prayed to God, who heard his prayer and freed the parents from their delusion.[65]

Job's experience provided fertile ground for exploring, on the one hand, the interplay between God and Satan in the lives of the saints and, on the other, the struggles to which God subjects them as they are afflicted by various sorts of evil. Luther preached on the festival of Saint Michael and All Angels in 1532 on the appointed lesson, Matthew 18:1–10, and Job's miseries form the setting for part of his explanation of the Christian experience of evil. Above all, Luther strives to assert God's total lordship, at times implying that God is too patient with evils. "When he wants to chastise, he withdraws his hand, takes away the protection and aid of his beloved angels, and gives the devil free rein and power over us." The resulting plagues are permitted "to serve as warnings for us and to draw us to himself so that we cling to him and obey him."

Luther rehearses the conversations between God and Satan in Job 1–2. God asks, "Where have you been?" The devil replies, "I have been going hither and yon on earth." Luther comments, "Undoubtedly, this would not have been without incident, without inflicting harm, for this pal prowls around, says Peter, like a lion looking for someone to devour." The Lord asks further, "Take a look at Job: a perfect man." Satan replies, "Yes, dear God! Job has reason to be upright, for you have protected his house and all his possessions." Luther observes, "The devil is saying, 'I would have gotten my way if you had not afforded protection.'" The story unfolds. With God's permission the devil

> sets to work at once, incites some evil scoundrels to carry off a thousand oxen and asses and kill the herdsmen. Next, he causes fire to fall down from heaven, burning up seven thousand sheep along with the shepherds and everything else. Third, he incites three bands of Chaldeans to make a raid and carry off Job's three thousand camels after killing the drivers. All this happened in one day, and that still was not the end of it. For Job had three daughters and four [sic] sons. As they were all together, happy, and in good spirits, what happened but the devil stirred up such a strong wind that the house collapsed on them, killing them all. The devil was capable of doing this but not until God had given him permission.

Then Luther warns, calling his hearers to repentance, "If our Lord should recall the angels, not a one of us would survive. We would all be dead in a moment."

God still could boast to Satan that Job had accepted all this: the Lord had given, the Lord had taken away, and blessed was his name (Job 1:21). Satan responds, "Let me have at his body, his flesh and bone. Then there will be no more fine talk. He will be making a different speech then since until now it

---

65. WA 45:261.27–264.15; EA² 6:246–47; HP 3:200–202.

has not been his own skin that is under attack." Luther concludes the telling of the story by depicting Job as sitting in ashes, covered with terrible sores from head to foot. Then he repeats his conclusion: God is calling people to repentance whenever the devil strikes, through fire, plague, drowning, falling to one's death.[66] Sin has made death inevitable and necessary: God elicits in believers the despair that turns them back from every false god that cultivates mistrust of their Lord in their lives. The gain of God's love is wrought at the price of dying, Christ's dying, and the death of the sinner's identity as sinner as well. That is the experience of God's people in Scripture, and the Wittenberg congregation could expect the same.

Satan not only attacks individual believers. Luther often discussed the warfare between the true church and Satan's forces, in the papacy, among the *Schwärmer*—those whose spiritualizing reforms undercut God's way of guiding and guarding his church through the Word in its oral, written, and sacramental forms—and within his own ranks, as false brethren challenged aspects of Wittenberg teaching. Using the device of calling to mind stories with which his hearers should have been familiar, in one of his last sermons (1546) Luther reminds the congregation that Adam's expectation that his church would be pure collapsed when Cain killed his brother, Abel. Noah believed that he had a pure church—until Ham mocked him and proved that sin still could raise its head within the people of God. Abraham had to contend with Ishmael, Isaac with Esau, Jacob with his wicked sons, and the strife continued. Augustine had to deal with the Donatists, who wanted to establish the pure church and separated themselves from the established church. Luther concludes that Judas will remain among the apostles and that he himself had to endure the presence of evil rascals in the church of his time, for as the reformer often said, "where God builds a church, the devil erects a chapel next to it."[67]

Suffering as Child of God and Enemy of Satan

One of the foremost characteristics of the pious or righteous believer was the presence of suffering in one of several forms, not as a result of one's own sin or Satan's attacks, or even God's mortifying, but simply in the course of answering the Christian's call to demonstrate God's love in God's world. God also tests faith and strengthens it when the faithful find his presence while bearing the burdens of their service to others. Suffering can involve a variety of ills that befall the believer, including sickness and misfortune of various kinds. But Gustaf Wingren correctly observes that Luther perceived a close connection between Christian suffering and the execution of God's call to serve

66. WA 52:716.28–719.12; EA² 6:433–36; *HP* 3:376–79.
67. WA 51:174.30–175.25.

him through serving others in the course of daily life.[68] Stories illustrate how God's people fall under the burden of affliction and distress while carrying out the works of love that God assigns to them. Luther taught people how to deal with all varieties of suffering that stem from faith by calling attention to how the ancient patriarchs had done so. Abraham offered a number of good examples that "the godly who are burdened with a cross and in various ways are hard pressed and groan under this weight have need of God's promises in order to be buoyed up by them."[69] Both confrontations with the enemies of their extended family and the continuing childlessness of Abraham and Sarah tested the faith of the couple, Luther explained to the Wittenberg congregation.[70] In the retelling of Isaac's encounter with Abimelech, Luther observes, "You see how kind the Lord is to his saints. To be sure, he tests them, sends them into exile, lets them be exposed to threats to their reputation and their life, and permits them to be afflicted with famine and misfortunes of every kind; yet he provides excellent, quiet, and safe hospitality and grants peace in the midst of their enemies." Luther confirms what he had shown on the basis of several of Abraham's experiences to the congregation in 1523 and to his students in his later lectures.[71] Isaac's example proves that "without a trial we learn nothing and make no progress. For this is the warfare and the exercise of Christians through which we learn that we are under the protection of the angels and that although we are plagued by severe and difficult trials, yet they do us no harm. This is our theology."[72]

Even before he had children of his own, in 1523 Luther sensed the distress that often accompanies being a parent. He found in Mary a good example of this. The Gospel lesson for the first Sunday after Epiphany, the story of the boy Jesus in the temple (Luke 2:41–52), provides "an example of the holy cross, showing how life unfolds for those who are Christians, and how they should act under the cross. Whoever is a Christian must expect to help bear the cross, for God will take him by the scruff of the neck and test him until he is worn out. No one comes to Christ apart from suffering." So it was with Mary. Despite her great delight with her child, "she had to endure much misfortune, pain, and anguish." First, she had to give birth far from home and in a stable. Then she had to go into exile in a strange country, Egypt. Luther

---

68. Gustaf Wingren, *Luther on Vocation*, trans. Carl C. Rasmussen (Philadelphia: Muhlenberg, 1957), 50–63.

69. WA 43:33.19–20; *LW* 3:221.

70. WA 14:231.23/36–222.24/30; 24:248.29–249.23.

71. WA 43:465.3–7; *LW* 5:53; cf. WA 43:436.37–437.8; *LW* 5:12. On Abraham, see WA 14:291.3/23–292.24/25; 24:361.29–363.30; 42:526.32–37; *LW* 2:369. WA 42:533.32–36; *LW* 2:378–79; and above all, on the call to sacrifice Isaac, see WA 43:200.30–268.10; *LW* 4:91–183. Similar incidents provided for good narrative and similar observations in Hagar's life: WA 42:599.29–36; *LW* 3:71–72; in Jacob's life, WA 43:526.32–529.17; *LW* 5:142–45. WA 44:174.30–175.8; *LW* 6:235–36; in Joseph's life, WA 44:287.35–289.29; 44:373.6–378.6; *LW* 6:384–87; 7:99–106.

72. WA 43:472.3–19; *LW* 5:63; cf. WA 43:476.22–29; *LW* 5:69.

ventures to the congregation that many of her sorrows and sufferings had not been recorded. The text found her scared and distressed, searching for her son in Jerusalem. Her heart felt the burden: "This child is mine alone, that I know, whom God has given me and placed in my care. God had him come to me, and now he is taking the child away from me." Luther comments, "Here we have the great anguish of the mother of Christ. She had been robbed of her child. In addition, her confidence in God was being taken away, for she had to fear that God was angry with her and did want her to be the mother of his son. No one can understand this who has not had the experience of enduring such a thing."[73] Every parent in the congregation must have recalled similar circumstances. The preacher encourages not only them but also all others with similar feelings to place their confidence in God when they feel afflicted and despair. Luther hazards that Mary too had perhaps said to herself, "Sure, God gave you faith in him up to this point, but perhaps he wants to take it from you so that you do not have it any more." But like Joshua, who despaired when the forces of Ai defeated his own troops (Josh. 7:7), and others in the Old Testament, God's unlimited grace turns despair to trust.[74] Luther's short summary of these Old Testament stories, designed to place Mary's struggles in a larger context, may indicate that he presumed the people were familiar with them; it may be that the editors or note takers felt free to omit details of the actual narrative Luther had presented.

By the time he preached on John 16:16–23 in 1531, Luther's wife had given birth three times. So he had some idea of what stood behind the comparison Jesus drew in verses 20–22 when he compared the disciples—who were suffering the pain of separation from their Master, compounded by fears of all kinds—with the emotional state of a woman about to give birth. "Her laughter is stifled; she sees no end to her pain, nor can she say for sure whether or not she will give birth to the child. Her thoughts and words run like this: 'May God help me, may God uphold me, may things go for me as God wills.' For she does not know whether the child is to come into the world or whether she will survive." She thinks on the Lord's word spoken in paradise that promised the sorrow of giving birth. But she also thinks that this will last only "a little while," as in the words of promise to the disciples. Their future and the futures of Luther's Wittenberg hearers were secure because of the utterly trustworthy concern of God for his children in a way that, because of his promise, a woman in labor cannot be secure as she experiences the pains of childbirth.[75]

The worst of these sufferings come from God's afflicting his saints—or, at least, seeming to be absent in the midst of afflictions—as Abraham experienced when he deceived Abimelech to protect himself (Gen. 20).[76] Luther explains

73. WA 12:409.20–411.3; CP 2:18–19.
74. WA 12:411.18–412.19; CP 2:18–19.
75. EA² 5:113–14; *HP* 2:92–93.
76. WA 43:111.28–36; *LW* 3:329.

to the parishioners in Wittenberg that God's delay in fulfilling his promises to Abram laid a cross and suffering upon the patriarch, alongside the difficulties caused by being a stranger in Egypt (Gen. 12). But God still was governing the course of Abram and Sarai's life and gave them consolation amid their trials.[77] God exercises and strengthens faith, and he provides comfort in the midst of these sufferings.[78] As he introduces Joseph to the congregation in Wittenberg, Luther labels the stories of this patriarch "the true 'golden legends,'" in which God "teaches how he boils and fries his saints, how he plays with them, as if everything he had promised was a lie."[79] God remained hidden for Joseph, but he continued to trust that God was with him even as Potiphar's wife tempted him and had him thrown into prison, the German version of his 1523 sermons explains to readers.[80] To his students, Luther spoke of God's playing with the saints in a similar way.[81]

Nonetheless, Luther took seriously the terror and confusion of the saints when God is at work in their lives "under the appearance of the opposite" of his true disposition toward them. In these situations Luther's appeal to God's reliability and steadfast loving-kindness remained the closest he came to a theodical address of the problem. Noah suffered because God seemed to be ignoring evil, or sleeping in the face of the wickedness of his day, and that conveyed comfort, Luther thought, to the Wittenberg students facing evil in their own time.[82] Jacob had to doubt whether God was on his side as he returned to his homeland and faced his brother, Esau (Gen. 32).[83] Joseph had to wonder why God was silent when he rushed into the disaster of being sold by his brothers (Gen. 37) and in his abandonment in Egypt.[84] But the experiences of the patriarchs also prove that God remains faithful when human faith becomes weak, as the German version of his sermons of 1523 makes clear. As Abraham and Sarah doubted that God would deliver the promised heir, God "took in those who were weak in faith," as Luther reshaped Paul's words from Romans 14:1. God leads his own from faith to faith, always open-

77. WA 14:224.13/32–23/40. On Luther's use of his "hidden God" concept in depicting Abraham, see Juhani Forsberg, *Das Abrahambild in der Theologie Luthers: Pater fidei sanctissimus* (Stuttgart: Steiner, 1984), 31–38.

78. WA 43:466.25–470.22; *LW* 5:55–60.

79. WA 14:467; 24:613.31–33.

80. WA 24:632.21–635.26.

81. WA 42:529.37–38; *LW* 2:373. WA 43:218.3–5; *LW* 4:115. WA 43:229.36–230.3; *LW* 4:131. WA 43:371.24–39; *LW* 4:326. WA 44:97.10–24; *LW* 6:130. WA 44:466.22–26; *LW* 7:225. WA 44:536.8–20; *LW* 7:319. See Ulrich Asendorf, *Lectura in Biblia: Luthers Genesisvorlesung, 1535–1545* (Göttingen: Vandenhoeck & Ruprecht, 1998), 387–409; cf. Forsberg, *Abrahambild*, 39–41.

82. WA 42:305.21–306.8; *LW* 2:61–62.

83. WA 44:99.22–101.24; *LW* 6:133–36.

84. WA 44:262.27–30; *LW* 6:351; cf. WA 44:303.38–304.19; *LW* 6:405–6. WA 44:341.5–342.21; *LW* 7:55–57. WA 44:375.32–376.31; *LW* 7:103–4. WA 44:429.24–430.10; *LW* 7:175–76. WA 44:582.29–585.38; *LW* 8:4–9. See Asendorf, *Lectura*, 139–46.

ing a new possibility for practicing, strengthening, and increasing faith day
by day.[85] God seems not to be acting according to human expectations when
he permits Rebekah to deceive Isaac and cause him to transfer the blessing
from Esau to Isaac. Yet, Luther informs the Wittenberg congregation while
referring to Genesis 27, "In all the stories of the Bible, God is faithful and at
the same time presents himself as unfaithful so that we can be smart enough
to learn to know him truly and how he carries out what he has to do on a
level beyond our imagination and reason."[86] In such biblical examples, Luther
found illustrations of his own and his contemporaries' honest appraisal of
God's way of working in his and their own lives. It is true that few perhaps
had experienced the precise kinds of conflicts and doubts as Luther had, but
he knew the Wittenberg citizenry well enough to sense that most recognized
a gap between their expectations of God's presence and providence and some
of their experiences.

Evil does not only invade the righteous and pious life from the outside. It
also comes from within, and therefore those who are sinful as well as righteous
simultaneously are constantly engaged in the mortification of the flesh, the
destruction of their own sinful desires and habits. In recounting the biblical
accounts, Luther also made it clear that the righteous children of God remain
at the same time sinners. Scholars have noticed that Luther's treatment of
the sins of the patriarchs differs from other commentators in the medieval
tradition and among his contemporaries,[87] but this approach to those who
were the saintliest saints and the most sinful of sinners conforms to Luther's
understanding of the Christian life as a life in constant confrontation with the
mystery of the continuation of sin and evil in the lives of the baptized.[88] His
treatment of Judah's intercourse with Tamar gave his students insight into the
larger context of the phrase *simul justus et peccator*. "The very saintly fathers
and sons of such great patriarchs, Judah and others, are described as men full
of the weakness and the very great blemishes to which this wretched nature
is subject. God guided them in a wonderful manner by his Holy Spirit, yet
in such a way that he permitted them to bare their own inclinations, that is,
the sin and fruit of the original evil." But these events have been recorded to
teach and console God's people. Abraham and Isaac "were lights, so to speak,
of the whole world and of the church of God. . . . They were perfect in faith,
hope, and love but at the same time outstanding and horrible sinners." This
was to serve "the preaching of repentance and faith or of the forgiveness of

85. WA 24:335.21–336.3; cf. WA 14:275.16/37–17/38; cf. also the summary of God's dealings
with Joseph in Gen. 42–45: WA 24:660.5–661.13.

86. WA 14:365.7–366.6/11; 24:478.32–479.27.

87. Roland Bainton, "The Immoralities of the Patriarchs according to the Exegesis of the
Late Middle Ages and of the Reformation," *Harvard Theological Review* 23 (1930); 42–43.

88. See Heinrich Bornkamm, *Luther and the Old Testament*, trans. Eric W. Gritsch and
Ruth C. Gritsch (Philadelphia: Fortress, 1969), 20–27.

sins, lest anyone be presumptuous because of one's own righteousness and so that those who have fallen would not despair."[89] These examples of struggling Old Testament paragons of faith served first to warn believers against falling into sin and to remind them of their inherent weakness and inclination toward wrongdoing, just as is seen in Rebekah's deception of her husband (Gen. 27), Luther reminded his parishioners[90] and his students.[91] These Old Testament stories of the saints' failings also served to comfort believers with the assurance that God will stand by them, forgive them, and restore them to proper, godly faith and love, as he emphasizes in lengthy discourses on Abram's lying to the king of Egypt (Gen. 12) and Abimelech (Gen. 20).[92] In treating Lot's intercourse with his daughters, Luther ventures closer to a definite theodical answer than he often did. He draws on the example of the strong faith that both Lot and his daughters must have had, not to excuse their sins, but rather to point out that Christians find comfort in the stories of God's faithfulness to those struggling with doubts as they themselves experience their own temptations to doubt God and his Word.[93]

Fifteen years later, in lecturing on Genesis 19, Luther asked, "Why does God permit his own to fall in this manner?" "Although we are not at liberty to inquire into God's doings with excessive curiosity, yet here the answer is easy. God wants us to be well aware of our feebleness, lest we lapse into overconfidence. . . . God wants us all to humble ourselves and to glory solely in his mercy." While acknowledging that Lot's daughters sinned out of a sense of necessity, not simple lust, Luther still treated their sin seriously and let it highlight God's reconciling nature.[94] In general, the reformer avoided answering the question "Why?" with regard to evil and instead focused on God's loving reprimands of sin and his merciful restoration of his people to trust and obedience.

Sixteenth-century Germans could not avoid recognizing what a significant role suffering played in human life. Christian theologians still wrestle with questions regarding why evil exists and why suffering strikes particular people. Luther's understanding of the person of the Creator required him to define God as the Lord of suffering, and at the same time he rejected any suggestion that God's will is anything but good. His disposition toward his human creatures,

89. WA 44:309.29–310.8; *LW* 7:10–11; on Isaac, cf. WA 43:446.37–447.41; *LW* 5:27.
90. WA 14:371.1/10–373.5/28; 24:483.19–34.
91. WA 43:511.33–513.8; *LW* 5:121.
92. WA 42:470.15–478.24; *LW* 2:291–303; also WA 43:104.3–116.36; *LW* 3:319–36; and WA 43:196.18–22; *LW* 4:85.
93. WA 14:286.13/33–288.18/36; and in an expanded German version, WA 24:352.17–355.25.
94. WA 43:98.10–16; *LW* 3:311; on the entire incident as an example of God's restoring the fallen believers, see WA 43:95.15–100.35; *LW* 3:307–14.

expressed in the atoning death of Christ on the cross, is one of steadfast mercy and love in spite of the reality of his wrath against the sin that harms these human beings. At the same time, Luther recognized the appalling and dreadful reality of evil, and his pastoral sensitivity allowed him to realize that "teaching people how to suffer" constituted an important part of what God calls the ministers of his Word to do for others. God's almighty grasp of his world made it so that he could use evil for his own purposes—though Luther strove to avoid labeling evil as good. Therefore in his sermons and lectures, Luther strove to cultivate trust in God along with confidence that God's rod of repentance, as it "mortified their flesh," drew vital lessons from the suffering behind which God stood and from the suffering inflicted by Satan. These lessons were intended to bring his hearers and readers the blessing of turning from sin and trusting alone in their Creator and Redeemer. The Holy Spirit would accomplish their dying to their sinful identity, using the various forms in which God's law expresses itself, including the message conveyed by their suffering. This laid the basis for their trust in God to produce good works— acts of praise to God and in service to God's other creatures.

5

THE LIFE OF FAITH
IN RESPONDING
TO GOD'S WORD
WITH PRAYER AND PRAISE

Active Obedience in the Sacred Realm

Obedience to God's commands within the context of one's calling posed the positive counterpart to the mortification of the flesh in the life of repentance for Luther. The life of repentance is lived out of a faith that God has given: "Christians cannot and must not talk about ethics without first and always making it an inquiry into faith."[1] Teaching what God has revealed of his own actions in behalf of his human creatures and what he expects of them provides, Kevin Vanhoozer argues, stage direction for faithful daily participation in God's drama of history and life. This metaphor helps pull the faithful into the truly human way of life by filling them with the trust that God is their faithful God and they are his own children.[2] Believers remain God's children and enjoy this identity insofar as they live by the trust that

1. Brian Brock, *Singing the Ethos of God: On the Place of Christian Ethics in Scripture* (Grand Rapids: Eerdmans, 2007), 183.
2. Kevin J. Vanhoozer, *The Drama of Doctrine: A Canonical-Linguistic Approach to Christian Theology* (Louisville: Westminster John Knox, 2005), 102–10.

holds fast to God's gift of his love and is anchored in the promise of this new identity. Therefore Luther rejected every effort to define what it means to be human in terms of performance.

> Luther does not set God on one side and humans on another, trying to define each and their relationship to each other; he simply looks for an opportunity to verbalize the story of God, the retelling of which involves him deeper in it. The story he tells is not outside his own search, pertaining to another independent actor, but is his [Luther's] story only because [he is] Christ's. Luther is not thinking about how to get in touch with a God somehow beyond and over him; he is verbally and methodologically thinking through the contours and categories of his own inclusion in Christ's own victory.[3]

This kind of life is always in flux as believers work in this world as agents of God, his coworkers within his structures for human life.[4] But it always reflects the basic relationship with God on which it is grounded, trusting in his promise in Christ and thankful for all that he has done. Luther viewed Psalm 111 as an attempt to "inflame the gratitude of the faithful for God's provision" of the Lord's Supper, Brock concludes, and because the relationship between God and his human children consists, on the human side, of the trust that takes form in feelings, "such 'gratitude inflammation' is essential for the renewal of the Christian mind, perception, and behavior."[5]

Luther pointed out to the Wittenberg congregation that the stories of Abram link the patriarch's identity as the chosen instrument of God to his love for the neighbor. "Faith and love for God govern love for the neighbor. . . . When love for God takes proper form, love for the neighbor will also [take proper form]. Love for the neighbor governs all external works: his people perform what love demands. All commands are directed by love." Luther believed that love for God coincided with love for the neighbor expressed in observing the first table of the law, that God's people serve one another in obeying the commands to honor his name and hear his Word by gathering for worship, deepening their understanding of Scripture, praying for neighbors and society, and telling others of God's love for them in Christ. Luther believed that loving the neighbor meant, first of all, converting others and bringing them to faith, and then demonstrating every other kind of love that truly benefits the neighbor and does no harm to faith, even beyond specific commands of the law.[6] This concern remained a constant theme also in Luther's later lectures. Faith produces a life of love that "advances daily when we gradually learn

---

3. Brock, *Singing the Ethos*, 208–9.
4. Ulrich Asendorf, *Lectura in Biblia: Luthers Genesisvorlesung, 1535–1545* (Göttingen: Vandenhoeck & Ruprecht, 1998), 436–68.
5. Brock, *Singing the Ethos*, 210.
6. WA 24:275.19–32; cf. WA 24:407.17–410.9.

more and more to hope, trust, and be patient. It is one and the same faith that begins, makes progress, and reaches perfection," Luther reflected as he placed the young Joseph before his students.[7]

As he considered sources for direction toward God-pleasing actions, non-Christian appraisals of virtue that coincided with biblical commands won Luther's commendation. He repudiated Aristotle's ethical system insofar as it tried to describe and circumscribe human life apart from its Creator, but he found the Stagirite's examination of what constitutes good human behavior useful on occasion. The reformer's list of virtues arises out of Scripture, to be sure, even when he uses ancient Greek and Roman thinkers to provide descriptions of these virtues. In addition, beyond what Aristotle could prescribe—and as a presupposition for all performance of vocation and virtue in the horizontal relationships of human life—stood the faith that exercised itself in study of God's Word and prayer.

Repeatedly Luther emphasized the dependence of the Christian life on listening to God. For his sixteenth-century contemporaries, even though God had spoken directly to the patriarchs, listening to God now meant hearing or reading God's Word from Scripture. Luther focused most often on preaching as a means of cultivating the Christian life, both because the vast majority of his contemporaries could not read and because he believed that oral communication addresses the receiver with the most effective and direct delivery of the message. But he also provided the literate with instructions for Bible reading and meditation on its words.

Listening to God through the Reading of Scripture

William Graham's observation that the central importance of Scripture for Luther consisted of its place in the Christian life leads him to comment further: "In his eyes this life demands that one keep constant company with scripture and use it as one's fundamental guide and support."[8] Graham cites Luther's

---

7. WA 44:401.30–402.7; *LW* 7:139. Luther clearly distinguishes between the justification by which God gives filial identity to the person he calls to be his child and the expectations that this newborn child of God meets through new obedience. Juhani Forsberg asserts that in depicting Abraham's justification, Luther taught that "incarnate faith" brings to the justifying of the sinner "secondly also the works, that is the love. 'In concreto' the human being is saved only through this incarnate faith" (*Das Abrahambild in der Theologie Luthers: Pater fidei sanctissimus* [Stuttgart: Steiner, 1984], 83). But Forsberg fails to appreciate Luther's insistence that only God's gift of righteousness justifies and that this gift of righteousness before God produces, distinct from itself, the renewal of humanity that lives in obedience to the God in whom the believer trusts. With this false interpretation of Luther, Forsberg in effect returns to the medieval understanding of salvation by "faith formed through love," *fides charitate formata*, a view that Luther specifically and repeatedly rejected.

8. William A. Graham, *Beyond the Written Word: Oral Aspects of Scripture in the History of Religion* (Cambridge: Cambridge University Press, 1987), 146.

admonition to his readers in the preface to Johann Spangenberg's postil: "Keep watch, study, pay attention to the reading: truly you cannot read too much in Scripture, and what you read, you cannot read too well, and what you read well, you cannot understand too well; what you understand well, you cannot teach too well; and what you teach well, you cannot live too well."[9] In a largely illiterate society, encounters with Scripture took place most often in the church service. But suitable stories for encouraging church attendance are hard to find in Scripture.

Indeed, in addition to Luther's burning concern that God's Word be preached to those who could not read it—as well as those who could!—the reformer rubbed shoulders daily with the small percentage of the population that could read and write, not only students and colleagues but also the burghers, in whom he hoped to cultivate a life of personal meditation and prayer, individually and in their families. Reading the Bible leads to understanding what God is saying, and Luther presumed that Christians will inevitably share what they gain there with others. Learning its teaching inevitably translates into daily living, Luther was confident. The wise men's encounter with God's direction through the star and the attempts in Jerusalem to interpret this experience on the basis of Scripture (Matt. 2:1–12) provides readers of Luther's postil with encouragement to read the Bible regularly. "Why did God not simply complete the star's task of leading the wise men by taking them all the way to Bethlehem?" he asks in commenting on the consultation of King Herod with his scholars in Matthew 2:4–6.

> He did this to teach us to cling to Scripture and not to follow our own presumptuous ideas or any human teaching. For it was not his desire to give us his Scripture in vain. He wants us to find him there and nowhere else. Those who have contempt for Scripture and let go of it will never again find him. As we heard before, the angels gave the shepherds a sign, and it was not Mary or Joseph or any other human being who in their holiness might have counted as a sign. It was merely the diapers and crib in which he was wrapped and laid. They were the vessels in which he is offered to us. So is Scripture his certain sign, as he himself said, John 5 [v. 39], "Search the Scriptures, in which you believe that you have life, for they are the very Scriptures that give witness to me."

Luther continues by citing the appeals of Jesus and Paul to the authority of Scripture (Luke 2:25–38; 16:29–31; Rom. 3:21).[10]

Luther also prepared guidelines for his readers' and hearers' use of Scripture. The priests and learned leaders of Israel knew the text of Scripture but failed to ponder and digest it. If they had, Luther concludes, they certainly would have run off to Bethlehem too, and not let fear of Herod shape their acceptance

9. WA 53:218.19–23.
10. WA 10.1.1:576.6–24; *LW* 52:171–72.

of the prophecies they found. Others, like Herod and his counselors, believed that God's Word is true but set about to defy and frustrate it. The third kind of reader, like the Magi, is prepared to leave homes and possessions, disregarding them so that they might find Christ. They confess him and his truth.[11] The wise men's paradigm for appreciating and studying Scripture portrays the pattern according to which Luther's readers were to approach the Bible. First, as a book whose message centers on Christ; second, as the Word of God that holds ultimate authority over every human opinion. The wise men arrived in Jerusalem and immediately got to the point, not asking first for Annas or Caiaphas or for someone's address: they wanted to know where the king of the Jews was. Luther's theology of the cross guided him to the certainty that God had been working under the appearance of opposites, under the guise of the modest and the unlikely. Jesus did not appear in the holy city, the city of power, Jerusalem. And his birthplace was revealed in Scripture, which is not a book full of obscurities for people of faith. Luther's confidence in the authority of Scripture led him into this early polemic against the authority of every kind of human teaching not in accord with Scripture, from Aristotle to the medieval church's inventions in the legends of the saints and glosses of the fathers.[12]

Preaching on Luke 11:27–28, Luther dramatizes the scene of the woman's acclaiming Jesus in order to focus on God's Word alone. It appears to the world as though this woman did a great thing by "striding before the people and praising the mother who had given her only son to the world." "Christ crumples up [her fine work] and throws it away." For "the woman speaks from her heart as a woman caught in the flesh." Such women of the sixteenth century would say, "Blessed is the mother whose son is a pastor," or when they hear a great preacher they pray, "Would that God make my son into a man like him." But Jesus directs the attention of his hearers to God's Word, and Luther elaborates on how best to hear God's Word: by placing human imagination to the side and focusing on Christ.[13]

To kindle Wittenberg hearts as Jesus's exposition of the Scriptures had kindled the hearts of the two disciples on the road to Emmaus (Luke 24:32), Luther concludes his Easter Monday 1523 sermon on their story with an admonition to Bible reading. He knew that Satan tries to prevent believers from turning to the biblical text, so he acknowledges the battle involved in the reading of Scripture. To repeat the experience of the disciples from Emmaus and be encountered by the Lord, the Wittenberg hearers are urged to "take the Gospel and the Holy Scriptures before you, the more the better, even if you already know them and have often read them. For it is certainly a

---

11. WA 10.1.1:593.7–595.8; *LW* 52:183–85.
12. WA 10.1.1:581.18–588.10; *LW* 52:176–80.
13. WA 17.2:280.29–282.12; *FS* 1:43–44.

suggestion of the devil, who tries to tear from you your delight in the Word. He hates to have you come to it, for he knows very well what fruit it bears in you. If you are thus busy with the Word and strive to live it the best you can, you will see that Christ is with you and a fire is kindled in your heart."[14] God addresses readers of the Bible directly, and hearing his voice there is part of the daily cultivation of trust in Christ. Luther urges his hearers to practice faith by "taking God's Word to yourself, and practice it, hear or read it and speak about it, and you will always find and prove something that pleases and moves you. You should in addition pray to God and say as the apostles did in Luke 17 [v. 5], 'Lord, increase my faith!'"[15]

The model of the disciples from Emmaus serves also to remind his hearers that Bible reading is not only for the individual believer; it is also a group activity.

> The best is for two or three earnestly to speak among themselves about it so that the living voice is heard. Then you will be much stronger and the devil must yield. Thus all evil lust and thoughts disappear, and thus there will ensue such a light and knowledge as you have never before experienced. The only trouble is that we fools have such a great treasure lying before our doors and do not know how to use it. And the devil deceives us in order to draw us away from it and make us indifferent because he cannot overcome it. Therefore we must prepare to resist the devil's suggestions and influence. Likewise, Christ will come and reveal himself even though at first you are not aware of it. The more you speak about it and discuss it, the more clearly you will recognize Christ and feel that he kindles your heart within you, as you heard in this Gospel of the two disciples' journeying to the village of Emmaus.[16]

Three years later Luther gathered his thoughts on Bible study in small groups and incorporated them into his plan for ideal life in the congregation. Acknowledging that many in the congregations of his time had little interest in studying Scripture, he dreamed of the day when congregations would have such small groups that would gather for prayer and Bible study. This reflects his confidence in the Holy Spirit and his use of the word found in Scripture and delivered by the saints from its pages.[17]

For the readers of his *Works*, in the preface to the first German volume (1539), Luther sketches an image of David in meditation. Here he does not recall a narrative so much as construct a concrete ideal, depicting the royal psalmist as a model for immersing oneself in God's Word. In his psalms David engages God's Word in the manner that Luther wants the Wittenberg hearers to emulate. He finds in David's practice a prototype for his own experience

14. WA 12:505.4–10; CP 2:280.
15. WA 12:503.5–18; CP 2:278.
16. WA 12:505.10–23; CP 2:280–81.
17. German Mass (1526), in WA 19:75.3–30; *LW* 53:63–64.

with the monastic pattern of "reading, praying, meditating" (*lectio, oratio, meditatio*), but he revises it to reflect his own experience with Scripture. To preserve the threefold form of the model, he presumes the reading of the text, and to prayer and meditation he adds the spiritual struggles (*tentatio*; in German, *Anfechtung*) that had accompanied his own life of repentance. He informs his readers, "This is the way taught by holy King David (and doubt-lessly used also by all the patriarchs and prophets) in Psalm 119. There you will find three rules presented in detail throughout the entire psalm." Luther continues, "First, you should know that the Holy Scripture is the kind of book that turns the wisdom of all other books into foolishness because it teaches only about eternal life." Readers could then imagine "how David continues to pray in this psalm, 'Teach me, Lord, instruct me, lead me, show me,' and many more words like these." Although "he knew well and daily heard and read the text of Moses and other books, he nonetheless wants to lay hold of the real teacher of Scripture himself, so that he may not pounce upon it with his reason and become his own teacher." David recognized that reading Scripture is not like reading about the legend of Markolf, a popular German folktale, or Aesop's *Fables*, which Luther held in high regard as a source of worldly wisdom.[18] David knew that, in contrast to such works, reading Scripture requires the Holy Spirit and prayer, Luther insists.[19]

David not only prayed over the text of his Bible reading; but he also medi-tated on Scripture. Luther comments, "You see in the same psalm how David constantly boasts that he wants to do nothing but speak, write, utter, repeat, sing, hear, and read God's Word and commandments day and night, at all times. For God does not intend to bestow his Spirit upon you apart from his external Word. Conform yourself to that. He has not given a vacuous com-mand when he commands you to write, preach, read, hear, sing, speak orally and in writing."[20] Luther's trust depended on this "external" Word, and he steadfastly opposed all spiritualists, such as Thomas Müntzer, who believed that they had received an "internal" revelation that could not and dare not be tested against the written Word of God. Luther's Ockhamist training had led him to believe that God works through the material order he has created and called good, as related in Genesis 1. He believed that God's power to establish a saving relationship with his chosen people lies in the externally proclaimed gospel (Rom. 1:17). Encountering the text of Scripture, Luther experienced the voice of God.[21]

18. WA 50:440–60.
19. WA 50:659.1–21; *LW* 34:285–86.
20. WA 50:659.30–35; *LW* 34:286.
21. Robert Kolb, "The Relationship between Scripture and the Confession of the Faith in Luther's Thought," in *Kirkens bekjennelse I historisk og aktuelt perspektiv: Festskrift til Kjell Olav Sannes*, ed. Torleiv Austad, Tormad Engelviksen, and Lars Østnor (Trondheim: Tapir Akademisk Forlag, 2010), 53–62.

Luther's own experience led him to see that encountering God's Word in Scripture always takes place for believers in the midst of spiritual struggles. He calls them the "touchstone" of understanding and experiencing "how correct, how true, how sweet, how lovely, how powerful, how comforting God's Word is." For David "laments so often regarding all kinds of foes, arrogant princes or tyrants, false spirits and factions, whom he must endure because he meditates, that is, continually is occupied with God's Word, as has been mentioned, in all sorts of ways." Luther applies David's experience to his own day, realistically appraising the difficulties his readers could expect in developing the habit of meditation: "As soon as God's Word dawns throughout your life, the devil will visit you and make you a real expert [on Scripture]." Luther reports that he had experienced that in his own conflicts with the papacy. He concludes his treatment of "David's rules" by saying that "if you study hard in accord with his example, then you will also sing and boast with him in the psalm: 'To me the law from your mouth is preferable to thousands of gold and silver pieces' [119:72]."[22]

Although in the previous year Luther had discouraged celebration of Mary's ascension, Luther preached on that designated day of August 15, 1523, on the text of Luke 10:38–42, Jesus's visit to the home of Mary and Martha. The story provided the framework for his affirmation of the priority of faith, out of which truly good works grow, and for admonitions to study Scripture as Mary had. For "works pass away and alongside God's Word are like ashes compared to fire. The word that the Lord speaks lasts forever. If we speak of faith, we will produce works out of it, but Paul says that the Word is God's power." Luther told the congregation that Martha was doing what the mistress of a household or a maidservant should do. Nonetheless, Christ was first of all concerned about trust in God. People lived under two kinds of regimes, Luther commented. Some try to live by keeping the law. Mary lived in the freedom that Christ gave, bound to serve others yet doing this spontaneously, doing "what is best" by beginning with God's Word, which then would lead her to do more good works.[23]

Reading the Scripture or hearing it applied from the pulpit should activate its use in daily life, as in testifying to others. Because Luther believed that the Holy Spirit works through the Word to change lives, he urged Christians to speak it to one another. He insisted not only that good parenting included leading children and servants more deeply into his Word but also that the power of the forgiveness of sins was delivered from one believer to another. Luther invented a scenario in which no pastor was available for absolution. In such cases, he told the Wittenberg congregation in 1537, "There is not always a sermon being given publicly in the church, so when my brother or

22. WA 50:660.1–19; *LW* 34:286–87.
23. WA 11:159.13–161.38.

neighbor comes to me, I am to lay my troubles before my neighbor and ask for comfort. . . . Again I should comfort others, and say, 'Dear friend, dear brother, why don't you lay aside your burdens? It is certainly not God's will that you experience this suffering. God had his Son die for you so that you do not sorrow but rejoice.'"[24] Luther had confidence in the power of God's Word. He believed that God calls pastors to proclaim the Word publicly, but that call granted them no exclusive franchise on the distribution of the forgiveness of sins. Furthermore, it excused no baptized believer from giving witness to Christ.

Hearing God's Word and Keeping It

Luther's audience consisted of many who could not read and write, who were dependent on the Word in the form of preaching. Scripture, however, offers few stories of people gathered to listen to the Word of God and therefore presents few opportunities for reinforcing this practice, which served as a major tool in the spread of Luther's reform and the cultivation of the new Wittenberg forms of biblical piety. However, in sketching Saint Andrew's concern for hearing God's Word—in his sermon for the saint's festival published in the House Postil of 1544—Luther fills in details omitted from Andrew's conversion story (John 1:35–42). Luther imagines that Andrew, like his brother, Peter, had a wife and children along with his calling as fisherman and wrestled with all the problems that accompany trying to support a household. But Andrew listened to John the Baptist, whose sermons of repentance led him to be baptized for the forgiveness of sins. He was not the type, apparently all too familiar in Wittenberg, whose worry about feeding the family and finding time to sleep left no time for going to church and hearing the preaching there. Andrew's chief concern was not how to find nourishment for himself and his family but how to enter the kingdom of God. He entrusted his physical life to God. This should serve, Luther asserts, as a paradigmatic narrative for his hearers and readers.[25]

In 1521 the need to encourage the habit of regular hearing of God's Word seemed, if anything, more pressing to Luther. In the Wartburg Postil, he uses the story of the wise men to encourage frequent participation in evangelical worship services. Allegorizing in part of his sermon for the festival of the Epiphany, he asks,

> What then is the star? It is nothing else than that new light, preaching and the Gospel, as it is orally, publicly proclaimed. Christ left two witnesses of his birth and his rule. The first is the Scripture, the word set down in writing. The second is the voice, the word that rings out orally. This Word Saint Paul and Saint Peter

24. "Sermons on Matthew 18–24," 1539–40, in WA 47:297.36–298.14.
25. WA 52:564.23–565.9.

also labeled a light and a morning star [2 Cor. 4:4; 1 Pet. 2:9; 2 Pet. 1:19]. For the gospel opened up the Prophets, and in the same way the star must rise first and be seen. Then in the New Testament the proclamation takes place orally, with a living voice, in public, and is presented as it is spoken and heard. . . . Therefore, apart from books there needs to be good, learned, pious, diligent preachers in every village who draw the living Word from the ancient Scripture and continuously inculcate the people with their message, as the apostles did. For before they wrote, people heard the proclamation and were converted with actual voices, and that is the genuine apostolic work of the New Testament. That is the true star that revealed Christ's birth, the message of the angels, which tell of his diapers and crib.[26]

Yet Luther strove to encourage more than merely listening to a sermon or reading the biblical text. If the preaching or reading did not produce an understanding of the gospel, a recognition of Christ as Lord and Savior, it would bring no profit.[27]

In order for God's people to hear his Word, the church needed preachers. Luther transformed the vision of the Christian life *from* a religion and piety centered on ritual performance of sacramental actions that supposedly provides grace to enable fulfillment of God's commands—*to* practice and piety that depend on the proclamation of God's Word and its reception through trust in God's promise. Luther's lectures to his students involve, above all, preparation for preaching, and he certainly did not neglect depicting the calling of the servants of God's Word, as in his treatments of Genesis.[28] Abram's building an altar at Shechem (Gen. 12:7) provides Luther the occasion to sketch "external service to God" for the Wittenberg congregation. Abram provided a place for his family to gather to hear the gospel, pray, and make sacrifices, as had taken place among God's people since the time of Cain and Abel.[29] Joseph and even Pharaoh had served the church and furthered the preaching of God's message. Luther imagines that Joseph had introduced the harsh discipline of limiting food during the years before the famine only because he had exercised power on the basis of God's teaching and the fear of God that he had cultivated among the Egyptian population. He envisages Joseph as proclaiming and preaching, bringing many of the Egyptians to faith in the true God, so that they would recognize God's blessings, live humbly, and repent. Alongside his proclamation, Luther speculates, he had undoubtedly prayed with fervor for the Egyptians.[30]

The calling of Andrew in John 1:35–42 is the basis for a number of Luther's comments on the nature and task of the public preaching office in the church.

26. WA 10.1.1:625.12–626.23; LW 52:205–6.
27. WA 10.1.1:628.3–8; LW 52:207.
28. WA 24:255.27–256.36; Asendorf, *Lectura*, 113–15.
29. WA 14:224.23/225.21–226.9/30; 24:255.27–256.36. See Forsberg, *Abrahambild*, 123–36.
30. WA 44:666.5–16 (cf. 44:668.22–24); 44:458.11–25. See Asendorf, *Lectura*, 277–82.

John the Baptist focused his preaching on the Lamb of God, Jesus Christ, and this model is what Andrew followed, as should every preacher.[31] Following the example of John, ministers of God's Word in the New Testament serve as proclaimers and preachers, not priests who make sacrifice. Priests were necessary in the Old Testament, before Christ made the one perfect sacrifice for human sin on the cross. He remains the church's only priest, and its public ministers are called above all to preach and absolve.[32] In choosing Andrew, Jesus indicated that his servants come from among the common and simple people of society, poor fishermen and sinful tax collectors like Matthew; even the betrayer, Judas, was numbered among the disciples whom Jesus gathered.[33] Luther fills in some details of the requirements that God laid down in Scripture for the conduct of his ministers and bishops, repeatedly emphasizing proper proclamation of the gospel of the forgiveness of sins.[34] For forgiveness brings life and salvation, initiating all that the Holy Spirit wishes to do among the people he has chosen and leading them to trust God and to respond in praise and prayer to God and in service and love for the neighbor.

Responding to God through Praise and Prayer

The God who speaks engages his children with his Word and expects to hear a reply. Scripture offers many examples of God's people turning to him in prayer. Luther presumes that he can mention their names and their stories would spring to mind, so familiar were they that he need not elaborate details. For instance, the mention of Elijah, Elisha, David, Solomon, Hezekiah, and others at prayer required no further details.[35] Luther does remind his hearers that contemporary believers should not expect that their prayers would necessarily produce the same results as those of saints in previous times: they should not assume that their petitions would bring the sun to stand still (Josh. 10:12–14), the waters of the sea to part (Exod. 14:1–31), or fire to come down from heaven (1 Kings 18:30–40). "But we are at least the equal of these [such as Joshua, Moses, or Elijah] to whom God gave his Word and whom the Holy Spirit has inspired to preach. Indeed, we are not different from Moses, Joshua, and Elijah." Therefore his readers, Luther concludes, should find in the prophets' experiences encouragement for their own prayers.[36]

Luther's expansive view of how believers praise God embraced all faithful service to him, but both formal and informal forms of praise and prayer in the

---

31. WA 52:565.33–566.9.
32. WA 52:566.10–567.31.
33. WA 52:567.32–568.14.
34. WA 52:568.15–571.40.
35. *Vom Kriege wider die Türken*, 1529, in WA 30.2:119.27–120.9; *LW* 46:173–74.
36. *Vermahnung zum Gebet wider die Türken*, in WA 51:598.33–599.30; *LW* 43:226–27.

Scripture also garnered Luther's commendation as instruction and example. Mary serves as an excellent pattern for praising God in singing her song of thanks and praise in reaction to being called to be the mother of the Almighty, the Son of God. "The tender mother of Christ [followed the exhortation of Ps. 44:7–8 that God's saints should praise God], and she teaches us, with her words and by the example of her experience, how to know, love, and praise God." For "she boasts, with heart leaping for joy and praising God, that he regarded her despite her low estate and nothingness."[37] The story of Mary's singing praise to God for the gift of the Messiah when she visits Elizabeth (Luke 1:45–55) offers a contrast to two examples of "false spirits who cannot properly sing" Mary's kind of praise. The first of the two characters whom Luther sketches responds with praise only in reaction to blessing; the second, "more dangerous still," tries to take credit, at least in part, for the good things God has given. Mary "had no thought but this: if any other young woman had gotten such good things from God, she would have been just as happy and would not have begrudged the other these blessings. She would have regarded herself alone as unworthy of such honor and all others as worthy of it." Such a pattern for praise, Luther notes, should find imitators in his readers.[38]

Mary Jane Haemig has effectively analyzed Luther's use of Abraham as a model for faithful engagement with God in prayer.[39] She points out that in 1520, in *On Good Works*, Luther explains that Abraham's prayer for the righteous in the cities bent for destruction exemplifies going to God with confidence in his love.[40] Abraham's struggling in prayer to God on behalf of Sodom presents a model of prudent but resolute and unrelenting prayer, both for the congregation in 1523 and the students in 1538, a pattern for bold beseeching that seemed to Luther to portray a prayer aimed at compelling God to forgive.[41] Lot's plea for another place of residence than that to which God instructed him to flee (Gen. 19:17–20) reminds Luther that God wants us to implore him for what we wish to have. Lot's pattern for prayer begins with thanks to God, next states the need at hand, and then makes his request clear. From such examples the professor teaches his students to pray and find comfort in God's answering Lot's prayer.[42]

Anna, the widow who had longed to see the birth of the Messiah (Luke 2:36–38), presented a good model for the prayers of sixteenth-century Germans. Thanksgiving to God filled her life. Luther explains that Luke's word

37. WA 7:548.29–33; *LW* 21:301.
38. WA 7:554.30–556.10; *LW* 21:307–9.
39. Mary Jane Haemig, "Prayer as Talking Back to God in Luther's Genesis Lectures," *LQ* 23 (2009): 270–95. The following discussion borrows extensively from her treatment.
40. WA 6:239.20–24; *LW* 44:66–67; Haemig, "Prayer," 270.
41. WA 43:282.1–283.3; 43:282.12–283.21; 43:282.27–34; 24:342.29–343.29; 43:41.30–44.9; *LW* 3:232–36.
42. WA 43:81.8–84.31; *LW* 3:287–92.

for her action in verse 38 embraces a confession of sins, a confession of faith, and a confession of thanks and praise. For thanksgiving to God confesses that believers receive his benefits; it acknowledges the goodness of the benefactor and the unworthiness of those who stand in need and are praying. Thus this thanksgiving to God flows into testimony regarding his goodness to other people.[43] This confession and her thanksgiving flow from her confession of the "redemption" for which she is waiting, the redemption of Israel through the Messiah. At the same time the faithful are always experiencing God's liberation or redemption from a variety of temporal evils and threats to their eternal welfare.[44]

Prayer, as the bold and confident pleading of children who are asking a dear Father, as Luther expresses it in his Small Catechism, takes place daily in Christian living, but particularly in times of trial and suffering. The *Anfechtung*, or *tentatio*, that formed an integral part of personal Bible study, according to Luther, also shapes the prayers of the pious. Abraham illustrates that a number of times. In Genesis 15:2–6 Abram pleads with God because no child had been produced to carry on the promise that he would become the father of nations. Luther points out that prayer is necessary because "God makes his saints sad again after they have been made glad, lest they become proud and smug. After they have been made alive, he leads them down to hell in order to lead them back from there."[45] In the midst of such doubts, believers are to follow Abraham's example of submitting to God's will, trusting him, and laying their requests and desires before him in prayer.[46] Luther sharpens his picture of Abraham's praying: "It is characteristic of sublime trials that they occupy hearts when they are alone. Therefore in Holy Scripture there is frequent mention of praying at night and in solitude; . . . because Abraham was occupied with these sad thoughts, he was unable to sleep, so he got up and prayed." And God came to converse with him "in a friendly manner."[47] While his hearers and readers might not expect God to chat with them in precisely the same way, Abraham's example was intended to encourage them to go to God in times of need and trial.

Jonah's prayer from the belly of the fish also gave Luther opportunity to reinforce the lessons of the catechisms regarding prayer. "Above all else we must pray and cry to God in time of adversity and place our wants before him. For God cannot resist helping the one who cries to God and implores him. His divine goodness cannot remain aloof. It must help and lend an ear."[48] On the basis of Jonah's praying, Luther also emphasizes that "our crying to God

43. WA 10.1.1:437.20–439.19; *LW* 52:141–42.
44. WA 10.1.1:439.20–442.3; *LW* 52:142–44.
45. WA 42:554.36–38; *LW* 3:9.
46. WA 42:557.1–559.20; *LW* 3:12–15.
47. WA 42:561.5–10; *LW* 3:17–18.
48. WA 19:222.9–12; *LW* 19:71–72.

is of a nature that God will answer," and the human heart will find solace in praying to God in trust.[49]

Haemig uses Luther's comments on Abraham's brief prayer that Ishmael function as the heir that had not come (Gen. 17:18) to illustrate two associated points in the reformer's teaching on prayer: (1) God gives more than we ask for or can understand; (2) neither the unworthiness of those praying nor the magnitude of what is being requested nor God's greatness should discourage God's children from praying. The reformer tells his students to courageously pray in the face of all that Satan throws at them and to confidently approach God with their desires.[50] Luther draws several conclusions from the ways in which Abraham prayed. Like Abraham, his hearers should pray in desperate and impossible situations.[51] Like Abraham, they should avoid the repetitious, ritualistic prayers of the monks and talk with God in the confidence that he opens his heart to and cares for those who come to him in faith.[52] No prayer of Abraham illustrates these principles more clearly than his "foolish" prayer for Sodom and Gomorrah, foolish because he acts as if God cannot count how many righteous people are in the cities. Its boldness makes it a "forceful and impulsive prayer, as if Abraham wanted to compel God to forgive."[53] The Wittenberg students are to imitate Abraham's love for others, especially his enemies and those caught in sin, as well as the patriarch's wisdom or prudence in approaching God with fervor and feeling, which led Abraham to shed tears as he sought God's mercy for the cities, Luther presumes.[54] From Abraham, however, students can also learn to rely on God's wisdom and not to expect that their every prayer would be granted. In this instance Abraham "went home full of sorrow and spent that night without sleep and in tears and sighs because of the destruction of so great a multitude."[55]

Abraham's nephew Lot also presents an exemplary prayer in his conversation with God's angels in Genesis 19:17–22. His plea to be permitted to flee to Zoar and find refuge there shows all readers of the story how to come to God with requests. As he had said in the Large Catechism,[56] Luther reiterates to his students that God has commanded prayer, attached his gracious promise to the practice of prayer, and in the Lord's Prayer provided them with a paradigm for their own praying. Lot did as well. His prayer begins with acknowledging God's goodness, implying his thanks and praise for God's protection to that point. Then he laments his situation and places himself at God's mercy because

49. WA 19:223.12–224.29; *LW* 19:73–74.
50. WA 42:661.1–36; *LW* 3:157–59.
51. WA 42:661.27–662.9; *LW* 3:158–59.
52. WA 42:662.32–663.27; *LW* 3:160–61.
53. WA 43:43.8–44.6; *LW* 3:234–35.
54. WA 43:40.28–33; 41.32–43.19; *LW* 3:231–35.
55. WA 43:45.29–31; *LW* 3:238.
56. *BSLK* 664–66; *BoC* 442–43.

of his need. Finally he makes his request to God. This prayer from a faithful believer caused God to change his mind regarding the destruction of Zoar.[57]

Haemig points out that the examples of Abraham and Lot exemplify the doubtful hesitancy that all believers often reveal when they approach God, but also encourage imitation of their bold assertiveness of faith in confidently calling on God to be merciful—appeals sometimes met with success, sometimes not. Haemig's analysis also demonstrates that prayer especially arises amid life's conflicts and tribulations. Prayer also brought home to Luther his conviction that as a God of conversation and community, God wants to talk with his people. "For Luther and his followers, prayer was conversation within a relationship between God and humans, a conversation started by God's Word, a conversation that respected the integrity and creativity of both parties. Prayer did not depend on human worthiness but on the nature of God, who had promised to hear prayer."[58] Anna in Luke 2 also serves as a paradigm for fervent prayer, which filled the life of this pious woman. "Of course, she had to eat, drink, sleep, and rest," Luther writes in the Wartburg Postil, but prayer and fasting constituted her way of life. That should not be understood as only including prayers with her mouth; she also meditated on Scripture and on preaching and gave God honor and praise in all her activities.[59]

In the early 1520s the problem of secret betrothals without parental knowledge and against parental wishes occupied Luther's attention. This topic sprang to mind as a good example for his readers in their daily lives. The confidence of the wise men admonishes the intended hearers of the Wartburg Postil's sermon on the Gospel for Epiphany, encouraging them to live a life that expresses its dependence on God through prayer. Luther urges young people to pray for a chaste life, follow the example of the wise men, and pray for God's counsel and guidance when choosing a husband or wife. This made concrete how his contemporary Germans could emulate the Magi's dependence on God and the prayers they must have continually offered as they made their journey and decided what to do after they found the baby Jesus.[60] From the pressing problems of everyday life to the crises of faith, prayer serves God as a tool for strengthening faith and a weapon against Satan, and so Luther made every effort to foster it. He was convinced that God's good gift of prayer gave believers the means of responding to God's goodness as they gained experience in his Word and in his direction of their daily lives.

Luther rejected humanly devised sacred works as the foundation for the human being's relationship to God, but he did not eliminate sacred works commanded or commended by God from the life of faith that he wished

57. WA 43:81.8–82.21; *LW* 3:287–89.
58. Haemig, "Prayer," 290.
59. WA 10.1.1:435.1–436.12; 52:139–40.
60. WA 10.1.1:724.11–725.22; *LW* 52:284.

to cultivate. His distinction between the vertical and horizontal spheres of human life placed works of prayer and praise within the context of the entire life to which God calls his people. It did not diminish the importance of such sacred works of piety but rather exalted all those works in the "secular" sphere of life that, he believed, the medieval church and particularly the monastic system had banished to second-class status.[61] The active righteousness that God calls believers to practice embraces both earthly and heavenly realms. For the Wittenberg reformer, therefore, the call to daily use of God's Word in Scripture and to response in praise and prayer formed an integral part of the life of the faithful.

---

61. Robert Kolb, "Die Zweidimensionalität des Mensch-Seins: Die zweierlei Gerechtigkeit in Luthers *De votis monasticis Judicium*," in *Luther und das monastische Erbe*, ed. Christoph Bultmann, Volker Leppin, and Andreas Lindner (Tübingen: Mohr Siebeck, 2007), 207–20.

6

THE LIFE OF FAITH IN SERVING THE NEIGHBOR

Luther's Ethic of Callings and Commands

From the initial efforts of his preaching career in the monastery, Luther's concerns about the conduct of his hearers in living out their faith had commanded his attention. In assessing the future reformer's earliest extant sermons, Elmer Kiessling emphasizes "their high ethical seriousness."[1] From the beginning of his career as reformer, the moral performance of his hearers in Wittenberg commanded his concern. His first postil demonstrates his zeal for offering instruction for living the Christian life to the people of early sixteenth-century Germany.[2] Luther found general public standards for behavior as lacking as their falsely directed trust in their performance of sacred rituals.

As noted in chapter 2,[3] some biblical stories are, at least at first reading, ethically ambiguous or, perhaps more accurately expressed, not examples of saintly virtues but of the moral vulnerability of God's faithful people. Luther continuously wrestled with the mystery of how sin and evil con-

---

1. Elmer C. Kiessling, *The Early Sermons of Luther and Their Relation to the Pre-Reformation Sermon* (Grand Rapids: Zondervan, 1935), 77.

2. The Wartburg Postil is found in WA 7:463–537; see Makito Masaki, "Luther's Two Kinds of Righteousness and His Wartburg Postil (1522): How Luther Exhorted People to Live Christian Lives" (PhD diss., Concordia Seminary, St. Louis, 2008).

3. See "Current Narrative Scholarship and Luther's Storytelling," in chap. 2 above.

tinued in the lives of God's chosen people; in dealing with the failures and foibles of the saints, he thus had less difficulty than some commentators in the history of exegesis. Gordon Wenham proposes three criteria that may help in sorting out the ethical values projected by biblical writers: "Obviously within Old Testament narrative we have all kinds of virtues and vices depicted. In some cases it is obvious whether the implied author approves or disapproves of the behavior described." He suggests that the repetition of a behavioral pattern in several contexts demonstrates the author's principles, either positively or negatively, indicated by the explicit or implicit judgment accompanying the story. Second, the context of the story may reveal the author's standard of evaluation. Third, "remarks in the legal codes, psalms, and wisdom books often shed light on Old Testament attitudes to[ward] different virtues and vices."[4]

Luther's childhood training and subsequent education had provided him with the standards that the medieval church had distilled from Scripture, traditional tribal values, and ancient Greek and Roman philosophers. Yet his own encounters with sin's deep penetration of human life and his insistence that the Holy Spirit guides believers through wisdom and love to interpret and apply God's commands in specific situations—all this led him to spend a good deal of time helping his hearers and readers think through the process of making ethical decisions for everyday life. For instance, he overruled the conventional wisdom of always telling the truth with the more primary concern to love others. Thus Christians should not repeat true rumors or reports if it is not necessary for neighbors to know such things. Through this kind of discretion, he aimed to promote the welfare of all. This illustrates his way of weaving together biblical commands with specific situations of everyday life, which do not always fall into neat categories of right and wrong, of benefiting or harming others. Nonetheless, in general his reading of the stories, as in Genesis, sorted out their intended ethical instruction according to criteria not unlike Wenham's.[5]

Christians live out their daily lives in the midst of the eschatological battle between God and Satan, between good and evil. In themselves they experience the conflict between desires born of their living with false gods and the Holy Spirit's fashioning them as children of God. Therefore they live in repentance and in the faith that turns back to God through killing contrary desires. Moved by God's love in Jesus Christ, they seek to do his will and, Luther expected, grow in their production of the fruits of faith. That growth takes place not in a religious environment set apart from this world but in the midst of daily life, Luther repeated with frequent polemical references to monasticism and

4. Gordon J. Wenham, *Story as Torah: Reading Old Testament Narrative Ethically* (Grand Rapids: Baker Academic, 2004), 88–89.

5. Large Catechism, eighth commandment, *BSLK*, 624–33; *BoC* 420–25.

other medieval religious observances.[6] God has liberated his people for the faithful performance of divinely ordained virtues within the believer's vocations in the home, in economic activities, in society, and in religious community. Luther presumed that the examples of the patriarchs, their families, and their contemporaries, as well as the New Testament contemporaries of Jesus and Paul, provided guidance for conducting daily life in the sixteenth century. Of the story of Rebekah and Isaac in Genesis 24, Luther could say in 1521, "There are several topics in this chapter that pertain to moral actions, for forming human life and training the spirit."[7] His sermon on this chapter two years later elaborates on the lessons to be learned as sixteenth-century Germans follow the example of their ancient fellow believers. These lessons include, for example, children's valuing their parents' planning of their marriages and all Christians' recognizing how God cares for his people, especially in governing marriage and married life.[8]

Even though Luther was convinced that many have only contempt for the common and ordinary details of family found in the stories of Abraham and Sarah, the Holy Spirit had intended to instruct all readers of Scripture in the proper way of conducting human life.[9] In elaborating on the covenant between God and Abraham in Genesis 17, Luther observes that God, as a special form of his favor, had given the patriarch assignments to serve him by serving other human beings.[10] In these callings people speak and act on behalf of God, as the story of God's communicating to Isaac gives Luther occasion to explain, lest his students think that they must wait for direct messages from God themselves and ignore his providential care in the help offered by his human agents.[11]

In his treatments of Genesis, Luther puts to use a host of examples that, rather than relating tales of extravagant religious performances, tell how "the fathers live in their households with their children, wives, domestics, and cattle. Here there is no outward show of religion, but there is only one coarse sack of household life."[12] God's gift of a relationship with himself freed Abraham

---

6. WA 43:30.20–34; *LW* 3:217. WA 43:108.18–109.11; *LW* 3:325. See also Luther's long critique of monastic vows, based on the example of Jacob's vow to God in Gen. 28:20–22, in WA 14:387.4/14–399.4/12/34; 24:499.29–510.21.

7. WA 9:369.17–18.

8. WA 14:317.14/34–320.13/29; 24:419.31–423.19.

9. WA 42:474.1–5; *LW* 2:296. On Luther's treatment of Sarah, see Mickey Leland Mattox, *"Defender of the Most Holy Matriarchs": Martin Luther's Interpretation of the Women of Genesis in the "Enarrationes in Genesin," 1535–45* (Leiden: Brill, 2003), 117–28.

10. WA 42:639.16–640.30; *LW* 3:128–30; Luther pauses a number of times in the stories of Abraham to explain that God places people in their vocations in the three situations that compose human society; cf. WA 43:20.31–42; *LW* 3:204. WA 43:30.13–19; *LW* 3:217. WA 43:74.37–75.8; *LW* 3:279; cf. Luther's similar lesson based upon Joseph's earthly callings, WA 44:259.20–260.32; *LW* 6:346–48.

11. WA 43:477.27–478.15; *LW* 5:70–71.

12. WA 43:432.38–40; *LW* 5:6.

to serve in the world. Luther places words in the patriarch's mouth: Because God is "gracious, ready to forgive, and kind, I go out and turn my face from God to human beings; that is, I tend to my calling. If I am a king, I govern the state. If I am the head of a household, I direct the domestics; if I am a schoolmaster, I teach pupils, mold their habits and views toward godliness. . . . In all of our works we serve God, who wanted us to do such things and, so to speak, stationed us here."[13] Because he trusted God, Abram could practice justice and righteousness toward other people, even to the point of setting aside his own rights, Luther affirms in commenting on his negotiations with the king of Sodom (Gen. 14:21–24).[14]

God uses his human creatures in their callings, such as in the filial concern Judah shows in aiding his father (Gen. 43:1–5).[15] These human callings are the masks behind which God cares for his world, as the examples of Jacob and Esau reveal.[16] In a strange bit of speculation, Luther conjectures that after all four of his wives had died and "Jacob had been deprived of the son he loved most," his daughters-in-law and his daughter Dinah "took the place of the mother of the household. . . . These women were without doubt very upright matrons, who administered Jacob's household diligently and faithfully, and it prospered under their care. They were not indolent and lazy, for managing livestock demands thoroughness and care." Luther then poses the question, Why does the Holy Spirit mention "such trifling, childish, servile, feminine, worldly, and fleshly things about these most holy people? . . . Why did he not write about things more serious and sublime? Why does he make so much out of the sweat of their working with the squalid matters of the household?" Because, Luther observes, "God hides his saints under such masks and matters of the flesh so that they may seem more wretched than everything else." For the people who trust in God live amid the troubles and afflictions of the world he created, which has now fallen from its created goodness. That is where the promises and commands of God are active and deliver his presence.[17]

Called by God to Love and Service

Luther believed that God had called people to serve their neighbors in specific walks of life, as the stories of the patriarchs' participation in family and economic pursuits, governmental life, and religious activities illustrates. Luther adopted the structure of medieval social analysis, which assigned individuals

13. WA 42:632.1–7; LW 3:117.
14. WA 42:548.3–549.19; LW 2:397–99.
15. WA 44:529.35–530.2; LW 7:311.
16. WA 44:129.23–26; LW 6:173. WA 44:166.42–167.8; LW 6:225.
17. WA 44:529.20–530.6; LW 7:510–11.

to three situations or walks of life (*Stände, status*). According to Luther, all three areas of human life have an integrity of their own, created by God for specific purposes,[18] and each brings blessings from God through those who exercise their responsibilities (*Ämter, officia*) in them. Luther affirms this when expanding on Lot's life in Palestine (Gen. 13:14–15)[19] and when explicating the blessing that Isaac gave Jacob (Gen. 27:39–40).[20] For Jacob exhibited this kind of faithfulness to God, content to serve the Lord in the lowliest of earthly tasks.[21] The patriarchs exercised callings in all three of the walks of life God had instituted: church, civil administration, and the family household.[22] God recognized the unique situations and gifts that he had given to every person, as opportunely illustrated in the stories of Joseph and his brothers.[23] Abraham's obedience to God's command regarding the sacrifice of Isaac lets Luther explore the unique case that made clear that almost always—this story being an exception!—God's people carry out God's assignments in normal vocational channels. In every case they do so under God's Word.[24] Luther repeatedly makes clear that the practice of vocation was to take place in subjection to God's Word.[25] Joseph and his family exemplified the nature of the Christian life: sojourners and wanderers on this earth but nonetheless with specific places given them by God to meet the needs of others.[26]

Called to Serve in the Family and Economic Sphere

God calls people into the situation of the household, defined as the economic as well as social and biological unit we today designate as "family." The stories of Genesis abound with details that demonstrate God's interest in that fundamental building block of society. Luther certainly treated the household on the basis of details in the lives of the patriarchs, but often the matriarchs gave him occasion to comment on what he regarded as the foundation of human society and human life. The very conception of Cain

18. WA 43:198.14–20; *LW* 4:88. See Robert Kolb and Charles Arand, *The Genius of Luther's Theology: A Wittenberg Way of Thinking for the Contemporary Church* (Grand Rapids: Baker Academic, 2008), 58–64; Robert Kolb, *Martin Luther, Confessor of the Faith* (Oxford: Oxford University Press, 2009), 172–96; and Gustaf Wingren, *Luther on Vocation*, trans. Carl C. Rasmussen (Philadelphia: Muhlenberg, 1957).

19. WA 42:516.33–517.18; *LW* 2:356–57.

20. WA 43:523.16–524.31; *LW* 5:138–40.

21. WA 43:617.36–619.4; *LW* 5:274–76; cf. WA 43:642.33–39; *LW* 5:310–11.

22. WA 42:378.5–13; *LW* 2:165.

23. WA 44:443.23–24; *LW* 7:194. WA 44:564.29–34; *LW* 7:356. WA 44:657.9–35; *LW* 8:106–7. WA 44:659.19–25; *LW* 8:110.

24. WA 43:209.8–212.32, esp. 210.3–11; 211.9–15; *LW* 4:103–7.

25. WA 42:341.32–41; *LW* 2:112.

26. WA 44:662.29–663.17; *LW* 8:114–15; cf. WA 44:706.8–17; *LW* 8:174.

(Gen. 4:1) propels Luther into a paean on marriage and family life for the Wittenberg congregation—against those who diminished the marital state.[27] The story of Rebekah in Genesis 26 leads Luther at verse 8 into a paean on the affection that God calls spouses to express toward each other.[28] Abraham's planning for the marriage of Isaac (Gen. 24) sends Luther on a long digression on various aspects of the patriarch's life, in which he often returns to the blessings of marriage and the example that Abraham and Sarah had set for a number of aspects of married life.[29]

The comments on Genesis 24 begin with a reflection on the report of Sarah's death in the previous chapter, comments that give a glimpse into Luther's own experience of marriage, some two decades long at this point: "When the woman who had governed his home died, Abraham lost his right eye. . . . For these people did not have hearts of stone, and the remembrance of the most delightful companionship and of the most attractive virtues of the wife he loved so much often set him to grieving again."[30] Luther imagines how pleasant their family life must have been. The visit of the three messengers in Genesis 18 provides the occasion for commenting,

> You will find everything most pleasant, with an atmosphere of openness and trust, in the house of Abraham. That this is true can be seen in the fact that the very angels of God seem to jest jovially with Sarah when she laughs and denies that she has laughed. Consequently the Word of God is continually heard there, and Abraham's home is nothing else than a kingdom of the forgiveness of sins and grace, yes, a very heaven in which the angels of God come to dwell and are received with reverence. In them he worships God, whom he knows and believes in as One in Three. In short, in Abraham's home there is nothing but grace and life.[31]

Yet Luther knew that Abraham and Sarah's married life was not only filled with laughter. As he muses on their life together in his lecturing on the birth of Isaac, Luther presents their relationship as a demonstration that in a sinful world, afflictions plague marriage even though God has instituted it. That should not discourage Christians, Luther counsels as he tells the story of these two. "Inconveniences, vexations, and various crosses are encountered in marriage. What does it matter? Is it not better that I please God in this manner, that God hears me when I call upon him, that he delivers me in misfortunes, and that he benefits me in various ways through my life's companion, the upright

---

27. WA 24:123.14–124.13.
28. WA 43:449.36–454.29; LW 5:30–36.
29. WA 43:295.13–314.33; LW 4:223–50; cf. similar comments when Isaac sent Jacob to find a wife, in Gen. 28:1–2; WA 43:558.6–564.37; LW 5:188–96.
30. WA 43:295.33–34 and 296.7–9; LW 4:223–24; cf. similar comments on Rachel, in Gen. 30; WA 43:655.24–659.7; LW 5:329–34. WA 44:199.5–201.38; LW 268–71.
31. WA 43:38.14–21; LW 3:228.

wife whom I have joined to myself?" For precisely in the trials of family life, God has hidden himself and through them brings blessings.[32] In discussing their life together, Luther uses the tensions over their failure to produce the promised son to drive home a number of points about Christian living. Sarai's advising Abram to seek the fulfillment of the promise of an heir through Hagar (Gen. 16:1–2) also serves as a model of Christian contentment and patience in bearing the burden of childlessness.[33]

Their quarreling about Abraham's treatment of Ishmael (Gen. 21:10–11) reveals honest and natural concerns in both the husband and the wife. Luther believes that their fighting about God's promises was conducted "in fear and obedience to God and true humility." "This account," he tells the future preachers before him, "is useful for comforting spouses, in order that they may not think it strange if disputes arise among even the most affectionate and the saintliest people. One should rather consider that in marriage there are such varied exercises in godliness and love."[34] Luther's treatment of the relationship of Isaac and Rebekah (Gen. 26:8) instigates a longer digression on how to conduct a marriage.

> No disagreement and discord is bitterer and more horrible than between spouses or between brothers. On the other hand, if there is mutual love, mutual play and kindness, that marriage is loved and praised everywhere by all, for it is rare because of the devil, who is its perpetual enemy, trying to disturb the divine union in whatever ways he can. . . . A husband should conduct himself in a kindly and gentle manner toward his wife, not only in the bedroom but also in public. He should not be capricious, irascible, and surly, for examples of dissensions and harm done to others are noticed by people and cause them to fall into sin. Especially when jealousy is added, there is hell itself. Therefore, it is useful if there are such examples of kindliness and amiability among spouses, so that others also learn the habits of being pleasant, affable, and patient if any offense or trouble occurs.[35]

The relationship of Abraham and Sarah leads Luther to think of Peter's exhortation for husbands and wives to love each other (1 Pet. 3:1–7), and that launches him into criticism of either spouse's attempt to play dictator in the household. "Husbands generally are lions in their homes and are harsh toward wives and servants. Similarly the wives generally domineer everywhere and regard their husbands as servants." Both are foolish and wrong, and the

---

32. WA 43:140.16–20; 43:140.28–141.3; *LW* 4:6–7.

33. WA 42:578.22–581.18; *LW* 3:42–46. On Luther's treatment of Hagar, see Mattox, *Defender*, 152–70.

34. WA 43:151.6–14; *LW* 4:21–22.

35. WA 43:450.30–451.9; *LW* 5:32; cf. the extension of these remarks, in WA 43:449.8–455.12; *LW* 5:30–38. In 1521 Luther had found in the examples of Jacob's family life in Gen. 30 a plan for marriage: WA 9:412.7–11.

people of the church should follow the example of Abraham and Sarah in loving and respecting each other.[36]

God uses the callings of wife and husband to continue his creation. Among Luther's frequent reiteration of the God-pleasing nature of conception, giving birth, and raising children are comments on the births of the offspring of Adam and Eve (Gen. 4:1),[37] Abraham and Sarah (Gen. 24:35–44),[38] Abraham and Keturah (Gen. 25:1–4),[39] Isaac and Rebekah (Gen. 25:21–26),[40] and Jacob and Leah and Rachel (Gen. 29:16–20, 32).[41] Sarah's death brings Luther to reflect on parenthood in general: "God has placed in woman his creative activity that brings human creatures into being, and along with it, the process of creating: conceiving, giving birth to, nourishing, and raising children; taking care of her husband; and administering the household. . . . God does not make human beings from stones. He makes them from a man and a woman."[42]

Luther also explicitly treats the mutual obligations of family members. He expresses some sympathy for Lot in his dilemma, under threat from the Sodomites, but after reviewing earlier interpretations, such as Augustine's, which argued that Lot had to choose between two evils, Luther grants the objections against that interpretation lodged by Nicholas of Lyra. However, he also contends that one cannot judge Lot's heart. Nonetheless, Luther impresses upon his students that this is one example of a biblical action by a presumably faithful believer that cannot be held up as a model for faithful service by others. For such parental irresponsibility is not in accord with God's plan for the calling of a father.[43]

The sixteenth-century German household often embraced servants as well as parents and children. Luther comments on the callings of both masters and servants. Abraham's servant Eliezer models the ideal of his calling, Luther observes when treating Genesis 24. There Eliezer faithfully carries out Abraham's commission to return to the land from which Abraham had come to find a wife for his son Isaac. Eliezer combines a pride at serving his master with humility and modesty as well as faithfulness.[44] His service commends all godly, Christian service. "Those who are placed more humbly in society should know that their calling carries with it the same honor and high regard as their masters and others placed more highly have, for whatever prestige or distinctions their superiors may command, the servants share with them;

36. WA 43:128.25–37; LW 3:354.
37. WA 42:176.29–179.37; LW 1:237–41.
38. WA 43:342.21–345.37; LW 4:289–93.
39. WA 43:352.10–353.9; LW 4:304.
40. WA 43:383.1–430.18; LW 4:342–78.
41. WA 43:627.18–630.24; LW 5:288–92.
42. WA 43:344.15–17, 24; LW 4:291.
43. WA 43:59.21–61.32; LW 3:258–60.
44. WA 43:338.27–340.10; LW 4:283–85.

they participate in the same renown as the heroes whom they celebrate."[45] To the end of his life Luther counted Eliezer as a model of faithfulness in serving others, a model also for pastors in their calling.[46] Jacob projects the paradigm of faithful service while he worked for Laban, in contrast to the shepherds of his own day, Luther remarks.[47] Joseph's service in Potiphar's house and in Pharaoh's government[48] permits the professor to depict for his students how to fulfill the calling of servant at various levels.

Called to Serve as Subject or as Ruler

Luther frequently emphasized the need for both justice and order in society, and that brought him to admonish rulers and subjects alike. For he believed, with medieval social theorists, that the responsibilities of both were written into the structure of human life by the Creator. Twenty-first-century Christians are so conditioned by their secular surroundings that they "easily overlook Luther's insistence on the theological importance of not understanding the secular political realm as *without* God. The secular political order is a particular kind of order, provided by God, which formally recognizes that even those who rage against him are given space to live. But this political space is received by Christians as a gift of grace that makes possible service to others."[49]

Luther's fear of the chaos that rebellion brings, with all its attendant suffering, stands behind his calling subjects to obey their rulers unless their governments command them to do something against God's law. His sense of what is both right and the will of God stands behind his sharp criticism of abuses of power by the powerful. Because the Bible contains fewer stories about the obedience of subjects, his references to the responsibilities of the governing and the governed tend to concentrate on the former. He described their general responsibility and the temptations they have to combat because of the nature of this responsibility. Luther sharply criticized counselors of princes but also exploitation exercised by rulers themselves, especially their misuse of the church and church property for their own benefit. He urged subjects to lodge appeals against political injustice even though they should not attempt to use violence in striving against it. Luther approved of passive resistance when rulers disobey God's commands for the proper exercise of their office.

45. WA 43:342.4–8; *LW* 4:288.
46. WA 43:300.10–29; 43:338.21–340.42; *LW* 4:229–30, 272–86; cf. Luther's reference to the service of Joseph and Eliezer in a sermon of December 13, 1545, in WA 51:96.20–25.
47. WA 44:51.1–21; *LW* 6:69–70.
48. WA 44:343.28–345.31; *LW* 7:58–61. WA 44:349.23–350.2; *LW* 7:66–67. WA 44:351.10–352.14; *LW* 7:69–70.
49. Brian Brock, *Singing the Ethos of God: On the Place of Christian Ethics in Scripture* (Grand Rapids: Eerdmans, 2007), 220.

Abraham exercises the calling of civil magistrate responsibly,[50] and Joseph serves as a model governor, Luther notes in detail in a brief "mirror of princes" on Genesis 41:40.[51] Luther recognizes that Pharaoh had acted uprightly in dealing with Abram and Sarai (Gen. 12:18–19) but through Abram's deceit had fallen into sin. Nonetheless, the reformer cannot resist noting how easily magistrates slip into a variety of sins, and that leads him to comment on the sins of the heads of households and subjects of rulers as well.[52] The irresponsibility and wickedness of the leading men of Sodom remind Luther of abuses by parents and masters of servants as well as civil officials.[53] Particularly the counselors of princes earn Luther's wrath from time to time. Phicol, Abimelech's military commander, has to be the source of that king's demand for a loyalty oath, the professor is certain; he expands on Genesis 21:22–23 with a critique of courtiers and a plea for sharp distinctions between administration of church and administration of civil government.[54] Nonetheless, subjects should appeal to their governments for the justice God has appointed them to administer, yet they must bear the wrong when civil magistrates fail at their vocation.[55] Even though Abimelech maintained peace and preserved justice (Gen. 26), "the majority of the princes and kings in the world always hate and persecute the Word, destroy the churches, and harass the godly." The Holy Spirit put forth Abimelech to comfort God's people that they might know of one who cared for the church and loved and learned God's Word.[56] But when rulers act in an ungodly way, Luther wants his students to know, God's Word trumps the word of the ruler. Rambling off from Rebekah's breaking the rules to deceive her husband and win the blessing for Jacob (Gen. 27), he reminds his students, "If the civil government tolerates me when I teach the Word, I hold it in honor and regard it with all respect as my superior. But if it says, 'Deny God; cast the Word aside,' then I no longer acknowledge it as the government. In the same way one must render obedience to parents."[57] God, not the obligations of the situation or position to which he has called believers in this world, remained the determining factor in the Christian life.

On the basis of Scripture, Luther did not hesitate to provide guidelines even for temporal rulers. David served as his prime example of how those called to exercise temporal authority should actually carry out this assignment from God. David could also, on rare occasions, typify for Luther the abuses

---

50. WA 42:629.18–22; *LW* 3:113–14.

51. WA 44:433.5–437.14; *LW* 7:180–86; cf. WA 44:670.27–671.37; *LW* 8:125–26.

52. WA 42:489.33–490.17; *LW* 2:318–19; cf. WA 42:524.26–35; *LW* 2:366–67.

53. WA 43:40.12–24; *LW* 3:230–31; cf. his critique of magistrates' corruption, in WA 43:110.35–111.12; *LW* 3:328–29.

54. WA 43:189.8–190.23; *LW* 4:75–77.

55. WA 43:192.8–195.23; *LW* 4:81–84.

56. WA 43:487.24–33; *LW* 5:84.

57. WA 43:507.6–42; *LW* 5:114–15.

of power that the reformer sharply criticized in those called to lead society. In the years between 1526 and 1534, Luther developed an image of the ideal ruler on the basis of psalm texts, which he interwove with—and interpreted in the light of—the David narratives that begin in 1 Samuel 16, continue through 2 Samuel, and conclude in the initial chapters of 1 Kings.[58]

In 1526 Luther preached on Psalm 112 in the presence of Ernst and Franz, dukes of Lüneburg, who were visiting Wittenberg at the time. This sermon reveals how Luther's presumption that David authored the psalm inclines him to present it as comfort for the persecuted faithful of God who face the might and repression of tyrants.[59] He did not often associate words in this psalm with David's own manner of governing, but on this occasion he does. In this case Luther's preface criticizes three vices of the rich and powerful: their striving for earthly might, fame, and pleasure. Regarding the second, he comments, "We shall never reach the point at which by our own efforts we will hang on to honors. God cannot tolerate that; he will blow them over. . . . David and the other patriarchs and prophets sought no honor in this manner."[60] In commenting on verse 2, "His descendents will be powerful on earth. The family of the upright will be blessed," Luther observes that David knew that the posture of the Jewish nation had confirmed that blessings continue to accompany the faithful. The Jews did "not seek wealth and fame apart from God's will." They let God give them honor, and therefore they received his blessing, as David reflected in the text.[61] Luther cites David's assertion in Psalm 37:25, "I was once young and have gotten old and have never seen a righteous person abandoned or his children begging for bread."[62] David's confidence in God's providence informed Luther's own faith.

The fate and course of governments and governmental authorities lay, according to Luther, in God's hands. He directed those whom he had called to civic responsibility to be faithful leaders, and he led to their fall from power when they disobeyed. God exalted David from the status of a commoner to being king, Luther points out, in an affirmation of God's control of human history and even the lives of those who exercise earthly power.[63] However, despite

---

58. The following material originally appeared as "David: King, Prophet, Repentant Sinner; Martin Luther's Image of the Son of Jesse," *Perichoresis* 8 (2010), 203–32.

59. Jaroslav Pelikan suggested that the printed version of the sermon contains contradictions due to editors rather than to Luther himself because Luther labels Psalm 112 a psalm of comfort and consolation at the beginning of the sermon but later turns to condemnation of the abuses of wealth and power; *LW* 13:xi. Pelikan's suggestion is probably false because it misses a fundamental principle in Luther's preaching, which captured a significant element in the worldview of the psalms: the consolation of the faithful rests in part on calling them as well as their foes to repentance.

60. WA 19:301.27–31; *LW* 13:394.

61. WA 19:308.12–17; *LW* 13:398.

62. WA 19:309.12–19; *LW* 13:399.

63. WA 19:310.19; *LW* 13:400.

David's avowal that "wealth and riches remain in the house of the upright" (Ps. 112:3), David was "driven out of his kingdom by his own son, and other saints have lived in great poverty." Luther meets the challenge: David and others who suffer among the people of God "have their treasury, their cashboxes, their storage cellars with God, in a place where no thief can steal them [Matt. 6:20]. They know that they have all they need in God [2 Cor. 3:5]. Although they do not have so much that their moneybags bulge and their cashboxes are full, they are certain that God will feed them. Although they suffer want for a while, and God is testing them, God will indeed not remain far away. They will have something to eat, even if heaven has to rain down bread."[64] For Luther, David's life and faith confirmed what the king had written in this text: that God rules the world in the interests of his own chosen people.

While at the Coburg Castle in 1530, Luther wrote a commentary on Psalm 118. Among his comments on the phrase first expressed in verse 1, "The steadfast love of the LORD endures forever," is a discussion of human dependence on God. "Scripture states that God made both lords and subjects, and temporal government belongs to him," as David had said in Psalms 18:48 and 144:2. "Here he does not boast of himself, that he wanted to rule his own people with power and wisdom, although he had the most wonderful laws and customs, established by God himself through Moses and the prophets who had anointed and confirmed him as king by God's command. He had learned by experience what the power and wisdom of kings and princes can do if God himself does not manage the household." The rebellions of Absalom and Bichri (2 Sam. 15–18, 20) proved to David that God was in ultimate control because he preserved David in the face of these assaults on his government.[65]

Twice Luther uses the exposition of psalm texts as the occasion for creating what could be viewed as a "mirror of the prince," an admonition to rulers to rule faithfully as servants of God and their people. In 1530 he did so with a commentary on Psalm 82, and in 1534 he turned to Psalm 101, which he reads as David's own description of himself as king. Luther likely wrote this commentary as an admonition to his own ruler, Elector John Frederick the Magnanimous, to live more piously.[66] Luther describes Psalm 101 as David's presentation of "the authentic image of the true ruler."[67] Luther is particularly worried about the abuse of power by courtiers in general and at the Saxon

---

64. WA 19:310.31–311.14; *LW* 13:400.

65. WA 31.1:81.8–82.22; *LW* 14:53–54.

66. Compare the comments of E. Thiele and O. Brenner in WA 51.198. On Luther's "mirrors of princes," see Robert Kolb, "Die Josef-Geschichten als Fürstenspiegel in der Wittenberger Auslegungstradition: 'Ein verständiger und weiser Mann' (Genesis 42, 33)," in *Christlicher Glaube und weltliche Herrschaft: Zum Gedenken an Günther Wartenberg*, ed. Michael Beyer, Jonas Flöter, and Markus Hein (Leipzig: Evangelische Verlagsanstalt, 2008), 41–55.

67. WA 51:227.37–38. This description stems from Heinrich Bornkamm, *Luther and the Old Testament*, trans. Eric W. Gritsch and Ruth C. Gritsch (Philadelphia: Fortress, 1969), 9. See also Wolfgang Sommer, *Gottesfurcht und Fürstenherrschaft: Studien zum Obrigkeitsverständnis*

court in particular. (His disclaimer that he has no experience at court and knows little of the trickery and deception that is practiced there is a pious, rhetorical exaggeration.[68]) In this psalm, Luther explains, "David, who was a king and had to keep servants at his court, cites himself as an example of the way a pious king or prince should treat his personnel." John Frederick should take note! In the service of his message, the commentator also carefully frames his picture of David. Governing officials should particularly "praise and thank God if they have a good organization and upright servants at home or at court. That should teach them to know that it is a special gift of God and not due to their own wisdom or capabilities."[69] Though he had forthrightly discussed David's sin when treating him as a model of repentance, in this commentary he ignores all the vices and transgressions of the king. "Dear David was so highly gifted. Such a precious, special hero is not only innocent of all deception and taking of life that took place in his kingdom. Indeed, he also actually opposed such liars and murderers, did not want to tolerate them, and acted against them so that they had to yield."[70]

In Psalm 101 Luther finds the virtues of the ruler and his responsibilities effectively depicted. He employs his own distinction between the two realms of human life to summarize David's way of ruling. "We hear in this psalm of many fine, princely virtues that David practiced. In this psalm he does not treat how to serve God, as in the first commandment, but how people should behave properly toward their neighbors. For just as the spiritual realm or responsibility shows how people should act properly in relationship to God, so also the earthly realm shows how people live in relationship to each other and how they do it in such a way that body, possessions, wife, child, home, land, and material goods remain in peace and security and how they can fare well on this earth."[71]

The psalm depicts David's practice of his powers as ruler, Luther contends, drawing on the many stories of David's rule of Israel in the two books of Samuel. In its first verse Psalm 101 records the king's praise for "mercy and justice." These terms are used here in the sense of the horizontal realm of human life. In this instance they do not relate to God's mercy and justice but to that exercised by earthly rulers. Luther explains that justice is almost always a synonym for punishment in courtly circles.

> If there is only mercy and the prince lets everyone milk him and kick him in the mouth and does not punish or express his rage [against wrongdoing], then

---

Johann Arndts und lutherischer Hofprediger zur Zeit der altprotestantischen Orthodoxie (Göttingen: Vandenhoeck & Ruprecht, 1988), 23–73.

68. WA 51:201.22–26; *LW* 13:147.
69. WA 51:201.30–34; *LW* 13:147.
70. WA 51:234.12–16; 51:235.10–16; *LW* 13:188–89.
71. WA 51:241.31–42; *LW* 13:197.

not only the court but also the land itself will be filled with wicked rascals. All discipline and honorable actions will disappear. However, if there is only or too much rage and punishing, tyranny will emerge, and then the upright will not be able to catch their breath because of the constant fear and worry. Even the heathen say this; it is an everyday experience: "Strict justice is the greatest injustice." But the opposite is said of mercy: "Pure mercy is the most unmerciful thing possible."[72]

Luther reads his convictions concerning good government into David's placing mercy before justice in this passage: "Moderation is good in all things. To achieve it is an art that must be attributed to God's mercy. To get as close to this goal as possible, it is better to give too much mercy than too much justice. That is why David mentions mercy first and then justice. Where this middle way cannot be achieved, it is better to practice mercy than punishment. For in giving mercy a person can draw back and give less, but when punishment is given, it cannot be taken back, particularly where it affects body, life, or limb."[73] David himself, Luther recalls, had practiced this principle with wisdom. The king did not punish his cousin and field commander Joab even though Joab had twice committed homicide (2 Sam. 3:27; 20:10). David cursed Joab because he had murdered Abner and Amasa, two rival field commanders more upright than he. But the king would have provoked severe dissension within his infant kingdom if he had proceeded against Joab, and so he waited and placed the punishment of this wicked servant in the hands of his son Solomon (1 Kings 2:6).[74]

Luther not only commends David's wisdom and upright conduct; but he also praises the king's reliance on God alone. "When David wanted to take the life of Goliath [1 Sam. 17], they wanted to give him instructions, put armor on him, and gave him real equipment. Yes, sir! David could not wear the armor and had another instructor in mind. He struck Goliath before anyone else knew what he was supposed to do. He was not an apprentice who had been trained in this craft. He was a master who had been trained in the craft by God."[75]

David models "fine, princely virtues" in the horizontal realm of human life, keeping the people within the law, "each person in relation to his neighbor. . . . The secular government should direct the people horizontally toward one another, seeing to it that body, property, honor, wife, child, house, home, and all manner of goods remain in peace and security and are blessed on earth." In providing an example of this, "David is the best of all."[76] Luther recognizes that in the horizontal realm of life, even those who do not trust God can be blessed

72. WA 51:205.24–206.3; *LW* 13:152–53.
73. WA 51:206.7–15; *LW* 13:152–53.
74. WA 51:206.30–207.11; *LW* 13:153–54.
75. WA 51:208.35–40; *LW* 13:158.
76. WA 51:241.31–42; *LW* 13:197.

by him with secular wisdom and insight into good governmental practices. He urges the reading of good pagan authors who wrote on effective administration of society, and he says that rulers such as Augustus and Alexander provided their people with good government.[77] But David recognized that God alone gives the power to rule well. Though the pagan rulers ascribe their success in ruling to "fortune" or "luck," David and other God-fearing rulers rule under God's guidance to serve God and the people he entrusts to them.[78]

Luther finds David's principles for ruling in the latter half of the psalm. "I destroy him who secretly maligns his neighbor," the psalmist writes (101:5a). Luther believes that David must have been speaking of courtiers, who, he was certain, generally malign others in their jockeying for power. This was the reformer's way of reading the biblical text into his own situation, applying it to the pressing need he was addressing. He commends David for destroying "royal, princely slanderers who sit in government offices, not only at court but also in the country. That is what I call the virtue of a David and an example of princely courage, a special impulse from God."[79]

David further rejects those of "proud demeanor and conceited in spirit" (10:5b). "Here David is speaking of the pride of governmental officials in relation to their subjects. He not only prides himself on the fact that he himself has not been proud in relationship to his subjects—which is itself truly a high, royal virtue—but also that he has not permitted it among those who served at his court." David provides a sterling example of the godly humility that too seldom graces the lives of ruling officials, an example that readers of Luther's commentary are urged to observe by reading his story in the books of Samuel.[80] Luther draws the contrast between David and Saul—the former remained humble, and the latter became proud and defied God—as an admonition to his Wittenberg hearers while preaching in 1532.[81] The next verse (101:6) expresses delight in the faithful and in devout servants, and Luther ventures, "Maybe David succeeded, as he boasts here, because he surveyed the entire land, opening his eyes, looking around for faithful, devout people wherever he was able to find them, and selecting without any discrimination among persons." Just as God had chosen the shepherd boy David, so David managed his kingdom.[82] Luther intends that the clergy among his readers convey this message to the government officials in their audiences and hopes that municipal officials and people at court will also take heed.

David closes the psalm with a vow to destroy the godless in the land. "Just as women are reluctant to hear someone call them whores when that is just

77. WA 51:242.20–243.9; *LW* 13:198–99.
78. WA 51:244.18–33; *LW* 13:200–201.
79. WA 51:246.13–29; 51:249.38–250.15; *LW* 13:203, 207.
80. WA 51:252.3–14; 51:253.20–39; *LW* 13:209–10, 211–12.
81. WA 36:332.29–333.14.
82. WA 51:255.24–256.5; *LW* 13:214.

what they are, so kings and lords are reluctant, and courtiers are even more reluctant, to hear someone rebuke them and punish them as unrighteous and wicked, because that strikes too close to home. David goes right ahead and minces no words. He does it rudely and indiscreetly enough. He wants to suppress nothing. In fact, he boasts of it as a good deed that he rebukes his own people at court so shamefully and even destroys them." That, Luther reminds his readers, had happened in relationship to Ahithophel (2 Sam. 17:23), Joab (1 Kings 2:28–34), and others of his officials. "David must have been not only a courageous hero with his fist but also an independent fellow with his tongue. It certainly was the same David who tore up the bear and slew the lion [1 Sam. 17:34] and smote Goliath [1 Sam. 17:50]."[83] Nonetheless, David had to suffer God's punishment for his own sin, in the defilement of his daughter Tamar by her brother Amnon (2 Sam. 13:1–21) and the slaying of Amnon by his brother Absalom (13:28–33), who in turn drove David into exile (15:13–37), ravished his "wife" (actually, his concubines; 16:22), and then died of a spear through his heart (18:1–18). Joab, Ahithophel, and all Israel rebelled against him (2 Sam. 16–17; 1 Kings 1). The narratives lend concreteness to the principle as Luther writes for the several groups of intended readers he envisions. Nonetheless, David did repent, and God remained faithful to him. David's rule took its course, and God forgave and blessed him.[84]

For Luther, David's trust in God and God's faithfulness to him forms the heart of the story of a successful political ruler. David's story contained many lessons regarding the pitfalls as well as the blessings of God's calling rulers; above all, Luther focuses on the virtues that David exhibited as he gives his readers a picture of the proper way to govern when God entrusts that task to an individual. In so doing the reformer uses the stories in the books of Samuel to create an idealized picture of David as king and shape it into a pointed critique of Saxon court life, the problem with which he was dealing in his own environment.

David demonstrates how to rule a kingdom in the vertical dimension as well as the horizontal dimension of human life. In Psalm 101:2–4 David speaks of his care and honesty in keeping the kingdom close to God's Word. He had restored divine worship and brought the ark to its proper place (1 Chron. 13:3). He obeyed God's command to refrain from building the temple himself (2 Sam. 7:2, 13). In Psalms 60:6 and 108:7 he expresses his delight in the fact that "God speaks in his sanctuary," which Luther interprets as the king's saying, "In my kingdom I have the true and pure Word of God and irreproachable and forthright teaching. I neither institute nor maintain any idolatry, factions, divisions, or any kind of false teachers,"[85] an obvious application of the verse

---

83. WA 51:261.34–262.11; *LW* 13:221–22.
84. WA 51:263.9–264.9; *LW* 13:223–24.
85. WA 51:216.22–34; *LW* 13:166–67.

to the reformer's own time and program for public life in Saxony. Following David's example requires God's guidance and support, Luther concludes. Among Israel's kings only three at most were highly praised, and "David is the only example that is presented as a model for them all, for the others ruled with idols and false prophets, and they persecuted and murdered the true prophets and condemned God's Word."[86] God had performed a miracle in giving David the capability of exercising his responsibility beyond even his great intelligence and ability.[87]

Luther's eschatological thinking exhibits itself continuously in his works as he observes how evil rages against God's faithful people, how Satan's deceptions are always attacking God's truth. He therefore is not surprised that "in David's story one can notice that many people were secretly extremely hostile toward him. When they had opportunity, they did their very best to strike out against him, to go after him, to cause him trouble, and to afflict him with every possible kind of suffering. In spite of this he continued to sing his song and ventured everything with God and his Word."[88] Implicit in his admiration of David's faithfulness amid affliction is Luther's admonition to subjects—particularly to the counselors who paralleled those who had undermined David's rule—to contribute to the common good by supporting good officials.

As is often the case in his appraisal of government, Luther's comments on Psalm 101 blame counselors rather than the king for the government's abuse of power. David's relationship with his own courtiers provides him with plenty of examples of how cautious rulers must be in the choice and use of their advisers. Ahithophel served as David's closest and best adviser but finally tried to undermine and overthrow David's rule. "The young nobles and courtiers want to be free. They want to be lords in the lands themselves. . . . When they are constrained to do something that they do not want to do, they know how to dissimulate and lie in wait until they see their opportunity. For a time they can hide their shifty eyes and deceiving faces very well." God can even call a David to repentance by letting Ahithophel deceive him, as if he were the voice of God (2 Sam. 16:23). "Thus it is very difficult at court to recognize and control the formidable masks of the devil."[89] Luther undoubtedly hoped that his words would be taken seriously at the courts of the Wettin princes who ruled Saxony and would produce repentance in some persons there.

In 101:3 the psalmist expresses his hatred for, as Luther translates the word, "transgressors." Luther regards it as truly miraculous that a ruler can recognize the necessity of hating transgressors, spiritual rogues, the "saints" of Satan, and to "separate them from himself in such a way that they do not stick to him or cling to him or remain in his presence at all." Luther imagines that

86. WA 51:217.14–18; *LW* 13:167.
87. WA 51:221.32–36; *LW* 13:173.
88. WA 51:218.20–24; *LW* 13:169.
89. WA 51:21.11–38; *LW* 13:170–71.

those surrounding David "sang very sweetly to him, praising one person here, one person there, extolling our cousin here or our brother-in-law there, in the hope of getting them a place in court or a promotion in the administration, regardless of their uprightness. . . . They succeed, too, unless God gives rulers a spirit like that of David so that they follow his example in constantly knowing how to avoid these false servants of God."[90]

David's assertion that he undertook no wickedness but hated lawbreakers (v. 3) leads Luther into another comment on courtiers. David could have easily hated some peasants in the countryside. "But to hate the lords at Jerusalem and in his court of Zion, that was indeed an accomplishment, even for David himself. But he was something more than the David of Bethlehem. He is a hero and an extraordinary man. He cuts through it all and lets God rule and be his Lord. Even if he lost a hundred Ahithophels, he would still prefer to keep his Lord and God, who is called Almighty and can create and bestow many, many kingdoms."[91] Luther was certainly hoping that his Saxon readers would take his admonition seriously.

David exercised self-discipline and throughout the psalms repeatedly admonishes others to guard themselves against temptation.[92] The king did more than exhibit virtues and freedom from vices in his own person. He also publicly waged war against deception and murder and especially false teaching. "David was highly gifted and a precious, special hero." "He sought, demanded, called, ordained, and commanded everywhere that the Word of God be preached in its truth and purity and that God be properly worshiped" (1 Chron. 15). His composition of psalms provided leadership for proper worship. David presented himself to all rulers as an example and perfect model of the way a person should seek God's rule and righteousness" (Matt. 6:33).[93]

Luther was conscious that his distinction between the realm in which the gospel proclaims and enacts God's gift of forgiveness and new life, and the realm in which the law prescribes the life of love toward God's creatures—that distinction was governing his interpretation of Psalm 101. This led him to acknowledge that his critics would say that his treatment of this text violated his own hermeneutic. He imagines them saying, "David is doing the very thing in this psalm that your interpretation talks about: he mixes the spheres of spiritual and secular authority and wants to exercise both." Luther rejects the criticism from two perspectives: "If a preacher in his official capacity says to kings and princes and to all the world, 'Give thanks to God and fear him, and keep his commandments,' he is not meddling in the affairs of secular government. On the contrary, he is thereby serving and being obedient to the highest ruler. Thus the entire spiritual government really does nothing else

90. WA 51:230.22–36; LW 13:184.
91. WA 51:227.33–42; LW 13:181.
92. WA 51:225.27–226.16; LW 13:178–79.
93. WA 51:233.39–241.28; LW 13:188–90.

than serve divine authority. That is why they are called servants of God and ministers of Christ in Scripture." Likewise, "if David or a prince teaches or commands fear of God and hearing his Word, he is not acting as a lord of that Word but as an obedient servant. He is not meddling in spiritual or divine rule but remains a humble subordinate and faithful servant."[94]

Luther's construction of this model draws together the narratives of the books of Samuel and the psalms attributed to Israel's second king. Luther found the basis there for sketching the conduct of the kind of person he believed God wanted to place in positions of power. The form of narrative again serves well to make concrete how government officials should carry out their God-given assignment to rule with justice and proper care for their subjects.

God's Commands and Human Virtues

This picture of David as ideal ruler demonstrates that Luther's vision of the Christian life required more than a discussion of the situations or structure of callings in home, workplace, society, and church. In addition, believers need directives to guide them in making God-pleasing decisions in the course of daily life. Luther discussed God's commands using concrete details in catechizing his hearers and readers. His sketch of Christian living placed God's commands alongside the callings that God gives; he used the stories of Genesis and the Gospels to depict and describe the virtues to practice and the vices to avoid within the context of vocation. The reformer's contrasting the lifestyles of the inhabitants of Sodom and of Lot's family (Gen. 19) led him to assert that God has provided a specific plan for human living even though he has given human creatures a good deal of freedom as well. "A human creature does not have such freedom that if God has commanded something, he can do it or not do it. So far as the commands of God are concerned, people are not free but must obey the voice of God or endure the sentence of death. Freedom is operative in regard to those things about which God has given no command."[95] Luther's use of the terms "freedom" and "to free" confuses some twenty-first-century readers accustomed to quite different usage. In Luther's first lengthy discussion of the justification of the sinner by God's word of forgiveness through faith in Christ, he defines justification as liberation: he titled the work *On Christian Liberty* in Latin and *The Freedom of a Christian* in German. But the freedom that justification effects in the sinner places the newly liberated person in bondage to neighbors, who need the love that the people who enjoy freedom from sin, death, Satan, and other evils are now bound to give.[96] At the same time Luther

94. WA 51:239.22–241.4; *LW* 13:194–96.
95. WA 42:512.21–24; *LW* 2:350; cf. similar statements in WA 43:29, 34–39; *LW* 3:216; and WA 43:477.29–478.21; *LW* 5:70–72.
96. WA 7:3–38, 42–73; *LW* 31:333–77.

reacted against what he saw as the excessive prescriptions of medieval ecclesiastical regulations for ritual and ethical life. He insisted that God's commands give specific prescriptions in many instances but also that they leave some things open to Christian judgment under their guidance. Therefore living a virtuous life and fleeing vices involves not only strict obedience to explicit commands but also the need for wisdom, to sort out the complicated situations of human life within the framework of God's callings and commands.

Although his Small Catechism provides a "chart of Christian callings," which children were to recognize as the situations in which God assigns them to serve each other in this world, Luther never compiled the list of virtues and vices he taught to children. In his teaching and preaching after 1520, he seldom employed those lists so prominent in medieval catechesis and preaching. He had no preferred virtue or virtues but rather depicted the Christian life as prepared for self-sacrifice and service, with the love demonstrated by Christ, who had come to serve rather than to be served (Mark 10:45). He presumed that the believer's new identity as child of God constructs a new character that lives out God's design for human life; he expected this godly character to produce its fruits in actions of love and service. Stories of God's people in Scripture depicted and modeled these virtues. The stories of the patriarchs and the disciples provided paradigmatic narratives that Luther used to cultivate the same character traits in his hearers and readers.

These virtues were the virtues of the Sermon on the Mount as well, expressed in Christ's command that we love our neighbor as we love ourselves (Matt. 22:39). Luther strove for peace among people as they encountered one another and exerted every effort to cultivate the kind of service he believed that God had designed human beings to render one another. Such a way of life would produce contentment or satisfaction in fulfilling one's calling to help other people and care for their needs. Practice of virtues according to God's commands provided a model for Luther's contemporaries as a "description of God, instruction in what he is and how he is disposed toward his human creatures."[97] Abraham's intervention on behalf of Sodom and Gomorrah also presented a "magnificent example" of love for the neighbor.[98]

Luther's admonitions regarding the living out of the Christian life presumed a general standard for human behavior that he found in the attitude described by Aristotle's concept of *epieikeia* ("reasonableness, fairness, or uprightness"). Although he harshly criticized Aristotle's *Ethics* for constructing an influential definition of what it means to be human apart from life's Creator,[99] in assessing Joseph's life Luther himself turns to the balance and wisdom expressed in

---

97. WA 44:591.26–39; *LW* 8:17.
98. WA 14:276.10/22/34–278.4/19/32; 24:337.15–28.
99. Compare *Confitendi ratio* (1520), in WA 6:166.32–167.4; *Wartburg Postil* (1521), in WA 7:514.5–14; *Ob Kriegsleute noch in seligem Stand sein können* (1526), in WA 19:632.7–24; and a sermon of October 1528, in WA 27:362.36–363.6.

Aristotle's term to describe God's will for the human disposition. This is to be understood in the context of his presumption that human beings are righteous in two ways, in two dimensions of life; they continue to be addressed both by God's promise of his gracious action on their behalf and by his commands for their own performance. Therefore "the law must not be cast aside because of the promise of grace but must be taught in order that discipline and the teaching concerning good works may be retained and we may be taught to know and humble ourselves after we have sinned." The goal of such teaching is that people may "govern and direct their conduct in a godly and prudent manner according to the norm of the law."[100] In this sermon Luther cites Aristotle positively when the Stagirite urges the practice of virtue, "the disposition to make choices consisting in the ability to find the proper balance by which, on the basis of reasoning of one kind or another, a person makes wise judgments. For instance, courage is the mean between rage and audacity or cowardice." Heads of household may well prescribe definite methods of managing the household but must always be ready to moderate commands when unforeseen changes in circumstance demand that they observe *epieikeia* and abandon the letter of the law.[101]

Often Luther's sermons aimed to cultivate specific attitudes or character traits that reflected God's way of doing things in the world and his design for human life. Relatively early in his career as reformer, his Wartburg Postil of 1521 reveals his concern that his hearers needed straightforward instruction in how to conduct themselves as children of God. This concern, present in his preaching a decade earlier, only intensified and deepened when he visited Saxon towns and villages in 1528.

Prominent among Luther's virtues was humility, an aspect of his conviction that trust in God produces contentment in the several situations of life, not contentment with evil and injustice, against which God's children always fight, but contentment with the callings that God gives at any particular time in life. In their stance toward their Creator, human creatures have every reason to be humble, and any number of biblical examples commend humility to God's people. As he fashioned the stories of Jacob and Esau's encounters, Luther saw a sharp contrast between the latter's smug pride and contempt for his brother and the former's modesty, humility, agreeableness, and guilelessness.[102]

100. WA 44:703.30–40; *LW* 8:170–71.

101. WA 44:704.13–42; *LW* 8:171–72. Luther here refers to Aristotle's *Nicomachean Ethics* 5.10 and also cites 2.6. On the debate over whether Luther's understanding of *epieikeia* is shaped by the biblical understanding of love or rather by natural law, see Gerhard Heintze, *Luthers Predigt von Gesetz und Evangelium* (Munich: Kaiser, 1958), 198–208. This passage supports the position of Franz Lau and Johannes Heckel that places Luther's concept of *epieikeia* in the realm of reason and natural law. See Franz Lau, *"Äußerliche Ordnung" und "Weltlich Ding" in Luthers Theologie* (Göttingen: Vandenhoeck & Ruprecht, 1933), esp. 42–44; and Johannes Heckel, *Lex charitatis: Eine juristische Untersuchung über das Recht in der Theologie Martin Luthers*, 2nd ed. (Cologne: Böhlau, 1973), 121–24, 164–66, 260–66.

102. WA 43:408.28–409.11; *LW* 4:379.

Luther freely idealized biblical figures and ignored their faults when he wished to construct models of virtues; he equally freely focused on their flaws and moral failures when he was attacking the lies of Satan that deny the identity of the child of God that Christ created through his death and resurrection and the Holy Spirit bestows through the Word in its several forms. As Luther recited biblical accounts of lives, he reminded his hearers how the humility practiced by Rachel[103] and Joseph[104] had produced a disposition to service and sacrifice for others. Luther sometimes used the related term "modesty" for this attitude that held self-glorification in check. Stories from the lives of Abraham[105] and Joseph[106] modeled this modesty for Luther's contemporaries.

David too furnished the preacher an example of humility in a sermon on Luke 14:1–11 from 1532. His predecessor, King Saul, had begun as a humble lad, taking care of his father's donkeys and obeying his father. "To this donkey-herder, poor and lowly, God sends the prophet Samuel to anoint him king." But, Luther points out, when he became proud and did not care about God and his Word, God cast him down, and Saul despaired and committed suicide. Then Luther turns to David. "David, too, was a humble man who tended his father's sheep obediently. Had he been proud, he would have said, 'Should I really tend sheep? That is highly distasteful to me. I deserve a higher place in life.' But he did not do that. He remained obedient and humble and cared for the sheep. He was really a fine, strong, intelligent young man, who might have said, 'What am I doing here tending sheep? I would like to advance and rise higher in the world.' But he dutifully remained a shepherd." And God loved this humble man and sent Samuel to anoint him king. Luther contrasts David to his arrogant brothers, who looked down on the youngest brother. "But God said to Samuel, 'You are to take no account of his person nor ask questions about those who have their heads in the air. You are to anoint the person as king whom I will indicate, and it will be the shepherd. I do not want the others.'" Luther comments that David remained humble after God had exalted him,[107] ignoring reports of David's actions that would seem to have presumed some arrogance. That did not serve his use of David's example at this point.

Luther's recitation of the humble conditions of Christ's birth gave ample occasion to teach humility at Christmas.[108] Mary provides a sterling pattern for Christian contentment amid humbling circumstances. She modeled the

---

103. WA 43:664.10–24; *LW* 5:341. On Luther's treatment of Rachel's faith, see Mattox, *Defender*, 198–211.

104. WA 44:615.25–27; *LW* 8:49.

105. WA 43:291.17–21; 43:291.38–292.10; *LW* 4:216–17.

106. WA 44:236.13–38; *LW* 6:316–17. WA 44:241.33–40; *LW* 6:322. WA 44:431.5–432.2; *LW* 7:177–79.

107. WA 36:332.19–333.2; 52:488.1–30; EA² 6:70–71; *HP* 3:42.

108. WA 52:40.12–41, 3.

sense of readiness to do the Lord's bidding as the angel came to her. Such contentment arises in the midst of difficult and disagreeable situations, Luther asserts, which Mary's background illustrates. He expands on her willingness to accept the Lord's gifts and will with the story of a godly woman who had a vision of three women near an altar. In the midst of the Mass a boy leapt from the altar, lavished caresses upon the first woman, and smiled at her. The second woman received only a smile. The third woman he slapped in the face, tore her hair, and pushed her away. The first virgin was one who insisted that she deserved blessings and wanted to dictate to God what he would do; such people hate and avoid suffering and lowly conditions. The second was willing to do some things for God but reserved time and blessings for her own desires. The third—Luther calls her a poor Cinderella—not only lived in want and misery but also was content to know that God is good, even without experiencing much of his blessing. She praised God despite her humble situation.[109] The actions of the boy reflected the world's attitudes toward these kinds of people. Mary also brought to Luther's mind another tale of one who accepted what the Lord had given him and recognized in his humble situation the richness of the blessings he had received. At the time of the Council of Constance a century earlier, two cardinals saw a shepherd in a field. The shepherd was weeping. One cardinal went to him and tried to comfort him, asking what the matter was. The shepherd finally pointed to a toad and confessed that he had failed to thank God for the blessing of being a human being rather than a toad. So moved by this reaction that he fell from his horse, the cardinal exclaimed, "O, Saint Augustine, it is as you said. The unlearned arise and enter heaven before us, and we struggle in our flesh and blood." Mary's confession in Luke 1:48 that the greatest thing in her life was God's regard for her concretely demonstrates this spirit of contentment, Luther argues.[110]

Jesus's demeanor toward Zacchaeus also demonstrates his own humility, a trait that Zacchaeus also demonstrates in his humbly searching for Jesus. Jesus could have had nothing to do with the despicable tax collector, going instead to the "exalted bishops in Jerusalem." But he ignored the prominent and pious and fixed his eyes on "this despised Zacchaeus, who wore no crown of roses around his head, was adorned with no bishop's vestment or authority, but rather only sincerely and earnestly wanted to see Jesus with a thoughtful and humble heart. That was his holiness."[111]

The parable of the Pharisee and the tax collector (Luke 18:9–14) provides another illustration of the contrast between pride and humility in Luther's August 1532 treatment of this text. "The Pharisee was a man of upstanding virtue, not a cheat or adulterer, but a man who fasted and tithed, yet in spite

109. WA 7:557.12–37; *LW* 21:310–11.
110. WA 7:567.20–33; *LW* 21:320–21.
111. WA 17.2:499.5–35; Church Postil, Luke 19, *FS* 2:212.

of this, he was arrogant and haughty." Then Luther turns from text to hearers
and comments that

> there are in our day as well people of excellent standing in our communities, high
> and mighty princes who rule well. . . . But then there are also arrogant jackasses
> who think they are the chosen of God, revel in themselves, parade and prance
> around proudly, idolizing their own persons. Such idolatry, presumption, pride,
> and haughtiness negate all good qualities. A housewife, too, can be good and
> efficient in keeping her house and raising her children, but if she is proud and
> boastful about how well she does it and looks down on her neighbor because
> she does not do half as much, her pride has soiled her fine virtue. A pretty girl
> who becomes proud of her beauty and looks down on others soils her beauty
> with her pride.[112]

In elaborating on this point, Luther anticipates John Milton's description
of the devil's rebellion as an act of pride. Summarizing his critique of the
Pharisee's pride, he concludes, "The Lord God is a God who cannot tolerate
arrogant presumption. He readily bestows talents, fortunes, nobility, prince-
doms, kingdoms, empires, but he will not tolerate presumption in anyone."
Luther continues by setting this example within the context of the story of the
creature's revolt against God. "What happened in Paradise? Lucifer was a most
excellent angel. God had endowed him above all the rest of the angels of God.
His legions were foremost among God's creatures. But when he thought about
this fact, that he was endowed above all the rest in wisdom and understanding,
he became proud and willfully despised God." Drawing on medieval tradition,
the reformer creates a scene in the heavenly prehistory. "God said, 'Lucifer,
listen to me. I did not endow you so highly in order for you to become proud
and scornful of me.' So God threw the devil into hell's abyss. Lucifer might
well have responded, 'Was I not more pious than the Carthusians and better
than all the others? Why have I been thrown into such a deep pit?' Lucifer
was better and more pious than the other angels, but because of his willful
disdain for God, he came to ruin."[113]

This entire sermon aims at cultivating a humility in individuals that will
strengthen the bonds of social support within the community. Luther concludes his sermon, "Let everyone humble himself before God, take care of
the neighbor and not despise him, serve and work faithfully to earn a living,
eat and drink. Let all be careful to avoid becoming proud and puffed up, for
every person sees that he too has unclean hands. To such people God gives
his grace, but those who do not hearken to him will be thrown out of his
presence. For God cannot endure pride, as Mary recounts in her hymn of
praise, 'He has scattered the proud in the imagination of their hearts. He

112. EA² 5:426–27; *HP* 2:281–82.
113. WA 36:234.30–235.2; EA² 5:428–29; *HP* 2:283.

has put down the mighty from their seats and exalted those of low rank' [Luke 1:51–52]."[114]

Humility fosters moderation, a virtue highly praised by both biblical writers and pagan philosophers such as Aristotle. Luther admonished the believers of his time to discipline their lives with moderation as did Joseph in his administration of power in the Egyptian government.[115] Luther also praised patience with others as well as with God through recounting examples of patient saints of the past. Abraham patiently waited on the Lord in the midst of his troubles with Pharaoh (Gen. 12:10–20).[116] Isaac as well waited with patience while the Lord was turning Abimelech's favor toward him (Gen. 26:16–29).[117] Jacob demonstrated his patience in the face of Laban's deception regarding Leah and Rachel.[118] The patriarchs displayed their faith in their contentment with patiently waiting on God.

God's people also demonstrate faithfulness in their relationships with other human beings. Joseph's faithfulness toward his own family in taking care of their needs and his reliability in carrying out the duties entrusted to him by Pharaoh commend personal loyalty and dependability to his students, Luther thought.[119] He also emphasizes Mary's faithfulness to family and to God in a 1532 sermon on the Gospel lesson for the festival of the Visitation of Mary, Luke 1:39–56. The lesson tells the story of Mary's trek to visit Elizabeth and Mary's singing her psalm of praise, the Magnificat. In his exposition, Luther emphasizes her faithfulness in trudging over the mountainous terrain, possibly in the company of Joseph and a servant, Luther believes. He views her making this trip "like a faithful servant, not impertinently, as on a lark or skipping off to a dance or some religious pageant, chatting along the way from house to house, eyes flitting here and everywhere. . . . She headed straight to her destination, without counting the trees or lingering along the way, for her heart was set on helping" Elizabeth. Luther makes explicit the contrary habits of the young people of Wittenberg, whose behavior was determining the way he recounted Mary's journey.[120] For "the purpose of this example is to teach everyone, especially the youth of our day, to serve willingly and humbly, irrespective of whether one thinks himself more deserving and important than the person whom he serves. Mary does this."[121]

Faithfulness means fairness in dealing with others, Luther believed. He called on his hearers to act fairly in their commercial dealings with other people, as

114. WA 36:235.7–236.20; EA² 5:432; *HP* 2:286.
115. WA 44:431.5–435.8; *LW* 7:178–83.
116. WA 42:484.1–16; *LW* 2:310.
117. WA 43:485.30–487.9; *LW* 5:82–84.
118. WA 43:632.36–633.24; *LW* 5:296. WA 44:268.39–269.30; *LW* 6:359–60.
119. WA 44:628.1–7; *LW* 8:66. WA 44:658.8–14; *LW* 8:108.
120. EA² 6:398–99; *HP* 345–46.
121. EA² 6:397–98; *HP* 345.

Joseph did when he priced grain for the Egyptians[122] (a generous estimation perhaps on Luther's part). However, when others make mistakes or fall into sin, believers should treat them with compassion, even as they strive to correct them. Jesus himself provided an example of the virtue of compassionate correction of those who make mistakes or sin. Preaching on the Gospel for the festival of Saint James, Matthew 20:20–23, Luther sketches the way in which Jesus treated the presumption of Salome when she sought special places for her sons in his kingdom. They were counting on their mother's being Jesus's aunt to win them the favor. Jesus did not shunt off Salome's request but acted like "any mother when her child soils himself. She washes the child off again, reveals her mother's heart, and does not send the child away." Jesus treated James, John, and their mother in the same way. Instead of saying, "I am good and you are fools. Get out of here," he "took them in great kindness and patience even as they were crudely stumbling. He hoped to improve them. This is the way of love."[123] Love also demonstrates the kind of compassion and readiness to forgive seen in the story of Joseph's encounter with his brothers (Gen. 42–45).[124]

Such love operates on a very practical scale in everyday encounters with others as well. Luther commended frugality, generosity, and hospitality to his hearers and readers. Joseph's feeding his family modeled the virtues of frugality and generosity as well as concern for others and stood in contrast with the gluttony, drunkenness, and wastefulness of the professor's own countryfolk.[125] Christians, he admonished, should practice the kind of hospitality demonstrated by Abraham when visited by the three angels (Gen. 18:2–5)[126] or by Rebekah when she first encountered Abraham's servant (Gen. 24:18–20).[127] Luther elaborates Mary and Joseph's difficulties in traveling and in finding a place to stay in Bethlehem in his recital of the Christmas story in the House Postil. "The evangelist undoubtedly wanted to depict this for us because we are so coldhearted, and this story would be able to warm those hearts a bit because our Savior had to suffer so miserably" at his birth. Readers should not curse the Bethlehemites for their coldheartedness but should repent of their own callousness.[128]

In his treatment of the Bethlehemites, Luther also teaches obedience to God's commands and the practice of the virtues he ordained in contrast to

122. WA 44:667.39–668.11; LW 8:121–22.

123. WA 10, 3:239.9–240.9; Church Postil for St. James, FS 2:127–28.

124. WA 44:598.1–11; 44:616.34–617.34; 44:630.29–631.14; LW 8:25–26, 51–52, 70; cf. Jacob's forgiveness of his sons, in WA 44:633.40–634.5; LW 8:74.

125. WA 44:664.3–12; 44:666.34–667.11; LW 8:116, 120.

126. WA 43:2.27–10.14; LW 3:178–89; cf. WA 43:15.5–17.33; LW 3:196–99. In 1521 Luther had made the same point in his Scholia: WA 9:357.24–39; cf. also his comment on Lot's hospitality: WA 9:7–8. In the 1523 sermons he also emphasized hospitality as he preached on this pericope: WA 14:275.29/38–276.10/33.

127. WA 43:329.27–331.15; LW 4:270–72.

128. WA 52:37.34–38.26.

vices. Because the reformer laid so much worth on contentment with what God gives, he warns against grumbling as he lectures on the relationships within Jacob's family.[129] His sharp words of criticism ring out as he observes how Joseph's humility stood in stark contrast to the pride so common in his own day, a "diabolical poison" that interferes with devotion to God and service to others.[130] The forgetful butler illustrates malice, treachery, and ingratitude for Joseph's help when he leaves Joseph languishing in prison.[131] With his frequently used sense of literary invention, Luther elaborated on the medieval understanding of Nimrod as a tyrant (Gen. 10:8–9), condemning exploitation of the powerless such as those with governmental power are sometimes wont to do.[132] Luther repeated his condemnation of greed and his warning against the dangers of being rich using the examples of the life he constructed for Esau[133] and the way in which Laban treated his daughters and their husband, Jacob.[134] The frugality of the Egyptians in Joseph's time that Luther imagined led him to contrast it with the exploitative taxes of the German princes, the conspicuous and luxurious consumption and usury of German merchants,[135] and the money- and goods-grubbing nature of the servants of both.[136]

Luther did not let himself be trapped in legalistic definitions of virtues and vices, however. In his sermon on Genesis 24, he speculates that the gifts brought by Abraham's servant when he went to find a wife for Isaac (Gen. 24:10) included gold, jewels, and other things that could better have been sold and given to the poor. But spending on such jewelry for a bride is pleasing to God, he argues, and that can be seen from his mentioning it in the story of the courting of Rebekah. Luther wanders further, pointing out that dancing, like jewelry, can evoke sin when it goes beyond proper limits. But neither dancing nor jewelry, when practiced or put to use without shameful words or actions, are to be condemned if they simply produce joy. The most praiseworthy jewelry that Rebekah possessed was her modesty (Gen. 24:65), the preacher observes.[137] In her callings as wife and mother, leader in her household, she demonstrated the virtues that God commands.

— ❖ —

129. WA 44:238.32–239.31; *LW* 6:320–21.
130. WA 44:432.3–433.32; *LW* 7:179–81.
131. WA 44:399.20–391.12; *LW* 7:123–24.
132. WA 42:400.26–402.34; *LW* 2:197–99.
133. WA 43:410.11–35; *LW* 4:381.
134. WA 9:583.24–26. WA 43:634.9–17; *LW* 5:297–98. WA 43:682.18–685.34; *LW* 5:367–72. WA 43:687.23–689.36; *LW* 5:375–78. WA 44:11.32–16.22; *LW* 6:17–23; cf. Luther's condemnation of the greed of Laban's sons: WA 44:2.24–5.17; 6:4–7.
135. WA 44:666.40–667.19; 44:673 .1–5; *LW* 8:120–21, 128.
136. WA 44:673.5–14; *LW* 8:128.
137. WA 14:315.16/29–316.15/35; 24:417.33–419.30.

Narratives serve as excellent vehicles for conveying instruction in the Christian life. Despite the gulf of time between the biblical figures and the circumstances of Luther's hearers and readers, the reformer firmly believed that these accounts provided his contemporaries with models and patterns for daily behavior. He retold and elaborated the stories of biblical saints, particularly those in Genesis and the Gospels, as concrete embodiments of how God wants his people to live—when the actions of the biblical figures corresponded to what Luther perceived to be God's design and plan for human living. He warned against taking every action of the saints portrayed in Scripture as a paradigm for living in sixteenth-century Germany, however, since he recognized that some of those actions reveal that even the greatest heroes among God's people still struggle against sin and evil and sometimes succumb to the devil's lies.

Luther recognized that human life is shaped by the experiences of children as they observe the behavior of parents and others in the village or town. He regarded the glimpses into the lives of God's ancient followers, as afforded by Scripture, as part of the family life of God's people. Luther therefore put these glimpses to use, sometimes with his own sharpening of focus through details imagined and added to the accounts. His goal was to cultivate a sense of vocation to serve one another in the various situations into which God calls people. Luther tested and gave direction to these biblical stories on the basis of God's commands to practice the good and reject the evil. That constitutes the good life.

7

LIVING WELL LEADS
TO DYING WELL

The Completion of the Christian Life

A life lived within God's callings in accordance with God's commands prepared the baptized to die well. In Luther's childhood environment, death's presence hung heavy over the village, taken for granted yet often interrupting and disrupting the equilibrium of family life and village structures. In the course of the fifteenth century, a genre of devotional literature developed, particularly under the influence of the Parisian theologian Jean Gerson's *Opus tripartitum* and the anonymous *Sancti Anselmi admonitio*, called the "art of dying."[1] Designed as tools for both parish priests and laypeople, these works on *ars moriendi* provided material that could be used, especially during a plague, to guide the dying to a spiritually satisfactory departure from life. Austra Reinis contrasts these medieval instructions on *ars moriendi*, which presumed that believers had to remain uncertain of their salvation to the very end, with the approach that Luther had pioneered in his *Preparation for Death* of 1519 (though there he tends not to use stories but rather straightforward

---

1. See Austra Reinis, *Reforming the Art of Dying: The ars moriendi in the German Reformation (1519–1528)* (Aldershot: Ashgate, 2007), 1–46. See also Rainer Rudolf, *Ars moriendi: Von der Kunst des heilsamen Lebens und Sterbens* (Cologne/Graz: Böhlau, 1957); and Franz Falk, *Die deutschen Sterbebüchlein von der ältesten Zeit des Buchdruckes bis zum Jahre 1520* (Cologne: Bachem, 1890).

proclamation of the resurrection hope).[2] His teaching on the justification of sinners "brought about profound changes in death culture."[3] He sought to comfort the dying with the assurance that God's promise, based on Christ's work, had restored them to God's favor. Throughout his preaching career Luther helped his hearers prepare for death. His letters also reflect his approach to bringing comfort to the dying.[4] He emphasized that when God promises to be the gracious and forgiving Father of a sinner in the baptismal form of his Word, he will remain true to his promise. To be sure, in line with his distinction between law and gospel, Luther proclaimed judgment upon the baptized who were indulging in sin. He afforded them no word of gospel and grace. But the repentant could without doubt trust in the faithfulness of Christ, who had died and risen to bring them to a life of trust and to the gift of salvation.

Biblical narratives supplied Luther with rich material for comment on various aspects of death. Also in these stories he often extended the text with his imaginative creations of possible scenarios. New Testament accounts, particularly of Jesus's raising of those who had died, and comments on death in the Epistles offered Luther a number of opportunities to help his hearers and readers with their own preparations for death.

The Reality of Death

Luther did not indulge in romantic pictures of death as a sweet escape. Death had invaded God's good creation as part of the curse upon sin. Luther frequently added death to his list of the enemies of the sinner and the believer, alongside the devil, the world, the sinful inclinations of the sinner, guilt, and other evils. Luther's refusal to mitigate death's threat may, in part at least, have been a reaction against the monastic ascetic contempt for the body he had experienced earlier in his life. It was also part of Luther's affirmation of the goodness of the natural order that God has created and called good, an attitude engendered by his deepening engagement with the Old Testament,

2. *A Sermon on Preparing to Die*, in WA 2:685–97; *LW* 42:99–115. See Reinis, *Reforming the Art*, 47–82.

3. Reinis, *Reforming the Art*, 6; cf. her extensive discussion, 69–129; and Werner Goez, "Luthers 'Ein Sermon von der Bereitung zum Sterben' und die spätmittelalterliche ars moriendi," *LuJ* 48 (1981): 97–114, here 114; cf. Helmut Appel, *Anfechtung und Trost im Spätmittelalter und bei Luther* (Leipzig: Heinsius, 1938), 105–13; and Ken Sundet Jones, "*Promissio* and Death: Luther and God's Word for the End of Life" (PhD diss., Luther Seminary, St. Paul, 2003), 1–107.

4. See also Neil Leroux, *Martin Luther as Comforter: Writings on Death* (Leiden: Brill, 2007); Ute Mennecke-Haustein, *Luthers Trostbriefe* (Gütersloh: Mohn, 1989), 113–34; Robert Kolb, "'Ein kindt des todts' und 'Gottes Gast': Das Sterben in Luthers Predigten," *Lutherische Theologie und Kirche* 31 (2007): 3–22; and Kolb, "'Life Is King and Lord over Death': Martin Luther's View of Death and Dying," in *Tod und Jenseits in der Schriftkultur der Frühen Neuzeit*, ed. Marion Kobelt Groch and Cornelia Niekus Moore (Wiesbaden: Harrassowitz, 2008), 23–45.

his increasing distance from Platonic ideas, and his Ockhamist tendency to see reality in earthly, created things. In explicating the story of the fall into sin, Luther tells his students:

> If Adam had obeyed this command [not to eat fruit from the central tree; Gen. 2:16–17; 3:3, 6], he would never have died, for death came through sin. . . . For us today it is unfathomable that there could be physical life without death and without all the incidentals of death, such as diseases, smallpox, stinking accumulations of fluids in the body, and so forth. In the state of innocence no part of the body was filthy. There was no stench in excrement, nor were there other execrable things. Everything was most beautiful, without any offense to the organs of sense. But there was physical life. Adam ate, chewed, digested. If he had remained as he was, he would have the other things physical life demands until at last he would have been translated to spiritual, eternal life.

Sin resulted in the loss of all this, and what would have been that blessed translation has become a horror.[5] Its horror casts a shadow over all of life.

As God confronted Adam and Eve in the Garden of Eden after their sin, his promise of deliverance in Genesis 3:15

> brought them back from death into the life that they had lost through sin. Nevertheless the life is one hoped for rather than one possessed. Similarly, Paul also often says [1 Cor. 15:31], "Daily we die." Although we do not wish to call the life we have here a death, nevertheless it is surely nothing else than a continuous journey toward death. Just as a person infected with a plague has already started to die when the infection has set in, so also because of sin and because of death, the punishment for sin, this life can no longer properly be called life after it has been infected by sin. Right from our mother's womb we begin to die.[6]

This is the lesson Luther draws from the narrative of Genesis 3.

In connection with his speaking of death, Luther also took occasion to admonish believers to take care of their bodies properly, finding middle ground between seeking death as an escape to heaven and hanging on to the things of this earth in idolatrous fashion. He warned against carelessness in caring for the body and other abuse of it. The story of Joseph in prison with the baker and butler elicits this warning from Luther against romanticizing danger and dying:

> We should not bring evils and dangers upon ourselves. When we are afflicted either by chance or by God's will, whatever misfortune there is must be borne steadfastly and with great courage, yet not in such a way that we neglect the plans and assistance by which we can be freed from afflictions. It is tempting God to have contempt for the remedies for evils that God has given. . . . The

5. WA 42:83.36–84.26; *LW* 1:110–11.
6. WA 42:146.18–26; *LW* 1:196.

body has been given to us by God, not that we should kill it with fasting or vigils, but that we should care for it with food, drink, clothing, sleep, and medicine. . . . We should be prepared for both eventualities: to protect and preserve our life and to meet death with equanimity according to God's good pleasure.[7]

The reformer's forthrightness regarding death also expressed itself in speaking of the physical repulsiveness that death produces. "Our bodies must waste away. Snakes and frogs have to chomp them down, as our experience each day demonstrates. The human body will become such a disgusting piece of rotting flesh that no one can stand the stench."[8]

Death is also to be recognized as the devil's tool: his "diabolical malice" causes death.[9] Luther summarizes the dire situation of sinners most clearly in sermons he preached in 1544 and 1545; these make clear how terrible the oppression of human beings is at the hands of every form of evil. As he exposits 1 Corinthians 15:56, he sketches a picture of his hearers as prey in the midst of a hunting expedition undertaken by death. Its "spear, sword, and blade" deliver "pestilence and misfortune and everything connected with them." "The three warriors, the law, death, and sin," make war against the Christians.[10] He continues:

> The sting of hell is sin. But the power of sin is the law. Sin is the sting of death. That means that the evil remorse in the heart, as it says, is genuine poison, which kills people. When sin awakens and remorse comes and says, "You are a child of death. You are lost and damned," then the person is a goner without outside help. Death strangles every single human being, using sin to do it. . . . Thus the human creature not only has to die, but also has to die in despair. Therefore that is what hell does. Death and hell would have no power over us if the sting, that is, the remorse, the vicious puppy, the sighing from hell, were not in our hearts.[11]

Christ's Triumph over Death

Nevertheless, a decade earlier in his lecture on Genesis 3:15, Luther had explained what God said and did when he confronted Adam and Eve after their fall into sin:

> Right from our mother's womb we begin to die. Through baptism we are restored to a life of hope, or rather to a hope of life. This is the true life, which is lived before God. Before we come to it, we are in the midst of death. We die and

7. WA 44:382.35–383.9; *LW* 7:113.
8. WA 49:765.19–21.
9. WA 36:346.18–26; cf. WA 47:714.1–3.
10. WA 49:773.14–15.
11. WA 49:776.28–38.

decay in the earth, just as other dead bodies do, as though there were no other life anywhere. Yet we who believe in Christ have the hope that on the Last Day we shall be revived for eternal life. Thus Adam was also revived when the Lord spoke to him. His Word did not revive Adam perfectly, indeed, for the life that he had lost he did not yet recover. But he received the hope of that life when he heard that Satan's tyranny was to be crushed.[12]

In a biographical invention of the reformer, the novelist and historian Richard Marius suggested that for his entire life he was beset by a fear of death. *Martin Luther: The Christian between God and Death*[13] is by implication a counterpoint to Heiko Oberman's serious biographical study, *Luther: Man between God and the Devil*;[14] Marius misreads Luther seriously. Luther's treatment of death is certainly not casual; confidence in the promise of resurrection and life eternal because of the work of Christ minimized his fear of death, which he regarded as natural and justified because death is the destruction of the goodness of human life.

Luther's trust in God's promise of new life for those who had thrown it away by sinning rested on his convictions about the very nature of God as a Creator, a Creator of life. The parallels between God's creation of the world and his resurrection of the dead were obvious to the Wittenberg reformer. Luther cited the first article of the Apostles' and Nicene Creeds as a confession of the omnipotence and creative power of God and his Word, and so "the article of faith on creation provides a strong and mighty basis for the article on the resurrection."[15] In 1533, while preaching on Luke 7:11–17, the raising of the son of the widow of Nain, Luther points out that Jesus raised the young man with a single word, "Arise!" without recourse to any medicines or other methods of healing, just as he (as the Second Person of the Trinity) had called the universe into existence out of nothing through his word in Genesis 1.[16] Luther's sermons on this text in both 1532 and 1533 argue a parallel: this restoration of life was possible simply because with God nothing is impossible.[17] In his treatment of 1 Corinthians 15 more than a decade later, Luther returns to the story of Adam and Eve's conversation about the curse that sin brought on them to elucidate the basis of Paul's affirmation of the resurrection of believers in Christ: "Because God, who has spoken this word

12. WA 42:146.27–35; *LW* 1:196.

13. Richard Marius, *Martin Luther: The Christian between God and Death* (Cambridge, MA: Harvard University Press, 1999).

14. Heiko Oberman, *Luther: Man between God and the Devil*, trans. Eileen Walliser-Schwarzbart (New Haven: Yale University Press, 1989; trans. from the original German, Berlin: Siedler, 1982). For a fuller critique, see Kolb, "'Life Is King.'"

15. WA 49:399.1–400.2; 49:399.38–400.27; cf. 49:436.32, 39.

16. WA 36:327.22–328.11; 37:536.35–537.11; 49:399.1–400.2; 49:399.38–400.27; cf. 49:436.32–39.

17. WA 36:327.22–328.11; 37:536.35–537.11.

[in Gen. 3:15, promising Satan's defeat and implicitly then the resurrection], is almighty and has made all things out of nothing, he is also able to make human beings who have died to be alive again. If God has created me from the earth, so he can awake me from the earth and bring me out of death."[18] Furthermore, God's majesty, his lordship over his creation, also offered a guarantee of his promise of resurrection.[19]

God not only creates life by nature; but he also accompanies his people through history. The raising of the daughter of Jairus (Matt. 9:18–26) reminded Luther of God's saving the children of Israel. He called on his hearers to trust in the one God, who will come to their aid and will liberate them, as he promised in the first commandment (Exod. 20:2).[20]

Luther anchored the comfort of the resurrection in the second article of the Apostles' and Nicene Creeds as well as the first. The person of Christ, as God and human creature, enabled him to redeem the dead and to awaken them from death.[21] Luther defined Christ's assignment from God the Father as the conquering of death, awakening the dead from death. He paraphrases Romans 4:25 in preaching on the raising of Lazarus in 1539: Lazarus came back to life because Christ died for the sins of the whole world and was raised so that those who die may live in God's presence and expect the resurrection of our flesh.[22] The story of the young man from Nain revealed why the Father had sent Christ into the world: he came to awaken the dead and to liberate his people from their misery, not only from death, but also from its cause, what had earned it. Christ was no sinner, Luther says, implying to his hearers his concept of the "joyful exchange" of Christ's resurrection and righteousness for the sinner's mortality and sin.[23] Christ had no guilt of his own. Death had no right to take him, no claim on him. But, as Romans 6 states, Christ carried the root sin of all human creatures into his grave and took its life away.[24] The resurrection of Christ is inseparably bound together with the resurrection of believers.[25] Luther mentions that Paul had spoken of two victories in Romans 5:12–14: "The first victory is that of death, which reigns and triumphs over all human children from the first human beings until now." "The other victory is the victory of life, which assumes lordship and triumphs over death."[26] Luther then describes this victory with the picture of a duel, which paraphrases and interprets 1 Corinthians 15:54:

18. WA 49:402.36–41; cf. 49:405.39–41; 49:406.29–30; 49:408.29–31; 49:412.29; 49:433.16–35.
19. WA 17.1:216.8–217.3; 49:737.16–18.
20. WA 36:347.19–348.42.
21. WA 49:50.5–13.
22. WA 47:712.21–25.
23. See Robert Kolb, "God Kills to Make Alive: Romans 6 and Luther's Understanding of Justification (1535)," *LQ* 12 (1998): 33–56.
24. WA 41:688.11–14; 41:691.3–8.
25. WA 49:762.29–35.
26. WA 49:767.30–32; 49:768.13–14.

Death is down for the count. It has lost its kingdom, its power, its victory. Indeed, it had the upper hand and because of sin the whole world was subjected to it. Every human being had to die. But now it has lost the victory. Against death's kingdom and victory our Lord God, the Lord of Hosts, has gained another victory, the resurrection of the dead in Christ. For a long time death sang, "Hurray! Triumph! I, death, am king and lord over all human beings. I have the victory and am on top." But our Lord God has him singing a little song that goes, "Hurray! Triumph! Life is king and lord over death. Death has lost and is on the bottom." Previously death had sung, "Victory! Victory! Hurray! I have won. Here is nothing but death and no life." But God now sings, "Victory! Victory! Hurray! I have won. Here is nothing but life and no death. Death has been conquered in Christ and has died itself. Life has gained the victory and won. . . ." That is the song that will be sung to us in the resurrection of the dead, when the mortal will put on immortality. Now death slays us human beings in terrible and various ways, one person by the sword, another by disease, this one by water, another by fire. Who can list all the ways by which death slays us human beings? Death lives, rules, dominates, triumphs, and sings, "I have won, I have won. I, death, am king and victor over all the world. I have power and dominion over everything living on earth. I spread death and slay all human beings, young, old, rich, poor, high class, low class, noble, commoner. I defy anyone to try to defend himself against me." But death will soon sing himself hoarse; death will sing himself to death. His "cantata" will soon be laid to rest. "Christ is arisen from the grave's dark prison. So let our song exulting rise. Christ with comfort lights our eyes."[27] Death, where is your victory? Where are you keeping the one who lay in the grave, whom you killed on the cross?[28]

Luther also sketches the confrontation between God and death, in his 1533 sermon on Luke 7:

God does not let this old grouch ruffle him but says to death, "Death, I am your death. Hell, I am a plague for you, . . . for your muskets and powder. Indeed, I will be your hell. You have terrified my people by having them die against their wills. Be careful! I am against you, and when you kill them, I will kill you. You have said, 'I have chomped down this man, I have wiped out this Doctor Martin.' Boast as you will, death. Those whom you have killed are not dead if they belong to me, but they are only sleeping. So speak softly, so that I can wake them with a finger."[29]

When he edited this text, Caspar Cruciger, Luther's former student and later colleague, rendered the words of Luther more freely: Christ "had strangled and chomped down both the devil and death, which had consumed him. Now he sits in eternal life and glory. That is our comfort and the ground of

---

27. From the twelfth-century hymn, translated for the hymnal issued in Wittenberg in 1524.
28. WA 49:768.25–39; 49:769.19–32.
29. WA 37:150.14–20.

our defiance, for we have been baptized in his name, we hear and confess his Word."[30] That God sees death as a sleep shows his power and is the comfort of those who hear his Word.[31] Christ is the one who gobbles down death, "whose righteousness and holiness are given freely to the sinner."[32]

Indeed, Luther drew his hearers and readers into the midst of the eschatological battle between death and life, between the "murderer" whom Jesus describes in John 8:44 and the creator of life himself. Luther depicts this battle in dramatically constructed stories of his own. In the series of sermons on 1 Corinthians 15 that he preached during the last two years of his life, Luther comments on verse 52, "For the trumpet will sound and the dead will arise and never decay." He cites 1 Thessalonians 4:16, "The Lord himself will come down with a battle cry and with the voice of the archangel and with the trumpet of God, and the dead in Christ will rise." In Poach's rendering the comment reads:

> The word for battle cry is *keleusma* [1 Thess. 4:16], when the soldiers in the army encourage each other and goad one another to fight boldly: "At 'em, at 'em, at 'em. Forward, forward, forward." The trumpets are the horns that are used when armies clash. That is the way it is on the field of battle. When the battle begins and you attack the enemies, you blow the trumpets or horns, beat the drums, and go forth with the taratantara. You call out a battle cry, "Let's go, let's go, let's go, let's go." The first lieutenant or captain, to whom the general has given command of the field, urges his soldiers to attack the enemies boldly. "Hui, hui, hui, hui." And the soldiers cry, "Stick it to them, stick it to them, stick it to them; strike them dead, strike them dead, strike them dead."[33]

Luther continues his examination of the text by returning to a description of the last day:

> For when God thunders, it sounds just like a trumpet, "Tutututu." And the bolts of thunder are not cracking jokes. Paul calls them the voice of the archangel. For God in his majesty speaks through thunder that shakes the entire earth and terrifies the world. Death is near! . . . Then the sun, moon, and all creation will scream, "Send death, dear God, send death. There are the godless, who do not know you. And the false Christians, who have not hearkened to the gospel of Christ. They all have blasphemed your name and persecuted and killed your saints on earth. Send death. It is high time. Bring that thing to an end." That will be the battle cry, and the taratantara of God, at which the entire heavens and all the atmosphere will be filled with the sound of "kir, kir, pumerli pum." Then a dreadful, unheard-of storm will take place, such as has not happened

30. WA 36:545.13–17.
31. WA 37:199.25–30; 47:713.31–33.
32. WA 41:690.10–12.
33. WA 49:735.25–35.

since the beginning of the world. . . . Then the last trumpet will sound, that is, the final bolt of thunder, which will collapse heaven and earth and everything in them suddenly into a heap. Then we will be transformed, that is, we will be changed from this mortal nature into an immortal nature, when heaven and earth pass away.[34]

This sense of triumph is combined with his sense of the awful reality and horror of dying to create Luther's approach to comforting the grieving that cannot be and ought not to be eliminated from human life. Believers react to the deaths of loved ones with grief that Luther regarded as a natural and justified reaction to the loss of loved ones, which confirmed the goodness of God's gift of life and the evil nature of death. However, confidence in the resurrection of the dead through Christ's own resurrection accompanied and mitigated that grief. The example of the patriarchs could also be put to use in instructing parishioners in the proper reaction to the death of a loved one. In 1523 Luther employs Abraham as such a model in his care for the burial of Sarah, a good work that the preacher commends to the Wittenberg congregation. He explains that Abraham's sorrow and tears had been recorded not as a bad example but because such sorrow and suffering is a result of the love for others that faith produces.[35] In 1540 he recounts Sarah's death to his students, recalls the blessings that she had experienced in her lifetime, and sensitively treats Abraham's profound sorrow over the loss of his wife.[36]

His sermon from autumn 1534 on Luke 7, the raising of the young man of Nain, delves into the emotions of the widow who had lost her son. Luther depicts her distress: "Among those people it was regarded a great misfortune if parents could not leave a name or children. They regarded this as a great disfavor of God. Hence the widow, who after the death of her husband placed all her hope and comfort in her only son, must have had great sorrow when her son was torn from her and she had nothing left on earth. Under such circumstances the thoughts were undoubtedly forced upon her: 'Behold, you are also one of the cursed women to whom God is such an enemy that they must pass from the earth without leaving any children.'"[37] Luther presumes that her broken heart produced many, many tears, and he ventures into her mind:

She doubtless cherished the secret wish and longing, "Oh, if only it could be the will of God that my son might still be alive or could again be restored to life." This was so deeply concealed in her heart that she could not see it herself. Indeed, she dared not even think of requesting this from the Lord, and yet her heart was filled with the thought. If she had been asked . . . what she would

34. WA 49:740.32–741.13.
35. WA 14:311.20/35–313.20/35; 24:408.29–411.35.
36. WA 43:270.17–284.28; *LW* 4:189.
37. WA 37:536.5–21; *CP* 5:142.

ask of God, she could have said nothing else than "Alas! What should I desire to ask more on earth than that my son might live." But her doubts triumphed, and her son came alive not because she had prayed, but only because the Lord met and had compassion on the poor widow—contrary to all human thought, hope, and effort her son was restored to her.[38]

Luther recognized that his parishioners had many questions about death, and on occasion stories helped answer them. The baptismal death and resurrection shaped the words Luther used to describe God's blessing of departure from this life to the better life with him, as is evident in Luther's description of God's promise to Jacob when he was about to depart for Egypt.[39] When death comes to God's faithful people, they will have the peace that God gave Abraham, so Luther interprets Genesis 25:8. Luther described death as a most pleasant sleep that holds no dread for those who know that Christ takes them from this life. Luther also knew the questions Christians ask, and so he poses for his students the query, "Where did Abraham go? What does it mean to be gathered to his people?" These words Luther found to be "evidence of the resurrection and the future life," "a comfort for all who trust in God." "We have a clear and extensive knowledge about death and life since we are certain that our Savior Christ Jesus is sitting at the right hand of God the Father and is waiting for us when we depart this life. Therefore, when we depart from the living, we go forth to the Guardian of our souls, who receives us into his hands."[40] The death of Ishmael in Genesis 25:17 occasions a briefer repetition of the assurance of resurrection after the believer falls asleep in the Lord.[41]

A saying that Luther occasionally quoted regarding the uncertainty of unbelievers in the face of death becomes half of a responsive chorus in his sermon on John 8:46–51 during Lent 1534: "The ungodly life's story is: 'I live. I know not how long. I die. I know not when. I pass away. I know not where I will go. I do not understand why I am rejoicing.' These are they who will see death, feel and experience it, for they have not believed Christ's Word, and as a result will be terrified by death. They will not be able to outrun it but must remain in everlasting death." The believers reply, "I live. I let God decide how long. I die. God wills when and what manner of death. I pass away. I know where I am going. I am mystified that I am still sorrowful." Such people, Luther says, "will fall asleep without terror or sorrow."[42]

---

38. WA 37:536.5–35; EA² 14:137–38; CP 5:152–53.
39. WA 44:637.37–640.26; LW 8:79–83.
40. WA 43:357.23–358.14; LW 4:309–10. Luther continues with consolation for the dying and the grieving on the basis of Abraham's death, and with an extensive treatment of questions related to death: WA 44:358.15–364.5; LW 4:310–18.
41. WA 43:373.19–375.32; LW 4:329–32.
42. EA² 4:383; HP 1:363.

Death has haunted humankind since the fall into sin. Christ provided new life through his own resurrection, Luther believed, for all who trusted the true God, before Jesus's time as well as afterward. For instance, Luther was confident that the patriarchs had trusted in God's deliverance through the Messiah. The brief account of Abraham's death and burial in Genesis 25:7–11 gave Luther the occasion to confess that Abraham's hope rested in Christ, whose promise of life in his resurrection extended to his hearers in Wittenberg.[43] The course of the regular system of lessons as well as his preaching, sermon series, lectures on Genesis, and speaking on other occasions provided him with opportunities to help his people learn to share that faith with Abraham.

Death is said to test the human spirit and show its true mettle. Luther's theology faced a test too, as it confronted death. There its sober and uncompromising realism found its place within the larger framework of his metanarrative that centered on Christ's death and resurrection. There Abraham and his Wittenberg hearers found hope. That hope they shared with the widow of Nain, the royal official who had lost a child, and Lazarus, who had experienced the power of Christ's resurrection. There they found reason to face death with confidence in God's promise of life everlasting.

Realistic about death, Luther also lived in that confident hope of the resurrection of his body because Christ had risen. Though he did not share his own grief publicly from pulpit or lectern, his deep sorrow over the death of two daughters and of his parents, expressed in letters and at table with his household, indicates his sober and unremitting estimate of death's curse. He reported to the friends gathered at the table on the demise of Magdalena, his fourteen-year-old daughter, that he had prayed, "I love her very much. But if it is your will, dear God, that you take her, I will gladly know that she is with you." The note taker reported that "as she lay dying, he asked her, 'Sweet Magdalena, my little daughter, would you rather stay with me, your father, or go to your other father.' Magdalena answered, 'As God wills,' and Luther said, 'You dear sweet daughter.' He added, 'The spirit is strong, but the flesh is weak. I love her so very much.'"[44] He wrote in an epitaph for her that she was born in sin, bound to die as a "child of death," but through her death had become "God's guest" because of Christ's death and resurrection. He comforted his wife with the hope of reunion with Magdalena in heaven.[45]

Such a faith shone through his preaching and lecturing as well. He was striving to help parishioners and students as well as readers far beyond Wittenberg to know how to trust God, endure suffering, praise God and pray to him, and show God's love to their neighbors. In all that, he presumed, they had also learned how to die well.

---

43. WA 43:357.13–364.13; see Ulrich Asendorf, *Lectura in Biblia: Luthers Genesisvorlesung, 1535–1545* (Göttingen: Vandenhoeck & Ruprecht, 1998), 133–39.

44. WA *TR* 5:189–92, §5494

45. WA *TR* 5:185–87, §5490–91.

CONCLUSION

Martin Luther began his efforts at reform on the basis of his conviction that the church had called him to the office of Doctor in Biblia, which committed him to bring the message of Scripture to the people of God. Their spiritual welfare, both in relationship to God and in relationship to one another, commanded his highest concern because in Scripture he found God's speaking his promises and his commands for all his human creatures. Luther's calling to teach the biblical message and his concern for the proper pastoral care of God's people led him to protest the practice of indulgences as he encountered it in Johann Tetzel's 1517 campaign that marketed them as a release from purgatory.

As Luther's reform found its sea legs in the next half decade, Luther came to realize that he was protesting in large part because the Christianity of his village and his university had undergone a transformation over the centuries. From a religion based on God's conversation with his people, initiated in his Word to them, it had become a religion that mirrored the pagan practices of its Mediterranean and Germanic predecessors, a religion of ritual aimed at pleasing God through specific ritual actions. He dedicated the rest of his life to proclaiming the God he found conversing with him in Scripture, preaching to all who would listen—or read, since he learned to take advantage of Johannes Gutenberg's invention.

As a professor of exegesis, he dwelt on both Testaments of the Bible, but his initial encounters with the Psalms and Romans shaped the development of his way of thinking. He recognized that the biblical account of reality differed from much of the theology he had been taught at the university, in part because of its forms. The concreteness of much of the biblical record had been placed into abstract forms shaped by Aristotle and others, who had not learned to define reality with the person of the speaking Creator God at its center. Luther strove to change that.

As a public communicator, he found many methods, including print. Luther believed that his own callings to teach and to preach essentially depended on oral communication, and he believed that human beings, made after the image of the speaking God, express themselves best in the oral exchange between speaker and hearers. He also believed that the God who said "Let there be" in the beginning continued to sustain the world with his word, in some fashion unfathomable to human beings, and that he re-created sinful human creatures through the very understandable, though also ultimately not rationally analyzable, word of forgiveness that the Second Person of the Trinity, who became Jesus of Nazareth, won for sinners by dying and rising to life again.

Luther also experienced life in terms of the passage of time. With recent emphasis on *kairos*, the right time, the proper moment, as an important element in the Greek understanding of human life, we sometimes lose sight of the importance of *chronos*, the routine, perhaps for the most part boring minute-by-minute, year-by-year, lifetime-by-lifetime passage of life. History, Luther found in the Scriptures, belongs to the very nature of the human situation, of the human creature. So he naturally turned to story, as he found the biblical writers had often done, to convey the conversing God to his audiences.

He used several kinds of communication in lecturing to students and preaching to congregations. For instance, Luther regularly catechized by bringing together a variety of Bible passages related to his texts in order to convey God's promise of life and his expectations for what human life should be. On occasion he could supply a careful analysis of the terms and context of the passage on which he was preaching or teaching. He also used narratives, retelling stories from the biblical text, often with his own elaboration, and sometimes other stories from the history of humankind, particularly of the church or, rarely, from his own experience. He could even invent a fantasy to convey the message he was pulling from the biblical text.

Luther used stories to console and comfort, and he used stories to instruct his readers and hearers in the proper way to live the Christian life. He himself described that life in several ways. In chapter one of this volume, readers can find some of these descriptions. His *Warning to His Beloved Germans* of 1531 reminds readers why his reform was worth dying for: "It has, praise God, come to this, that men and women, young and old, know the catechism and how to believe, live, pray, suffer, and die."[1] Twelve years earlier he had described the active righteousness that the Holy Spirit enables believers in Christ to live out with words from Titus 2:12: it consists of living soberly (crucifying the flesh), justly (in regard to the neighbor), and devoutly (in relationship to God).[2] Between these two, in 1525, he advised parish pastors that their call-

---

1. "Aber nu ists / Gott lob / dahin komen / das man vnd weib / jung vnd alt / den Catechismum weis / Vnd wie man gleuben / leben / beten / leiden / vnd sterben sol"; *Warnung an seine lieben Deutschen*, 1531, in WA 30.3:317.32–34; LW 47:52.

2. WA 2:147.4; LW 31:299.

ing dictated that they preach the law to reveal sin and terrify the conscience; preach the gospel to bestow the forgiveness of sins; aid hearers in putting to death the sinful desires that disrupt the good life; encourage works of love toward the neighbor; and continue to emphasize the law for those without faith.[3]

This volume sketches Luther's way of cultivating such a life by examining how Luther used narrative to accomplish the task. His stories strove, first, to build faith in Jesus Christ and his atoning work as the foundation and orientation for all of daily life; second, to foster a life of enduring suffering and of killing sinful desires, in part through that suffering; third, to encourage reading and hearing the biblical message and responding in prayer and praise; fourth, to lead his readers and hearers to fulfill God's callings in accord with the virtues God commands as they care for other human creatures and God's world; and finally, to prepare those he addressed to die trusting in Christ, that is, to die well.

Luther's reform was all about cultivating proper faith and life in the people of God. His use of stories arose out of his convictions about the nature of God and of his human creatures, out of his belief that as persons, human beings learn effectively through the concrete depiction of the structures God has written into humanity. Because Luther believed in the consistency of human nature and also in a fallen world, and despite his recognition of the historical uniqueness of every time and place, he moved easily between the biblical world and his own. In both he found God eager to speak and desiring community with his human creatures. Luther dedicated his life and his stories to making that happen.

3. WA 18:65.9–66.11.

SUBJECT INDEX

184

SCRIPTURE INDEX